SOPHIA

SOPHIA

Aspects of the Divine Feminine

PAST & PRESENT

SUSANNE SCHAUP

NICOLAS-HAYS, INC.
York Beach, Maine

First published in 1997 by
Nicolas-Hays, Inc.
P. O. Box 612
York Beach, ME 03910-0612

Distributed to the trade by
Samuel Weiser, Inc.
P. O. Box 612
York Beach, ME 03910-0612

Library of Congress Cataloging-in-Publication Data

Schaup, Susanne.
    [Sophia. English]
    Sophia : aspects of the divine feminine past and present /
Susanne Schaup.
        p. cm.
    Includes bibliographical references (p.   ) and index.
    ISBN 0-89254-036-2 (paper : alk. paper)
    1. Femininity of God. 2. Women and religion. 3. Feminist
theology. I. Title.
    BL458.S3313 1997
    291.2'114--dc21   97-9189
                                                                      CIP

MG

Cover art is Andy Warhol's *Details of Ren. Paintings: Botticelli's Venus*
© 1997 Andy Warhol Foundation for the Visual Arts / ARS, New York
Art Resource, New York used by permission

Cover and text design by Kathryn Sky-Peck
Typeset in Granjon with Trajan display

Printed in the United States of America
03 02 01 00 99 98 97
10 9 8 7 6 5 4 3 2 1
*The paper used in this publication meets the minimum requirements of the
American National Standard for Permanence of Paper
for Printed Library Materials Z39.48-1984.*

First published in German as *Sophia - Das Weibliche in Gott.*
Copyright © 1994 by Kösel Verlag GmbH & Co., Munich.

CONTENTS

Sophia

NOTE TO AMERICAN READERS

TRANSLATING MY BOOK into English was not an easy task. If the original has any merit, part of it is linked with the spirit of the German language. I may say that my heart went into it, and while I was working to express complex matters simply, the words came forth to bring home the truth of Sophia as I see it. A struggle of this kind in one's native language results in style. This I cannot hope to achieve in any other language.

There was one advantage, however, in translating the book myself. As the author, I was able to take liberties not permitted to the translator of someone else's work. I took the opportunity to make amendments suited to an English-speaking readership. If Sophia is a living reality, and not just a figure of speech, insights into her nature are bound to change and develop. With some touches here and there, I brought her up to my present state of reflection. The last chapter has been rewritten, so that in the end this book has been reborn in the English language.

My thanks are due to some friends who assisted me with research in America and supplied me with books that I could not get easily over here. Sigrid Bauschinger, Sara Hudson, and Carol MacKnight were most resourceful, and provided unfailing help. I also thank Betty Lundsted, publisher and experienced editor, who gave me the same assistance and mended linguistic deficiencies which escaped my attention.

This book is a modest contributioin to our knowledge of Sophia, and it is also an affirmation of Divine Wisdom in our time. May a spark of the sophianic spirit, which moves so many of us today, ignite readers on the other side of the ocean.

Susanne Schaup
Munich, October 1996

INTRODUCTION

For the great goddess . . . whose forehead is crowned with the
Turrets of the Impossible, moves through the generations from
one twilight to another; and of her long journeying from . . .
revelation to revelation, there is no end.

—John Cowper Powys[1]

THE CONTROVERSY ABOUT A NEW image of God has reached a point in our time which may be compared to a landslide. It represents the last stage of the so-called "gender question," which in Western civilization has been an issue for at least two hundred years. It is the last step of a movement which began as a struggle for women's rights and expanded during the last three decades into an "ontological revolution."[2] In countries where women, to a certain extent, have attained legal equality with men, much more is at stake today. A civilization which in global perspective has not only oppressed women, but minorities and weaker members of any kind, which can only solve conflicts with lethal weapons, which exploits nature and destroys our environment, brings up the inevitable question of the ultimate cause of this failure of mankind. It is a question raised

---

[1] John Cowper Powys, *A Glastonbury Romance* (Woodstock, NY: The Overlook Press, 1987), pp. 1118–1119.
[2] This term was coined by Mary Daly; see *Beyond God the Father* (Boston: Beacon Press, 1973); also *Gyn/Ecology* (Boston: Beacon Press, 1978).

---

with anxiety, despair, outrage, anger, and resignation. How did we get into this scrape? Was it really inevitable? Has the principle of might over right been the prevailing concept since the dawn of humanity until today, even when legislature ordained differently? Why has the central message of Christianity, the commandment of love, not been able to prevent this disastrous development? What was it that turned the blessing of scientific and technological progress into a curse, at least into a terrible predicament? All philosophical systems for the salvation of mankind have to resign in the face of the condition of the world. Has religion failed?

Various names have been attached to this last century before the turn of the millennium—"Century of Woman," among others. Women worldwide should protest against this label, considering the outstanding events of this century: two World Wars, the second one with the "holocaust" as a new dimension of horror, the atomic bomb, the destructive potential of nuclear power even for peaceful purposes, the explosion of poverty in various parts of the world, the mass rape of women—always practiced, but formerly taboo—as an additional atrocity of common warfare, not to mention irreparable ecological damage. Has it not rather been a "Century of Wolves"?[3]

However—and in that sense we may stand at the end of a century of women after all—the most radical inquiry into the causes of our troubled world was made by women during the past decades. They pointed out and analyzed with painful clarity the connection between patriarchal religion and a society of violence. The undreamed-of unfoldment of the mental faculty, the development of the power of reason occurred

---

[3] The title of Nadezhda Mandelstam's famous memoirs of the Stalinist era, *Jahrundert de Wölfe* [Century of Wolves], has become a slogan in Germany and Austria. Publisher's note: We were unable to locate a translation of this book.

with the blessings of a God in whose name untold acts of violence and destruction were committed. We may contemplate the reverse side of Western culture, we may have a grasp of the complex historical reasons, and yet stand perplexed by so many contradictions. What has made and still makes them possible? The many causes, which may explain one particular event in history, are drowned in a deluge of impenetrable complexities when we try to get a view of the whole. Is there a final cause at the basis of all explanations? The frequently quoted paradigm shift, the promise of the future, should be able to expose and to transcend this ultimate cause.

That which gives a culture legitimacy is ultimately its underlying concept of God. If this concept does not change, nothing can actually change, as all revolutions in history have demonstrated. No scientific, ecological, or social paradigm shift can take effect, as long as the theological paradigm does not change along with it. In other words, there is a need for a transformation in the way we refer to God and our image of Man as reflected in this discourse. The image of God in Western religion, including Judaism and Islam, is a masculine one, despite all protests to the contrary, and as such is a direct cause of the devaluation of the Feminine and feminine priorities in our culture. Jesus, himself, was known to be kind to women in flagrant violation of the customs of his time, but his example was overshadowed by the sanctions of worldwide patriarchy, which preceded Christianity by thousands of years and retains a formidable staying power to this day. Nothing else was to be expected. Patriarchy is the prevailing world order. If this system is to change, if a more just, more humane and ecologically sound world order is to be introduced, we need more than a reform of institutions, including established religion. It takes a new way of feeling and thinking, a new sense of being-in-the-world, as well as a new perception of God. Nothing short of this profound change will be able to uproot one of the most vicious patriarchal myths: the legend of the natural, preordained and never-ending conflict of the genders.

In the face of these facts, it is difficult to stay clear of the polemical trap. Polemical argument has a tendency to hypnotize and to narrow one's vision to either black or white. Ultimately it does not lead anywhere, no matter how true or plausible from a particular point of view this may be. However, we need to grasp, and this also means that we have to feel deeply, that there is no subject of greater importance, since it is basic to all the glaring problems of our world. Today it is imperative that we listen to the call for Wisdom. Wisdom goes beyond Knowledge. It asks questions about the meaning and the purpose of knowledge, about the responsibility of our accumulated knowledge to a higher authority.

Wisdom, one might say, is ethically responsible knowledge, but this is not enough. Wisdom considers everything, weighs all things with a view to the greater Whole and does not exist apart from Love. Wisdom is concerned with the well-being of all creatures, of every aspect of creation, including the animal and plant kingdoms and all the elements. Wisdom takes a look behind the surface of things and perceives the truth underlying the phenomena. Men and nature, sentient beings, and so-called inanimate objects, reveal their secrets to the eye of wisdom. A good doctor, a good therapist, or a good counselor must have wisdom, just as a good mother is not only loving, but also wise. If you wish to inquire into the secret qualities of plants or minerals, you will have to adopt the loving and humble attitude of wisdom.

How did it happen that an entire culture came to disregard wisdom? If a civilization pursues knowledge for its own sake, if it puts it to reckless use and banishes love from public life, although love is the central message of its religious tradition, something went wrong. There has to be something which led to this course. If, in our houses of worship, we often do not feel the life-sustaining wisdom and love of God, there must be a reason for it. If women experience discrimination in the churches and have been made invisible by many injunctions and the exclusive address as "brethren," there has to be a justification for this in our image of God. Many women, as well as an increasing number of men, no longer accept the traditional image of God, because it lacks the Feminine. It is small comfort to be told that the masculine gender of the Holy Trinity is not to be understood in a sexist way, or that the personhood of Father, Son, and Holy Spirit transcends the polarity of male and female.

If God is personal, as we are taught, the human mind can only grasp this concept in terms of masculine and feminine. Any other interpretation is bound to lead to theological abstractions which a woman may understand in her head, but not in her heart and her sensibility. This is not, and can never be, "knowledge of the heart." It is of little help that the Virgin Mary—at least in the understanding of the Catholic Church and in Eastern Orthodoxy—has been elevated as "Queen of Heaven." The figure of Mary, the blessed virgin and obedient servant of God, however gracious and comforting she may appear to many, has become a problem. Women are no longer willing to identify with Mary's humble obedience, which has been imposed on them for so long. They are no longer able to identify with Mary's disembodied femininity. Even the fact that the Hebrew word for Holy Spirit—*Ruah*—is feminine, is poor compensation. The Holy Spirit, as "he" migrated from Hebrew to Greek and Latin to our modern languages, became more masculine along the way, and is definitely referred to as masculine in our grammatical usage. But is the dove, a symbol of the Holy Spirit, not conceived as a female animal? Certainly, but the gulf which separates us from the time when the dove still was the symbol of the Feminine Divine, has become too deep and wide.

Sometimes an artist found ways to smuggle in surreptitiously what the official discourse of God prohibited. In the little Romanesque church of Urschalling in Upper Bavaria, we see a fresco (see page 26) in which the Holy Spirit appears in unmistakably female form. Standing between Godfather and Son in a close embrace, so that their robes merge into one at the bottom, held lovingly at the shoulder by the two male figures on her side, a female person of charming gracefulness is revealed as part of the Holy Trinity. An unknown artist of the ninth century dared to project the feminine aspect of God onto the Holy Spirit. Centuries later, Mathias Grünewald created his famous altar at Isenheim, showing two mysterious female beings in a blue aureola hovering above a concert of angels. One of them, a figure with blazing head, is often interpreted as *Maria aeterna*, but also as the primeval Wisdom of God, *Sophia* in Eastern tradition. To give one more example of a work of art which, like all great art, is in touch with the deep well of the unconscious: in Michelangelo's world-famous painting of the creation of Adam on the ceiling of the Sistine Chapel, Godfather is seen to embrace a nude female figure with his left arm, while his right hand is ushering Adam into life. Some suggested that the female figure represents Eve, but this is unlikely, because according to Genesis, Eve was not created before Adam, but after him. Another reading is in fact much more plausible: God is imagined as embracing Wisdom, his "darling," as she is described in the Old Testament. In other words, artists are more daring and less inhibited than theologians. They may anticipate needs which only later centuries may acknowledge to be of universal significance. They are able to take a deeper look, from their own vision or the intuition of their souls, than the discourse of God of their time permits. Thus, artists may challenge the patriarchal image of God and bring in the Feminine Divine in a way no theologian would have dared. In our time, images like this acquire a new significance as witnesses of an original intuition of God unfettered by patriarchal doctrine.

From a deeply felt need women, as well as men, started a quest for a new image of God. They searched the traditional image for hidden feminine elements and traces of motherhood, which were disregarded in exegesis, or overlooked due to faulty translations of the Scriptures. The question was raised whether the concept of a monotheistic Fathergod were not preceded by an older tradition shared by all nations of antiquity under various names as the Great Goddess. The people of Israel lived in close vicinity of nations where the faith of the Goddess was still alive. The prophets, Jahve himself, and also Saint Paul, rant and rave against the ancient faith, condemned as idolatry under pain of severe punishment. In the struggle over thousands of years between the older feminine and the new masculine concept of God, based on a shifting historical reality, Jahve came out victorious. However, gods may be attacked and defeated, but they cannot be eliminated altogether. In the so-called Wisdom Books of the Old Testament, a female figure appears in close proximity to God, Wisdom—"Frau Weisheit" in Martin Luther's translation of the Bible. Under her Greek name "Sophia," her life in Western Christianity remains a hidden one, whereas in the East she was always more manifest. Especially in the rich iconography of the Orthodox Church she has always been a figure of divine stature.

Theologians have developed their own ways of dealing with her. There is no doubt as to her feminine nature, but by her identification with Jesus Christ and the Holy Spirit on the one hand and the Virgin Mary on the other, she became integrated in the circle of the most sacred personae of Christian doctrine. She is an entity of uncertain definition and various interpretations, but there have always been passionate souls who dedicated themselves to her service, keeping her memory alive under the adverse condition of a patriarchal religion.

Sophia

Was the Great Goddess totally absorbed in Lady Wisdom, or Sophia in the Eastern Church? We shall see that she developed into a being of divine stature and for centuries fulfilled the need of the human soul for the Feminine in God. She is being rediscovered in our day, as Divine Wisdom with many echos of the ancient Goddess. In biblical times, she was deprived of all her ritual functions, but she retained her most characteristic and endearing features—her wisdom, and her love of human beings. Having had to surrender the power of creation to Jahve and to yield precedence to the persons of the Trinity, she could never again claim the stature of the Great Goddess, yet she is there and was always revered as divine by a deep instinct of the soul, which longs for wholeness.

For many contemporaries in search for the Feminine in God, traditional Sophia is not sufficient. *Ich brauche die Göttin* ["I Need the Goddess"] is the title of a book by the German feminist scholar Gerda Weiler.[4] Merlin Stone, an American author, spent ten years visiting excavation sites in the Near East and wrote her pioneering book *When God Was A Woman*.[5] Other investigators, women and men, reached the same conclusion by different approaches, for instance by studying the cave drawings in Southern France or in Spain. More recently, we had the monumental work of Marija Gimbutas,[6] who presented an enormous amount of evidence that there was a Goddess-centered period of peace and high culture before the patriarchal order took over. The first

[4] Gerda Weiler, *Ich brauche die Göttin* ["I Need the Goddess"] (Basel: Mond-Buch-Verlag, 1990). Gerda Weiler died in 1994, shortly after completing her Feminist Anthropology in 2 vols: *Eros ist stärker als Gewalt* ["Eros is stronger than Violence"] (Frankfurt: Ulrike Helmle Verlag, 1993); *Der aufrechte Gang der Menschenfrau* ["The Upright Gate of the Human Female"] (Frankfurt: Ulrike Helmle Verlag, 1994).

[5] Merlin Stone, *When God Was A Woman* (New York: Harvest, 1976).

[6] Marija Gimbutas. *The Goddesses and Gods of Old Europe, 6500-3500 B.C.* (Berkeley: University of California Press, 1982).

conception our ancestors had of the Divine was female. Overawed by the forces of nature, prehistoric man observed how the Earth miraculously produced plants and crops, just as the bodies of women and female animals gave birth to new life. With the striking correspondence between the female cycle and the phases of the moon, the female power of reproduction was recognized as closely linked to the creative powers of nature. The old thesis that the cult of the Goddess was nothing but a fertility rite has been invalidated.[7] The discovery of thousands of female figurines from the Stone and Bronze Ages, with their prominent sexual attributes, seemed to corroborate this thesis, but today these characteristics are understood as representing not only the biological, but the comprehensive creative potential of women. An ancient Sumerian prayer invokes the Goddess Nana—or Innana—as "Mighty Lady, the Creatress."[8] On another tablet the Goddess Nammu is addressed as "the mother who gave birth to heaven and earth." The Egyptian Goddesses Nut and Isis, or Hathor, command the highest rank, and about Isis it is written: "In the beginning there was Isis, the Oldest of the Old. She was the Goddess from whom all Becoming Arose." Asherah or Ishtar, the Goddess of Canaan, was even worshipped as the "Progenitress of the Gods." The Goddess, or the Great Mother, not only was the source of procreation, the visible cycle of growth and decay, but she held in her hands the entire cosmos. She joined human life mysteriously with the works of nature to form a unity of all Being. Thus, since time immemorial a cosmic dimension was attributed to the Goddess. Without this fea-

---

[7] Riane Eisler, "The Goddess of Nature and Spirituality," *In All Her Names*, ed. by Joseph Campbell and Charles Musès (San Francisco: HarperSanFrancisco, 1991). See also by the same author: *The Chalice and the Blade: Our History, Our Future* (San Francisco: HarperSanFrancisco, 1987).

[8] This and the following citations are quoted in R. Eisler, "The Goddess of Nature and Spirituality," p. 5.

ture, the cult of the Goddess could not have developed. It is part of her nature that she is not a jealous, monotheistic goddess. Her work is inclusive, not exclusive. She tolerates other gods and goddesses next to her, but she stands above them all, and embraces all as the feminine principle of divine creativity.

Today we conceive of these ancient times as women-centered, rather than matriarchal, in the sense of female dominance. Women were not necessarily the rulers, but the feminine life principles prevailed. Female power implied the capacity to produce and nurture life, not the power to rule and dominate others. A number of authors from antiquity—such as Hesiod, Empedocles and Ovid, to mention just a few—tell us about a legendary "Golden Age," in which warfare and blood sacrifice were unknown and when men lived in peaceful enjoyment of the gifts of nature, which provided sustenance for all creatures. The sensational excavations of Catal Hüyük in Anatolia, and at other places, confirmed this lore. The relics of human settlements discovered at these ancient sites suggest that prehistoric society was a peaceful and cooperative one. Women held high positions as priestesses and craftswomen, and there is no indication that any section of society, including men, were suppressed. No weapons were found, and in the extant works of pictorial art there is no representation of violence.[9]

With these new insights a change of paradigm took place in archeology. Whereas formerly it was assumed that men initiated all culture, it now turned out that it was women who stood at the cradle of civilization.[10] In the center of early human culture stood the Great Goddess or Mother Goddess as a divine symbol of life and of the unity of

[9] For a descriptive reconstruction of the Goddess culture, see R. Eisler, *The Chalice and the Blade*.

[10] Richard Fester (ed.), *Weib und Macht* ["Woman and Power"] (Frankfurt: Fischer, 1979).

humankind and nature. Until the Indo-Aryans, with their gods of war and their weapons, uprooted the goddess culture and established a hierarchical order, society was peaceful and our relation to nature as the life-giving Great Mother was one of harmony and reverence. The same applies to the women-centered culture of Minoan Crete. The archeologist Nicolas Platon, who directed the excavations on the Mediterranean island of Crete for fifty years, stated that this society was "remarkably peaceful," and that "the whole of life was inspired with an ardent faith in the goddess Nature, the source of all creation and harmony."[11]

In the paradigm shift which is emerging today, humanity seeks to treat nature gently. The exploitation and reckless destruction of nature resulted in one ecological disaster after another, but the necessary change of attitude takes hold only gradually. Even today there exist cultures, for example some of the native American traditions, in which nature is held to be sacred as a mother who must never be exploited or harmed. Such cultures, marginalized and nearly eradicated, are being rediscovered and studied for the healing of the Earth. Even science is beginning to develop a new image of the planet as a living organism and restored to it the ancient Greek name of Gaia.[12] Gaia is a living entity, a Mother, who brings forth and sustains life. She will expel the species that upsets her balance in an intolerable way.

The quest of our time for the Wisdom of the Goddess longs to overcome the alienation between human and nature, man and woman, human and God. We have been careless in our dealings with nature, with each other, with ourselves—and with God. When all is said and done, we have to accept responsibility for the dead end where we got stuck. If a patriarchal God has been imposed on all other concepts of the

---

[11] R. Eisler, "The Goddess of Nature and Spirituality," p. 15.
[12] James Lovelock, *Gaia* (London: Oxford University Press, 1979).

divine, mankind has made this choice and will be held responsible for it. History might have taken a different course, even in the period of the Old Testament, even more so in the Christian era. But we drove away Wisdom, as we banished Eros from religion[13] and are horrified to see how devoid of love this world, how fragmented our lives have become.

One way to approach Wisdom is to trace her in our own tradition, in the biblical sources and the testimony of individuals who were in touch with Divine Wisdom. The immediate, personal experience of Wisdom, divine Sophia, was always an exceptional condition in an emergency, a spiritual crisis, but also a state of grace difficult to communicate and invariably suspected by the Church. Yet there have been such persons almost at all times, women and men with an inner vision of Sophia. Whether they were aware of it or not, they were witnesses of a tradition that goes back to the Great Goddess, and never did these visionaries see Wisdom in other than female shape. As children of their time, they were restricted by patriarchal prejudice, as we shall see, yet they all beheld Her with eyes of love and reverence. Today the patriarchal prejudice is losing ground, and we are lucky that our broadened view permits us to look at Divine Wisdom with all her implications. Human consciousness is aching to expand on all levels. For the first time in history, we are called to synthesize past, present, and future and to develop a "diaphanous consciousness," as the late philosopher Jean Gebser termed it.[14] The present links up with past phenomena, sunk in oblivion for ages, to design a future in the "Eternal Now" of becoming.

---

[13] See Walter Schubart, *Religion und Eros* (Munich: C. H. Beck, 1966); Rudolf Steiner, *Die Suche nach der neuen Isis, der göttlichen Sophia* ["The Search for Isis, the Divine Sophia"] (Dornach: 1980).

[14] Jean Gebser, *The Ever-Present Origin: The Foundations & Manifestations of the Aperspectival World,* trans. by Noel Barstad and Algis Mickunas (Athens, OH: Ohio University Press, 1985).

In this book, I propose to highlight several strands of sophianic tradition in our culture and in non-Christian civilizations. This can only be done in brief outline, focusing on particular developments or representatives of sophianic vision. We shall, in succession, look at Lady Wisdom, or *chokhma* in Hebrew, in the Old Testament, in order to appreciate her complex physiognomy within the biblical environment. The special case of Lilith is intended to show what may become of the Great Goddess, if she is maligned and misinterpreted, and what kind of revenge she takes. The perverted Goddess, the female nightmare, the men-murdering and child-slaying demon is seen to haunt humanity to this day. Next I would like to focus on some inspired visionaries of Christian history, and demonstrate their struggle to restore Sophia to the Christian intuition of the Divine, and to show the lack of wisdom which by necessity contaminated her image. Chapter Four is dedicated to Otfried Eberz, the great German sophiologist of this century, who is little known even in his native land. With remarkably clear perception this scholar and lifelong student of mythology, history, and religion, penetrated the ancient myths to locate the origins of Sophia, and devoted all his work to her recovery. No feminist of our day could be a more ardent admirer of the Feminine Wisdom of God, or address a more radical appeal to modern women to reclaim consciousness of the Goddess. Otfried Eberz is a prophet of an emerging Feminine Age, which does not mean the advent of a new matriarchy (if there ever was one), and he knows the sophianic principles too well even to consider a shift toward matriarchy as a sort of reverse patriarchy as desirable.

A brief look at non-Christian traditions will show that the Feminine Divine is a universal intuition and in some cultures has been maintained to this day. Under different names and shapes the Great Goddess has remained the same, the *Magna Mater*, the Source of all life. Accordingly, one invocation of the Egyptian Goddess Isis was: "In All

Her Names!" We can only spell out some of these names and give only a few examples of her infinite variety, but if she has a message for our time, we are listening. She is already proving to be a powerful inspiration in our search for a transformed image of God. We know that her existence is not confined to prehistory, but that she is an eternal power notwithstanding her different shapes, as she strides "from revelation to revelation."

One does not have to leave the church or any formal religion in order to attract Sophia in a shape suitable for our time. No one has to turn their back on Christianity in order to be inspired and blessed by Sophia. She is unaffected by theological controversy and political setbacks. Such conflicts inevitably turn up wherever an old paradigm becomes brittle and a new one is beginning to take shape; wherever old patterns of thought cling to received doctrine, whereas new ways of thought claim the Spirit that "bloweth where it listeth." The struggle of women on the political front is important, but it cannot be fully liberating, because any political struggle is restricted to the immanence of its socio-political framework. Still, we need our sisters on the visible battlefront, just as we need feminist theologians and spiritual leaders. Some may be called to build or rebuild a vision of Sophia, to make her image come to life. This needs experience and a certain "sophianic" frame of mind. It needs the inward look and a familiarity with the sophianic tradition. To search for Sophia is a spiritual quest. When we are able to overcome the alienation from our inner sources, when in this predicament of estrangement from the patriarchal God of tradition Sophia is building a bridge to connect us again, because she does not divide body and soul, nature and spirit, the feminine and the masculine, Heaven and Earth, I and Thou, the sophianic movement of today may be of the greatest consequence. It is a liberation of God, of authentic creativity, of "Power of Being," as American feminists use the term, and as German lovers of Sophia have found it independently and given it exactly the same name—"Daseinsmacht." This coincidence is just another evidence that there is a sophianic movement today across national boundaries, despite the general backlash against the women's cause. This movement is all-embracing, it is concerned with every issue in our private and public lives. We have learned the lesson that "the private is the political." The modern sophianic movement, as the final stage of women's liberation, was initiated in the United States, and many of us in Germany were inspired by American feminist authors, our valiant and learned sisters who took the first step. I would like to add that the message of Sophia has deep roots in German culture, although it was forgotten like everywhere else. What we needed to do was to rediscover our own Sophianic visionaries, like Hildegard of Bingen and other mystics of the Middle Ages, Jacob Boehme after the Reformation, and most recently, Otfried Eberz, this solitary prophet in the wasteland of the '30s and throughout the nightmare of the Nazi era. Sophia is One, yet she will manifest in every culture with some difference, as we reclaim and recreate her in our imagination and in our hearts. The world needs Sophia. In her return, the original source of the past is transformed into the present and becomes a promise for the future.

Meditation

IT IS WELL TO RETURN TO THE SOURCE. It is well to trace what is hidden in our tradition, to bring back to light what has been forgotten, to recognize the great in what is small and barely noticed, to liberate the faded image from the dust and rubble of ages. Male cannot do without Female. Where the feminine element became invisible or distorted, it was cut off, driven underground, suppressed, and misrepresented. It was denied its rightful place. Why? How did it happen? There are many reasons we can think of, but ultimately they are but speculations, never conclusive evidence. What really happened, and how it happened in every instance, is buried in history. Besides, what would be the use if we knew for certain how, by what acts of violence, where for the first time and through whom, this transition from one world order to another, from one image of God to another was accomplished? A paradigm comes into being and has validity, until a new impulse calls for a change. It is like a ship changing course. For a long time it steered into a certain direction, until it got into troubled waters or ran aground. The charts no longer apply, the equipment is outdated and needs repair or replacement. The crew is tired, disoriented or—worst of all—intoxicated, and doesn't know what it is doing.

In this emergency, a vision is born to save the ship. The rediscovery of Sophia as Divine Wisdom is a creative response to the need of our time. In this age of transformation we have the choice either to take the final step toward destruction or to re-orient ourselves. For hundreds and thousands of years life has been wasted and violated, while new life was blossoming forth all the time. Today we reach out for the forces which honor life and preserve the creation.

Our image of God, so abstract and remote, has done us harm. The Divine withdrew from the Earth, the feminine creative power was neglected, so that the Earth that nurtures all of us, was raped and exploited, and human beings are violated, mistreated and murdered by their own kind until today. So that everything which is weaker or was weakened and exposed to contempt—like woman, the body, or nature—has been marginalized as inferior, and excluded from full participation in the likeness of the Divine. Life may be confusing and painful, history is full of contradictions, but there is also a measure of justice, beauty, love, and reverence in the present as in the past. Beauty seems to be fading from our world, just as the possibility of leading a peaceful life in a sound environment is decreasing steadily, whereas there is more violence and destruction everywhere. The end of the Cold War did not bring the desired world peace. How could it have?

We approach the sources of our tradition with a sense of mourning for what has been lost, but also with passion. What human license, often camouflaged as the will of God, has suppressed, may be brought to light again. We read the Scriptures with fresh eyes in our endeavor to distinguish historical contingency from genuine revelation. Our search is for a complete, holistic image of God, not in his maleness, not as a ruler, but as all-embracing motherliness and creativeness, so that all human beings, women and men of all races, may recognize their likeness in the image of God. If God is not within us, if God is not on Earth or in any particle of creation, he is not anywhere. We search for God in Wisdom, and what we find is exciting. It fills us with a sense of wonder and joy.

Chapter One

LADY WISDOM

FOR A LONG TIME EXEGESIS HAD little to say about Wisdom, who makes such a splendid and extraordinary appearance in the Old Testament, in the books of Proverbs, Ecclesiastes and the Book of Job. The apocryphal books, featuring the Wisdom of Solomon, Ecclesiasticus (or Wisdom of Jesus, son of Sirach) and Baruch, are part of the hidden or spurious tradition which does not belong to the proper canon of Holy Scripture. These books were not admitted to the Hebrew and the Lutheran Bible, and therefore theology paid comparatively little attention to them. Not until this century did interest in this remarkable figure of Wisdom arise on a large scale. During the last two decades, feminist theology rediscovered her with passion. In Wisdom—"Sophia" in Greek, "Chokhma" in Hebrew—as revealed in the Old Testament, there is an element of what women today, and not only women, fervently seek: the "grounding," as it were, of a God lost in abstractions, his proximity to human beings, the motherliness which was appropriated by Jahve in a rudimentary form, but embodied more convincingly by Jesus Christ. However, the fact that Jesus was a male has been used as an argument against women, to deny them their full share in the likeness of God.

1

It has been said that Auschwitz, or Hiroshima, shattered once and for all the traditional image of God. Where was God almighty, all-knowing and all-kind in the face of these unspeakable atrocities? Is our image of God, passed on by tradition and interpreted in official doctrine, reflected on a level of abstraction which only initiates, professional theologians, are able to follow, not hopelessly deficient? A search for new images of God has set in. Lay people, not academic theologians, started to read the Bible with fresh eyes, to find what is missing, what was lost during two thousand years of Christian history and even for many centuries before that period. Many of us who hardly knew the Old Testament discovered the beauty, as well as the ambiguity, of a tradition, which is the Jewish as well as the Christian heritage. We experienced the tremendous power of the Word, the passionate drama enacted between man and God. In these biblical battles and crises, in wars and calamities, a God was born, "revealed" in biblical language: "I am; that is who I am,"[1] who refuses to be named or to be represented by an image, a God of law and order. Israel, his chosen people, could not have lasted or preserved its identity in any other way. Surrounded by alien nations who worshipped other gods, threatened and defeated time and again, this people had no choice but to exalt God as the supreme Ruler, the Lord and the King, who commands obedience and metes out punishment to those who offend against his law. Moses, the man of God, constantly has to mediate between the angry God and his unfaithful people and to hold it to the law and the commandments of the Lord, and "thereby you will display your wisdom and understanding to other peoples" (Deut. 4:6).

After the exodus from Egypt, Moses led the people of Israel through the desert for forty years, a long time of preparation and antic-

---

[1] Or: "I will be what I will be" (Exod. 3:14). All quotations from the Bible are from *The New English Bible* (Great Britain: Oxford University Press/ Cambridge University Press, 1970).

ipation, a time of learning and discipline. It needed heavenly signs and miracles to keep this stubborn and unsteady people in line. They worshipped heathen gods, especially goddesses; in the golden bull-calf they paid tribute to Baal, who was part of the goddess cult; they complained and hankered after the fleshpots of Egypt. It was a tough job to persuade the Israelites to keep the covenant with God: "For the Lord your God is a devouring fire, a jealous god" (Deut. 4:24). This God appears at times more like a tribal chief or warlord, ranting and railing, administering justice and punishment, but he can also be forgiving and bountiful. This is a harsh and eminently masculine God, a severe, but just Lord. The love he bears his people is demonstrated in acts of kindness, but it remains the love of a patriarch to his children. To his minor *sons*, it should be added, because the partners in this dialog with God are only the sons, not the daughters of Israel. They are "included" in his address, as they were "included" in Christianity more than three thousand years later.

Why is this people so stubborn and unfaithful to God? The tribes of Israel and Judah lived in close proximity with heathen peoples. They had spent a long time in Egypt, one of the most highly-developed cultures of the ancient world, where a different order prevailed. Here, the Goddess Isis was the creatrix of the world, and together with her brother-consort Osiris, she integrated the process of becoming and decaying, the secrets of life and death, in the loving union of woman and man, the *hieros gamos*, the sacred wedding. In all cults of the ancient Goddess of the Orient, the sacred wedding, the union of the Goddess with her male partner, plays a central part. In Sumer it is Innana and her Son-Lover Dumuzi, succeeded by the Assyrian-Babylonian Ishtar and Tammuz. In Asia Minor the principal Goddess was Kybele, who was worshipped in Rome as Magna Mater, the Great Mother. The Great Goddess of the Phoenicians, Philistines, and Moabites was Astarte or Asherah, and some of the Israelites still adhered to these cults from time immemorial.

Alexander the Great pushed the influence of Greek culture as far as Egypt, and with Greek philosophy also the myths of the Greek gods spread throughout the Mediterranean. Besides Zeus, the "father of the gods," there was Demeter of much older lineage, the goddess of fertility and transformation. The Eleusinian mysteries, performed until the fourth century of the Christian era, were dedicated to her and her daughter Persephone. Demeter is a powerful goddess. She stands for life, itself, and knows the secrets of death and resurrection, but—as the myth shows—her power was already broken by male violence. We only mention the Goddesses Pallas Athene, the Greek Goddess of Wisdom, and Hera, the consort of Zeus. Both can be traced to pre-patriarchal religion, but became so deformed by the Greek influence that it is hard to recognize their original character. Especially Pallas Athene, who sprang from the head of Zeus, is very masculine in character and hardly represents Wisdom in the ancient sense.

Something similar happened to Isis, next to Demeter the most important Goddess of the Hellenistic era. Seth, her adversary, abducted and killed Osiris, and Isis set out to find him, and restored his dismembered body to life. There are other great goddesses at her side, like cow-horned Hathor or Maat, the Goddess of "Truth, Law and Order." To this category of female deities belongs also Nut, the "Goddess of Heaven," who arches her body over the disk of the earth and feeds the earth with milk flowing from her breasts. Corresponding to these powerful goddesses, women in Egypt held positions of honor. Their lives were largely self-determined. Women could be traders, craftswomen, artists, priestesses, and of course there were queens. By comparison, the daughters of Israel did not do nearly so well.

Jahve had to fight the matriarchal system, or rather: the woman-centered order. He never tires of ranting against the cults of the Goddess, and to condemn them as harlotry, an abomination in the eyes of the Lord. On the other hand, he cannot prevent that ideas from the old myths enter into the concept of Wisdom, which—as we have seen— is a feminine intuition in Hebrew (Chokhma) as well as in Greek (Sophia). In this environment, Wisdom emerges as an autonomous person. Her physiognomy is a complex one due to the long history of her development and various influences from outside.

The Wisdom tradition bearing witness to her emerged after the Babylonian captivity of the sixth century B.C. and took centuries to be recorded in written script. The deportation to Babylon was a time of great existential insecurity for the Israelites. The highest class of the population, including craftsmen, but not the priests, were deported by Nebuchadnezzar. This exile did not necessarily threaten the lives of the Israelites, but it was a shattering experience, and the loss of their home and their religion was a calamity. In their new environment, they were confronted with the cult of the Goddess, and without the spiritual guidance of their priests they were continuously tempted to adapt to foreign customs. It is in this context that Wisdom raised her voice.

In Proverbs, the oldest Book of Wisdom, she at first represents instruction, reprimand and fear of the Lord. It is wise to avoid evil. Wisdom calls for penance. She admonishes fools, simpletons and sluggards to keep to the path of righteousness. Those who do not heed her advice will have to bear the consequences, and Wisdom will withdraw from them. She addresses herself to her "sons" and to "men" in general. The seeker of wisdom, the good and the just will find her. It is wisdom in the aspect of prudence and shrewdness, the bestower of good things. As such, she is "more precious than red coral" (Proverbs 3:15). She reveals herself in her own person:

> I am Wisdom, I bestow shrewdness
> and show the way to knowledge and prudence.

Pride, presumption, evil courses,
subversive talk, all these I hate.
I have force, I also have ability;
understanding and power are mine.
Through me kings are sovereign
and governors make just laws.
Through me princes act like princes,
from me all rulers on earth derive their nobility.
Those who love me I love,
those who search for me find me.
In my hands are riches and honour,
boundless wealth and the rewards of virtue,

. . .

my path is the path of justice;
I endow with riches those who love me
and I will fill their treasuries.

(Proverbs 8:12-21)

We note in this text that Wisdom *loves* human beings. Not only does she reward the good as they deserve, but she likes to be with human beings and enjoys their company. She mediates between God and men; her dwelling place, her joyful residence is on earth amid human beings—provided she is well received.

In the same chapter there is something entirely new: Wisdom, pervading all spheres of profane life, suddenly acquires a theological quality:

The Lord created me the beginning of his works,
before all else that he made, long ago.
Alone I was fashioned in times long past,
at the beginning, long before earth itself.

Where there was yet no ocean I was born,
no springs brimming with water.
Before the mountains were settled in their place,
long before the hills I was born,
when as yet he had neither made land nor lake
nor the first clod of earth.
When he set the heavens in their place I was there,
when he girdled the ocean with the horizon,
when he fixed the canopy of clouds overhead
and set the springs of ocean firm in their place,
when he prescribed its limits for the sea
and knit together earth's foundations.
Then I was at his side each day,
his darling and delight,
playing in his presence continually.

(Proverbs 8:22-30)

Wisdom, unmistakably female, is seen to maintain a close, in fact a loving relationship with God. She is his "darling" and his "delight." She watches over his creation, because she was there, before God made the earth—before all time. The Hebrew word *amon* (darling) was also rendered as "confidant" or "beloved" or "lover" in German translations. Martin Luther lost this intimacy by using the word "Werkmeister" ("foreman," or "master mechanic") in his translation of the Bible, following the Greek and Latin versions. In this interpretation, Wisdom as helpmate of God is emphasized, but the love relationship, which Michelangelo portrayed so naturally in his fresco in the Sistine Chapel, is lost. The artist's nude female figure suggests more the lover than the master mechanic or "[W]isdom, who sits beside thy throne" (Wisdom 9:4). God and Lady Wisdom, as a pair of lovers, are an uncustomary image in biblical tradition. It does not fit in with the spirit of law and discipline and the fear of the Lord. There is no doubt that Lady Wisdom as God's beloved was inspired by an older conception of the Divine from the environment of the goddess cult, as it is preserved in the Song of Songs.

In the old religion, God was conceived as a divine couple, and the Goddess had precedence over the male God. He was integrated in her love and her works on Earth. There was no hierarchy of power in this relationship, but it was based on love, and the primary creative force was beyond dispute the Feminine Divine. The authors of the Old Testament could not go as far as this, but the Feminine conceived as Divine Wisdom is indeed close to God. In some way not precisely defined, she has a share in the act of creation. Furthermore, she loves human beings and blesses them with her bountiful gifts.

Besides this highlight of Lady Wisdom's self-revelation there are frequent attacks on the "foreign woman" and "Lady Stupidity," the shadow of the positive feminine archetype. We read, for example:

> The Lady Stupidity is a flighty creature;
> the simpleton, she cares for nothing.
> She sits at the door of her house,
> on a seat in the highest part of the town,
> to invite the passers-by indoors
> as they hurry on their way:
> "Come in, you simpletons," she says.
> She says also to the fool,
> "Stolen water is sweet
> and bread got by stealth tastes good."
> Little does he know that death lurks there,
> that her guests are in the depths of Sheol.
>
> (Proverbs 9:13-18)

Gerda Weiler called attention to the patriarchal devaluation of ancient matriarchal rituals.[2] The woman in the window or in front of her door represents the high priestess who invites the lover to the sacred ritual. Through her, he used to receive divine initiation, because the mysterious force which is at work in all life, in all processes of becoming and growing, is opened up through love. "Love wove human existence into the cosmic order and ensured the maintenance of life . . ."[3] The "seat in the highest part of the town" may indicate yet another tradition.[4] From ancient Egypt there are reports of a ritual race around the walls, which ended with the triumphal entry of the king through the city gate. The queen received him in priestly robes and adornments. As Gerda Weiler says, the "queen in the window"—or, as in our biblical text on her "seat in the highest part of the town"—is the "ritual gesture, which since archaic times carried the message of an invitation to the sacred marriage."[5] In many cultures, the queen offers a drink to the newcomer. Also Lady Stupidity entices men with a drink: "Stolen water is sweet." This implies that the drink which she has to offer is not hers, but "stolen." In the biblical text the sacred rite is defiled as an act of prostitution, the queen or priestess is degraded as a harlot, and what once was supreme wisdom is now called "stupidity." The new Wisdom is still splendid in her closeness to God, but she is definitely no longer the autonomous Feminine who gives her love as a free gift to her chosen consort. The new Lady Wisdom turns away from eros. She favors those who keep the law and live in the fear of the Lord.

The "foreign woman" is forever associated with harlotry and idolatry, and there are constant injunctions against the worship of idols:

---

[2] Gerda Weiler, *Der enteignete Mythos* ["The Disinherited Myth"] (Frankfurt-New York: Campus, 1991), pp. 152-157.

[3] Weiler, *Der enteignete Mythos*, p. 154 (translation mine).

[4] *Der enteignete Mythos*, p. 155.

[5] *Der enteignete Mythos*, p. 155 (translation mine).

"The invention of idols is the root of immorality"(Wisdom 14:12). The foreign woman meets incautious men "dressed like a prostitute." She is "full of wiles, flighty and inconstant," she kisses the stranger and lures him into her house: "I have spread coverings on my bed in colored linen from Egypt" (Proverbs 7:16). The Egyptian coverings are reminiscent, of course, of the cult of Isis, which the Israelites came to know during their Egyptian exile, and which still flourished for centuries.

Not only the idolatress and harlot is castigated in the Proverbs, but woman as such. It is a tedious litany:

Like a gold ring in a pig's snout
is a beautiful woman without good sense (11:22).

The wisest women build up their homes;
the foolish pull them down with their own hands (14:1).

A capable wife is her husband's crown;
one who disgraces him is like rot in his bones (12:4).

[A] nagging wife is like water dripping endlessly (19:13).

Endless dripping on a rainy day—
that is what a nagging wife is like (27:15).

Better to live in a corner of the house-top
than have a nagging wife . . . (21:9 and 25:24).

Better to live alone in the desert
than with a nagging and ill-tempered wife (21:19).

The words of an adulteress are like a deep pit;
those whom the Lord has cursed will fall into it (22:14).

A prostitute is a deep pit,
a loose woman a narrow well (23:27).

Conversely, there is not a single commentary on what a disgraceful man may do to a woman. It is remarkable how often "nagging wives" are blamed and lashed out against. Up to this day, it is a patriarchal topos that women, especially wives, are "nagging." As this is mentioned so often in Proverbs, one might ask the question just what made women in ancient Israel so shrewish? It is conceivable that this habit, if it was one, was due to their general condition of life. A woman in Israel was not entirely without rights, but compared to male prerogatives, her rights were greatly limited. He, at any rate, had the right to dispose of her.[6] Furthermore, we might ask if women, living in a cultural environment where the old faith of the Goddess was still alive and where women held a high social position, did not suffer from this subjection to patriarchal law and order. The tragedy of women in a male-dominated world, the continuous violence against women, still exists. Her complaint, which is not heard in a man's world, which is ridiculed and trivialized, has not ceased. Many a "nagging wife" feels deserted in a world in which her deepest concerns are despised and betrayed. Did the women of Israel, who were much closer to the radical change of a woman-centered society to a male-dominated order than we are today, not have every reason in the world to complain?

The greatest part of Proverbs (chapters 10-30) consists of rules to live by in pointed aphorisms. Often, Wisdom does not appear to be more than a pragmatic shrewdness as opposed to foolishness. The godless person will be castigated. If necessary, wisdom has to be whipped into the young and foolish. This kind of wisdom comes to resemble more and

---

[6] The most horrid example of unexpiated male violence against women in ancient Israel is the fate of the Levite's concubine (Judges 19:22-29). The retribution for the crime against this woman—gang rape resulting in her death—does not consist in punishment of the guilty, but in a wild massacre, in the robbery and rape of yet more women. There are other passages in the Old Testament where women are turned over by their husbands or fathers to be raped (see Genesis 19:18).

more simple obedience and piety. She appears as moral law, not as that high spiritual entity that raised her voice in those magnificent verses of chapter 8 in Proverbs. The Book ends with the praise of the capable wife. She keeps herself busy from morning to night and increases her husband's property. She applies herself to her household duties with vigor and industry. She provides against the lean season of winter and is generous to the poor. "When she opens her mouth, it is to speak wisely, and loyalty is the theme of her teaching"(Proverbs 31:26). Divine Wisdom has been turned into a chaste and thrifty housewife for her husband's honor and glory. She certainly is impressive and commendable in many ways, but can narrow virtue and the fear of the Lord really express feminine autonomy, her former playful participation in the works of creation and her unquestioned divine status?

The interpretation of Wisdom as practical prudence in the affairs of daily life predominates to a degree that makes us wonder what this striking discrepancy really means. The utterance of Divine Wisdom looms sky-high above those qualities which are called "wisdom" in the greatest part of Proverbs. There are similar highlights in other books of the wisdom tradition, as in the Wisdom of Solomon. This is considered the youngest Wisdom Book and was composed in Greek by a Jewish teacher of wisdom in Alexandria, the great center of Hellenistic culture, about 100 B.C. By that time, Wisdom-Sophia ranked highly in Greek philosophy as an ideal with a long tradition. To attain wisdom was the highest aspiration of a Greek philosopher. The term "philo-sophy" itself means "love of wisdom," and consequently the philosopher is a "friend of wisdom." In the course of time Sophia was elevated to the sublime realm of ideals, which can only be approached, but never completely realized by man. In Greek thought she had withdrawn to the region of Platonic ideas, spiritual entities which humans can only approach by reflection.

We may assume that the author of the Wisdom of Solomon, a Hellenized Jew, was familiar with this tradition. Solomon, the prototype of all seekers of wisdom, prays for Wisdom, and he attains her. Wisdom is "a spirit devoted to man's good" (Wisdom 1:6); she is a "holy spirit of discipline" (Wisdom 1:5). Solomon loves Wisdom so much that she means more to him than all other goods, more than scepter and crown, wealth, jewels and gold, health and beauty of appearance, even more than the light, the source of life. She does not only bestow these goods, but she is also their creatress. She leads the seeker of Wisdom to knowledge of all things: "I learnt it all, hidden or manifest, for I was taught by her whose skill made all things, wisdom" (Wisdom 7:21). Wisdom does not reveal herself here, but the philosopher, her friend, knows her by her very nature:

> For in wisdom there is a spirit intelligent and holy, unique in its kind yet made up of many parts, subtle, free-moving, lucid, spotless, clear, invulnerable, loving what is good, eager, unhindered, beneficent, kindly towards men, steadfast, unerring, untouched by care, all-powerful, all-surveying, and permeating all intelligent, pure, and delicate spirits.
>
> (Wisdom 7:22f)

Wisdom appears as a truly divine power. In fact, she is "initiated into the knowledge that belongs to God, and she decides for him what he shall do" (8:4). She sits beside God's throne (9:4), and "the Lord of all things has accepted her" (8:3). She is the beloved sharer of his throne and directs his hand—so it appears. However, this would be too daring, and so another passage states: "For even wisdom is under God's direction" (7:15). She is like a fine mist that "rises from the power of God, a pure effluence from the glory of the Almighty" (7:25); she is "the flawless mirror of the active power of God and the image of his goodness" (7:26). This is Platonic thought: Behind and above the idea of Sophia, there is God, as an idea even more elevated, and she is but his reflection and flawless mirror. According to Greek thought, she might remove herself to an unapproachable realm, if it were not for her manifold works, her love of human beings and men's love of her. The relationship of the seeker of wisdom to Sophia is an openly erotic one:

> Wisdom I loved; I sought her out when I was young and longed to win her for my bride, and I fell in love with her beauty.
>
> (Wisdom 8:2)

The seeker of wisdom is determined "to bring her home to live with me" (8:9). From the battlefield and the turmoil of the world he will come home to find rest with her, "for there is no bitterness in her company, no pain in life with her, only gladness and joy" (8:16). Indeed, he speaks of her as of a dearly beloved wife.

On the other hand, Wisdom is associated with the fear of God, as in other Books of Wisdom, and people are divided into two categories, the just and the godless. Also in this book there is strict warning against the folly of idol worship as an abomination in the eyes of the Lord. Idolatry is identified with human sacrifice, prostitution, general looseness of morals, and every kind of debauchery and crime. So great is the need, even in this book, for setting up a defense against the heathens and their goddess cults, that any accusation may be brought forward. There is an allusion to suspicious, secret services, "frenzied orgies of unnatural cults" (14:23).

It may be assumed that the author had the ancient Mysteries in mind. As a Hellenized Jew he would have known about the Eleusinian Mysteries, the spiritual center of the Hellenistic world. Thousands of people participated in the annual event. The rites were kept secret, and

no initiate came away without a profound change of character and outlook on life and death. As initiates were prohibited on pain of death to
disclose anything about the rites performed in the temple of Eleusis,
wild rumors must have spread about the Mysteries, especially on the
part of those who, like the Israelites, had no access to this cultural world.
Today we know that an intoxicating potion of the ergot of rye, water,
and mint evoked a vision of the resurrection of Persephone in the consciousness of the initiates and led to a deep experience of the mysteries
of life and death.[7] The key figures in the Mysteries were Demeter,
Goddess of Fertility, her daughter Persephone and Hecate, the old
Moon Goddess. Together, these three form the Trinity of the Greek
Goddess myth: virgin, mother and crone (wise old woman). This divine
feminine triad must have been abominable in the eyes of the God of
Israel, just like the goddesses of Egypt and the Near East. As we have
seen, the people who succumbed time and again to the temptation of
idolatry had to be reprimanded harshly and kept away from the cult of
the "foreign woman" by all means of deterrence, including slander.

Wisdom, however, is revealed as a totally different entity. There is
still something of the Divine in her, but it remains unclear just to what
extent she is divine. In no instance does she receive the name of a
Goddess, even though the passionate, poetical glorifications in the
Books of Wisdom practically confer the status of Goddess on her. By
and by she takes on the qualities of other Goddesses, especially the
Egyptian Isis and Maat, as feminist theologians have suggested.[8] The
utterance of Isis in an Egyptian song of praise bears a striking resemblance to the self-revelations of the biblical Lady Wisdom in her co-cre-
ative, cosmic aspect, as the following text shows:

---

[7] See R. Gordon Wasson, Albert Hofmann, Carl A. P. Ruck, *Der Weg nach Eleusis* ["The
Way to Eleusis"] (Frankfurt: Insel, 1984).

[8] See Joan Chamberlain Engelsman, *The Feminine Dimension of the Divine* (Philadelphia:
Westminster Press, 1979).

I am Isis, the mistress of every land . . .

I gave and ordained laws for men, which no one is able to change.

I divided the earth from the heaven.

I showed the paths of the stars.

I ordered the course of the sun and the moon.

I divised business in the sea.

I made strong the right.

I brought together woman and man.

I revealed mysteries unto men.

I made the right to be stronger than gold and silver.

I ordained that the right should be thought good.

I established penalties for those who practice injustice.

I decreed mercy to suppliants.

With me right prevails.

I am the Queen of rivers and winds and sea.

I am the Queen of the thunderbolt.

I stir up the sea and I calm it.

I am the rays of the sun.

I overcome Fate.

Fate harkens to me.

Hail, O Egypt, that nourished me![9]

Isis claims absolute and unrestricted divinity as creatress of the universe.

In the praise of Wisdom in Ecclesiasticus (Wisdom of Jesus, son of Sirach), Sophia reveals herself yet another time as an independent divine power. The book dates from the second century B.C. and is thus a relatively young document. The most voluminous of all the Books of Wisdom, it is first of all a compendium on the right conduct of life. We

---

[9] The text is actually much longer than this excerpt, quoted in Engelsman, pp. 64-66.

are told in the beginning that the author, a man well-versed in Hellenistic and heathen lore with its multitude of deities, was an ardent student of the law, the Prophets, and the other Books of the Fathers, and from their knowledge he drew wisdom, for wisdom is acquired by *study* (Sirach 9:1). The seeker of wisdom relies on the authorities, not on the voice of his own heart or of his conscience. These maxims convey a great sense of security and serenity, and we are frequently reminded that the beginning of all wisdom is the fear of the Lord and "includes the fulfilling of the law" (Sirach 19:21). This kind of wisdom is largely mundane. It is prudence as shown in the right way of life. "Wisdom raises her sons to greatness and cares for those who seek her. To love her is to love life; to rise early for her sake is to be filled with joy" (Sirach 4:11-12). In the middle of the book, Wisdom suddenly reveals herself as a higher entity:

> I am the Word which was spoken by the Most High;
> it was I who covered the earth like a mist.
> My dwelling-place was in high heaven;
> my throne was in a pillar of cloud.
> Alone I made a circuit of the sky
> and traversed the depth of the abyss.
> The waves of the sea, the whole earth,
> every people and nation were under my sway.
> Among them all I looked for a home...
> I took root among the people whom the Lord had honored
> by choosing them to be his special possession.
>
> (Sirach 24:3-6,12)

Once again, this testimony stirs memories of the Great Goddess. In her comparisons with a variety of trees, the old dwelling-place of the Goddess, Wisdom aligns herself with the ancient goddesses.

There I grew like a cedar of Lebanon,
like a cypress on the slopes of Hermon,
like a date-palm at Engedi,
like roses at Jericho.
I grew like a fair olive-tree in the vale,
or like a plane-tree planted beside the water.
Like a terebinth I spread out my branches,
laden with honor and grace.
I put forth lovely shoots like the vine,
and my blossoms were a harvest of wealth and honor.

(Sirach 24:13-14, 16-17)

Hills and groves used to be the favorite sanctuaries of the Goddess. Trees, symbols of fertility and the eternal cycle of becoming and decaying, were sacred to her. To the Lord, who gave his law to the people through Moses, these places of worship and tree sanctuaries were execrable, and he ordered them to be destroyed "on mountain-tops and hills and under every spreading tree" (Deut. 12:2). Yet Wisdom holds on to trees and proclaims her beauty and fruitfulness through this metaphor.

Apart from these peaks of a direct utterance of Wisdom, the book Ecclesiasticus is very patriarchal. The warnings and admonitions to embrace Wisdom are addressed exclusively to men, and there is no dearth of invectives against women as the origin of all sin (25:18,32; 26:9-14). There are also affirmations of the value of a good woman (36:24-27), but the overall impression is that of a sharp split of the Feminine into a divine being on the one hand, elevated as God's consort in the sharing of his throne, his beloved and co-creatress, and of the concrete, human woman on the other hand, the source of evil. A strange contradiction is being established: The ancient Goddess, once the measure of woman's high ontological rank, has to be fought relentlessly, but her divine attributes enter with almost literal accuracy into the revelation and the concept of Wisdom. Concrete womanhood is suspect, to say the least; it has to be put down and subjected to men's rule. The fear of the "wild, untamed" woman is palpable, especially of the kind who still adheres to the old religion, the autonomous woman, the "sorceress," who, according to the law of Moses, is to be put to death.

In this heterogeneous milieu, deeply split by patriarchal thinking, Lady Wisdom makes her appearance as a divine person, furnished with attributes of regal power and sublimity. Consciously or unconsciously, she has absorbed the qualities of the old Goddesses, and simultaneously, as the younger wisdom texts of the Old Testament show, the spirit of the Greek philosophical concept of *sophia*. She wavers between a godlike figure and the homely housewife, faithfully fulfilling the law, a model of virtue and industry. On the one hand, the Great Goddess continues to exist in Wisdom, but on the other, she is reduced to profane prudence and narrow morality. On the one hand, the feminine is divine; on the other, it is rotten and "the beginning of all sin." This split has run its fateful course in Christianity. It lifted the Virgin Mary into heaven, whereas the ordinary human woman fell prey to male prejudice and misogyny. Three hundred years of persecuting women as witches are the most terrible proof of this schizophrenia.

However, the manifestations of Wisdom are still more varied. Although she loves to associate with humans, she is also seen to withdraw from them. In the Book of Job, one of the oldest wisdom texts, she is hidden, out of man's reach like happiness or God himself, who strikes the just with calamity and refuses to justify his actions. As obscure as God's ways, as impenetrable for man, is the dwelling place of Wisdom. In verses of imperishable poetical beauty, the places are stated where she is *not*:

Sophia

There are mines for silver
and places where men refine gold;
where iron is won from the earth
and copper smelted from the ore;
the end of the seam lies in darkness,
and it is followed to its farthest limit.
Strangers cut the galleries;
they are forgotten as they drive forward far from men.
While corn is springing from the earth above,
what lies beneath is raked over like a fire,
and out of its rocks comes lapis lazuli,
dusted with flecks of gold.
No bird of prey knows the way there,
and the falcon's keen eye cannot descry it;
proud beasts do not set foot on it,
and no serpent comes that way.
Man sets his hand to the granite rock
and lays bare the roots of the mountains;
he cuts galleries in the rocks,
and gems of every kind meet his eye;
he dams up the sources of the streams
and brings the hidden riches of the earth to light.
But where can wisdom be found?
And where is the source of understanding?
No man knows the way to it;
it is not found in the land of living men.
The depths of ocean say: "It is not in us,"
and the sea says: "It is not with me."
Red gold cannot buy it,
nor can its price be weighed out in silver . . .

(Job 28:1-15)

20

Wisdom is more precious than gold and gems, but "no creature on earth can see it" (28:21). Only God knows the way, because he saw her, as he was creating the world. In an unspecified way, she is his creature too: "Even then he saw wisdom and took stock of it,/ he considered it and fathomed its very depths" (28:27). These words waver curiously between a created and an uncreated figure existing in her own right before creation. An important point is made at the end of the chapter:

> The fear of the Lord is wisdom,
> and to turn from evil is understanding.
>
> (Job 28:28)

The chapter about Wisdom, thrown into the tragic conflict between man and God out of any recognizable context, leaves a strange impression. Why is wisdom mentioned at all at this point in the story? What sense does it make to clamp down on Job in his plight and to tell him jeeringly that he knows nothing and, indeed, can never know anything about wisdom except through God, who remains obscure and unintelligible? Could it be that Wisdom made herself invisible because Jahve usurped dominion over her, whereas formerly she lived freely on mountain tops and in trees, visible to all who would find her?

Despite magnificent imagery, Wisdom in the Book of Job remains as alarmingly obscure as God, himself. However, for humanity today, there is a clear and very definite message: to dig up the bowels of the earth, to turn her upside down, to trample upon her and destroy her, does not lead to Wisdom. On the contrary, the frenzied desire for gold and metals will induce Wisdom to withdraw and make herself invisible, so that she cannot be found anywhere on Earth, nor in the depths of the sea. The text admits a variety of interpretations.

The book Baruch gives clear reasons for her obscurity. This very slender book was written during the Babylonian captivity which God had imposed on his rebellious people as a penance for "sacrificing to demons" once again (Baruch 4:7). They had deserted the source of Wisdom, and so she left them. "Has any man discovered the dwelling-place of wisdom or entered her storehouse"(3:15)? The hidden wisdom is described in similar images as in the Book of Job. God, who knows all things, also knows Wisdom. As the "whole way of knowledge," he bestowed her on "Jacob his servant and to Israel, whom he loved" (3:36). "Thereupon wisdom appeared on earth and lived among men" (3:37). She withdrew, because men deliberately deserted her. She can be regained, if the heart seeks her earnestly. A return to wisdom is called for, and if Israel will hang on to her, it will fare better.

Then follows the Letter of Jeremiah with his harangue against idolatry, forever associated with loose women. He tries to convince the Israelites by all means at his disposal that those foreign idols have no power and are nothing but a fraud. He would hardly put himself to so much trouble, if the danger did not appear terrifying to him. What makes idolatry especially obnoxious is its association with women. Wherever there is idolatry, women are involved, and in the view of the prophet, this means prostitution and every kind of immorality. The ritual impurity of women, defined by law, was not shared by the neighboring peoples. In their society women held a high rank as priestesses. The *hierodules*, the maidens consecrated to the temple, were degraded as temple prostitutes by the monotheistic father religions, and this interpretation is prevalent even today. The contemptuous term "temple prostitution" obscures the venerable ancient cult of *hieros gamos*, the sacred wedding, the center of all goddess cults. If the old religion is to be devalued, the thrust must be aimed against this center, and the women involved in it must be given a bad name. Jeremiah does his best to accomplish this goal. His best argument, in the effort to expose the idols as non-existent bogeys, is the fact that unclean women and mothers fresh from childbed are allowed to touch the offerings. "Be assured by all this that they are not gods, and have no fear of them" (6:29). Unclean women, as defined by Mosaic law, are those who have "a discharge of blood," and this state of impurity lasts for seven days (Leviticus 15:19). Unclean is everything the woman touches, and unclean is everyone who touches her or any object she has touched. The strongest injunction is on sexual intercourse during this time.

> If a man lies with a woman during her monthly period and brings shame upon her, he has exposed her discharge and she has uncovered the source of her discharge; they shall both be cut off from their people.
>
> (Leviticus 20:18)

The meaning of the verb "cut off," so frequently used in the Law of Moses, is somewhat ambiguous, but generally the Hebrew word *karat*, "cut off," implies capital punishment. To mingle masculine semen, or potency, with female blood, is the greatest sacrilege. Blood is not the same as blood. There is no way to overlook the fact that in the Old Testament there is constant shedding of blood. Brother slays brother, murders are committed, bloody acts of revenge take place, there is the constant threat of the "keenness of the sword," and the Lord himself eradicates nations in order to make room for his chosen people in the Promised Land. Not to mention the blood of sacrificial animals, which must be shed according to meticulously prescribed rituals.

More than other laws, the laws about offerings and sacrifices are specified in minute detail. The altar and the curtain of the sanctuary are to be sprinkled with blood; the horns of the altar are to be smeared with blood, and the rest has to be poured at the base of the altar. There is no denying that the sanctuaries of the God of Israel are fairly dripping with blood, decreed by himself by irrevocable law. The only blood, however, which is not shed by an external act of violence, which flows naturally, the blood of women during their period of menstruation and in child-birth, in other words: the life-giving blood, is sanctioned by the greatest taboo.

This sanction against female blood is continued in Christianity and prevails even today, after the most profound reason for this taboo, the replacement of the goddess-centered world order by patriarchal rule, has been brought to light.[10] It reveals a downright hysterical fear of the female body, and its natural functions, in the service of its numinous ability to produce life. The mystery of the blood still divides those who cling to the patriarchal image of God from those who embrace a more holistic view, with disastrous results for humanity—and for God.

When considering Wisdom-Chokhma-Sophia, as she is revealed in the Wisdom Books of the biblical tradition, we cannot leave the concrete woman in this tradition out of the picture. "Lady Wisdom" is seen against a gradually fading matrifocal milieu, as she enters the patriarchal age. From the depth of the human spirit she is conceived as feminine. In the tradition of the Old Testament, where disruptions, the struggle of the new against the old, are so apparent, Wisdom in her physical and spiritual appearance is definitely a feminine figure. The realism of the people of Israel and their sensuous power of speech saved them from those lifeless abstractions which finally absorbed the Feminine into the patriarchal image of God and consolidated the split between the Feminine Divine and the concrete earthly woman.

---

[10] As can be seen by the controversial reception of *Das Schwarzmondtabu* ["The Taboo of the Black Moon"] (Stuttgart: Kreuz Verlag, 1988) by Jutta Voss, a Lutheran minister and psychotherapist. Three years after publication of the book, the Protestant Church of Germany saw fit to take disciplinary proceedings against the author, which resulted in the loss of her ministry and the right to teach religion. Jutta Voss now runs her own wellness center for women.

Wisdom survives as Divine Wisdom, potent, gracious, lovely, powerful-in-action, beloved by God and mankind. Wisdom is the link between God and creation. She is rooted in God, but she dwells with men, unless they drive her away.

Let us call to mind just once more the wealth of images and readings of biblical wisdom. In the highest vision she is not simply an attribute of God, but a divine person in her own right of undefined origin. (Only once, in the passage already quoted from Sirach 24:4, do we find the statement that she is "the Word which was spoken by the Most High.") She is initiated into his knowledge and leads his hand. She is the sharer of his throne and his works, his darling and confidante. On the other hand, the wisdom texts emphasize that she is but the "fear of God." In this vision, she is divested of her divinity. She is made to represent duty and loyalty to God's law. Gone is the freedom of her self-revelation, her playful and creative aspects. Since the law is harsh to women as the source of temptation and evil, Wisdom is estranged from women. She condescends to embody worldly prudence and virtuous housewifery, "laden with merchandise" like a ship (Proverbs 31:14). The tendency is obviously to absorb her into patriarchal law and to tie her to morals in a narrow sense. Solomon embraces her as his bride and beloved wife, but woman, as such, is morally unreliable and needs to be admonished to follow wisdom as guide to a virtuous conduct of life. The taming of woman involves the taming of Divine Wisdom, and both are degraded in the process. Wisdom and woman alike are subjected to male supremacy.

One of Wisdom's particularly endearing qualities is that she is never concerned with the power principle. She cannot be invoked, like Jahve, in the name of destructive power: "Rouse thy wrath, pour out thy fury, destroy the adversary, wipe out the enemy . . ." (Sirach 36:7). She is tied to mankind by love, and when her love is not returned, she simply

The Holy Trinity *(a fresco from the early 9th century) by an unknown artist, found in the Romanesque country church in Urschalling, Upper Bavaria, Germany. The artist dared what theologians throughout Christian history did not: to give the Holy Spirit a female shape. Thus, Sophia is integrated in the Trinity. The little church has become a place of pilgrimage in recent years for the sake of this fresco.*

withdraws. She does not punish, but when man digresses from the path of righteousness, he will have to bear the consequences of his deeds. She stands on the crossroads and in the streets, she admonishes and calls out to men, but she does not impel (Proverbs 8:1-7; 32-36). She warns and laments, but she will not resort to violent means to bring mankind back under her guidance. Such is the rule of Wisdom who knows herself at one with the highest mystery of life.

Despite her intimacy with God, a certain dividing line is carefully preserved. She never attains the cosmological stature of a fully-fledged Goddess like Isis, Maat, or Demeter. Her existence is defined by her relationship to Jahve. In a way never explicitly stated, she, too, is his creature, and is confined to certain limits, although these can be stretched and are open to interpretation. Nevertheless, she is grand and beautiful, and men will never cease to love her despite all patriarchal distortions.

Meditation

How beautiful is Lady Wisdom in her closeness to God, to humanity, to everything in creation. We recognize her in the weaving of Nature, in her sacred trees (which today are diseased), in the living water (which today is polluted), in the fertile earth (which has been uprooted and poisoned by human beings).

We find her in our souls, although her image was mutilated, cut off, distorted, if not rendered invisible. She was bound to the law, forced into the fear of the Lord, so that her playful breath, the great liberator of the human soul, was crushed by the angry voice of God and his constant exhortation to obey the law. As if one initiated in her wisdom would not know what is right, would not hold sacred the great law of life, which is the law of love. Therefore, the ways of love degenerated into mere morals, and the fear of the Lord did not include reverence for His creation, her earthly body.

Once, the deepest mysteries were revealed to seekers. Once, we knew that love is more powerful than death, because when the Divine Mother descended into the realm of the dead to demand her child, no power of darkness could resist her forever. Then death brought forth life, and we knew that Life is greater, that death is part of life as its polar opposite, that death can only exist by virtue of the other, which is Life. We did not have to *believe* this; we experienced it in sacred ritual. We witnessed it in the Mysteries, in *hieros gamos*, which releases divine power through the union of female and male, the creation of new life and the glorious affirmation of one in the love of the other. We recognized the divine in times of old—God within us, and above us, and in all things. We do not blame tradition. It surrounded Sophia with the luster of divinity according to the possibility of the times—wisely calling on the ancient tradition when wisdom was still a Goddess. Under different names, she dwelled with human beings and never ceased to enflame our souls.

Chapter Two

THE CASE OF LILITH

I F THERE IS ONE SYMBOLIC FIGURE that during the past decade responded more than any other person of mythology to the need of the soul for the suppressed Feminine, it is Lilith. She is the archetype of the Dark Woman, and her history is as old as that first twilight of the gods, when the Great Goddess, the source of all life and wisdom, was overthrown to make way for the Fathergod. After millennia of continuous devaluation of the Feminine Divine, the Dark Woman is returning today, because the time is ripe to restore the wholeness of the many-faceted archetype of the Feminine. The split between an elevated figure of light, ever more abstract and removed from earthly life—in Christianity symbolized by the Virgin Mary—and her dark, elemental "shadow," symbolized by the witch, is crying out for healing.

For a hundred years psychology has attempted to trace the hidden residues of the unconscious, in order to explain the malaise of contemporary humanity. A culture demanding the suppression of natural drives (*Triebverzicht*) in the name of religion, admitting only domesticated eros, and a culture that is, at the same time, built on violence, becomes sick and makes human beings sick. At the dawn of modern psychology, pioneers like Sigmund Freud, C. G. Jung, and others, as well as the poets of all ages who dared to enter the realm of the "Mothers," were aware of a feminine part of the psyche, but today it is mainly women who call for the integration of the feminine aspect of being. The last phase of the women's movement has embraced this concern as an existential need. For many women, Lilith has become the symbol of their own wholeness. On the other hand, when men dream of the Black Woman, such dreams often release intense fear. The split-off, dark Feminine is often experienced as threatening by men. She represents the Unknown; she refuses to be co-opted by male thinking habits. The Swiss psychologist Siegmund Hurwitz described such a dream of one of his male clients and embarked on a search of many years to discover the origin of the dream figure he interpreted as Lilith.[1]

When women dream of the Black Woman, something very different may happen: they may recognize in her an autonomous part of their own self, which they were never allowed to acknowledge. The Father in his threefold potency—as God in the Judaeo-Christian tradition, as cultural "father," and as head of the patriarchal family—expelled from the consciousness of both men and women the dark aspect of the Feminine. For a woman, a dream of this kind may become a liberating experience.[2]

In the '80s, a veritable Lilith cult broke out on both sides of the Atlantic. At first, Lilith became a figure of identification for the Jewish women's movement in the United States. In the USA, as in Germany, there was an outburst of creative writing with a focus on Lilith, magazines with her name in the title were founded, academic studies of the prolific Lilith tradition appeared. Women defied the convention which gave Lilith an exclusively negative image as a destructive female spirit, a creature of evil. They saw in her the rebel against male domination,

---

[1] Siegmund Hurwitz, *Lilith: The First Eve* (Santa Rosa, CA: Daimon, 1991).

[2] See Ingrid Riedel, "Wandlungen der Schwarzen Frau" ["Transformations of the Black Woman"] in *Wendepunkte Erde—Frau—Gott* ["Turning Points Earth—Woman—God"], ed. by P. M. Pflüger (Olten-Freiburg: Walter, 1983).

they sought the Great Goddess whom she once represented. They wished to evoke her image within their own minds and hearts, beyond all historical interpretations and distortions, as an archetype of divine feminine potency. Lilith is indeed one of the most fascinating of all the goddess figures of popular mythology. She is the only one who has survived over the centuries, in Jewish mythology and various popular traditions, as well as in literature, for the very reason that she was so far removed from her origins. She has been handed down to us as the monstrous destroyer of men—beautiful, seductive, evil, rustling through 19th-century fiction and poetry like a snake through dry leaves. She is the blood-sucking vampire, the nightmare, the demon of unrestrained sexuality, who assaults men during the night and persecutes them in their dreams up to this day.

Who is she? Who is Lilith really? German readers may know her from Goethe's *Faust: Part One*. In the night of Walpurgis, when all sorts of weird spirits are released, Faust turns to his companion to identify a certain young witch who caught his eye, and Mephistopheles replies:

> "Observe her with some care,
> For that is Lilith."

Faust asks who she is, and Mephisto tells him:

> "Adam's first wife.
> Beware of her resplendent hair,
> The one adornment that she glories in,
> Once she entraps a young man in that snare,
> She won't so quickly let him out again."[3]

---

[3] Johann Wolfgang Goethe, *Faust, Part One & Part Two,* trans. by Charles E. Passage (Indianapolis: Bobbs-Merrill, 1965), p. 144.

When Lilith haunts the Brocken, a spooky mountain in Germany, as a seductive young witch, she is in reality as old as time. Her origin goes back to Sumer in Mesopotamia, where a great civilization flourished around 4000 B.C. The name Lilith appears for the first time in a Sumerian version of the epic of *Gilgamesh* as *ḳi-sikil-li-la-ke*, "maiden, beloved, companion of Li-la," that is, Gilgamesh.[4] In Jewish mythology, where Lilith flourished as the "Queen of Demons" longer than in any other tradition, folk etymology related the name Li-la to the Hebrew word for "night," *laila*, for Lilith is a demoness of the night. She belongs to the circle of Sumerian-Babylonian mother goddesses Inanna and Ishtar, with the twofold aspect of the nourishing, benign and the terrible, devouring mother. From Ishtar, the Babylonian mother goddess and queen of heaven, she inherited the feature of sensuous eroticism, whereas the dark aspect is derived from the goddess Lamashtú. Amulets with incantations against Lamashtú have been preserved, like the following:

> Dreadful is she, headstrong is she, she is a goddess, terrible is she. She is like a leopard (?), the daughter of Anû. Her feet are those of (the bird) Zu, her hands are dirty, her face is that of a powerful lion. She rises out of the reedbed. Her hair is loose, her breasts are bare. Her hands are caked with flesh and blood. She forces an entry through the window, she slides in like a snake.[5]

Her father is Anû, the Babylonian god of heaven. Part of her image are her wild, streaming hair, mostly burning red or raven-black, and her

---

[4] Irmgard Roebling, "Lilith oder die Umwertung aller Werte" ["Lilith, or the Re-Evaluation of all Values"], in *Lulu, Lilith, Mona Lisa* (Pfaffenweiler: Centaurus, 1989), pp. 57-97. This is a well-researched, very informative study.

[5] Hurwitz, *Lilith: The First Eve*, p. 43.

---

naked breasts. She can be seductively beautiful or ferocious like a wild beast, as in the following ancient text of incantation:

> Her abode is on the mountains, or in the reedbeds. Dreadful is her appearance. Her head and her face are those of a fearsome lion, white as clay is her countenance, she has the form of an ass, from her lips pours spittle, she roars like a lion, she howls like a jackal. A whore is she. Fearsome and savage is her nature. Raging, furious, fearsome, terrifying, violent, rapacious, rampaging, evil, malicious, she overthrows and destroys all that she approaches. Terrible are her deeds. Wherever she comes, wherever she appears, she brings evil and destruction. Men, beasts, trees, rivers, roads, buildings, she brings harm to them all. A flesh-eating, bloodsucking monster is she.[6]

This figure is truly monstrous, the incarnation of evil. From her derives Lamia of Greek mythology, a mistress of Zeus, whose children are killed by jealous Hera. To take revenge, Lamia now murders the children of other women and sucks their blood. Lilith is also related to the *stringes,* the child-abducting sorceresses, still remembered in Greek folklore and fairytales. She entered the *striges* of Roman mythology and developed into the *strega* in Italy, the witch allied with the devil and feared to this day for her power to cast the evil eye. Other female monsters of Greek mythology—Medusa, Gorgo, the Sirens—as well as dangerous water spirits, like Undine, Melusine, and Lorelei in German folk tradition, all these female vampires and witches may be considered descendants of Lamashtû-Lilith. Even the myth of the *femme fatale*,

---

[6] Hurwitz, *Lilith: The First Eve*, p. 36.

which became a literary fashion toward the end of the 19th century, is a reflection across millennia of the Babylonian goddess.

It is difficult to trace the features of the dreadful demon in the only representation of Lilith preserved from Sumerian times. It consists of a terracotta image in relief, identified as Lilith and dated to 2000 B.C. (see page 60). The image shows a nude female body of great beauty in the prime of her youth. Her feet in the shape of birds' claws stand on the back of two mild-looking lions. From her shoulders issue two powerful wings, repeated exactly in the plumage of the two owls by her side. The similarity of the birds' legs with their talons and the feet of the female figure is striking, but this resemblance to the animal world is neither disturbing nor ugly, but indicates a close relationship and familiarity with fellow creatures of the animal kingdom. Lilith carries rings in her hands, which remind us of the rings of eternity in Egyptian mythology. Her countenance is flawless and lovely, like the full moon. She wears a peculiar headdress in the shape of a spiral. It is of the same ornamental design as the headdress of the kings of Ur. The spirals resemble snakes, animals dedicated to the goddess, and the upward turn might indicate sacredness. As the feminist scholar Gerda Weiler explains:

> We find such whirls of energy in all places where earthly power strives to unite with cosmic energy. Spirals or concentric circles point upwards to the sacred hills. Double spirals, the "cosmic eyes of the Goddess," are found in the decoration of cult objects and sacred stones placed in geomantic power points. The crown of Lilith resembles an energy whirl, pointing toward the cosmic flow of power as her "third eye."[7]

---

[7] Gerda Weiler, *Der enteignete Mythos* ["The Disinherited Myth"] (Frankfurt-New York: Campus, 1991), p. 137 (translation mine).

Wings and birds' claws suggest an inner relationship between the goddess and the bird nature. As the bird surges upward toward the sky, the Goddess dwells in Heaven and spreads her wings in protection over the Earth. In later times the wings of the divine bird-woman transmute into the protecting cloak of the Virgin Mary, so familiar in the Catholic tradition of Southern Germany. Representations of Nut, the Egyptian Goddess of Heaven, are called to mind, as she bends her body over the Earth, stretching her hands toward the Earth in a gesture of blessing, before patriarchy raised the Fathergod to heaven and banished the Goddess to the lower realm of the Earth. The owl figured as the wise companion of the Goddess, before the patriarchal world order turned her into a messenger of disaster, a sinister bird of misfortune. The powerful lions are emblems of the sun. Both celestial bodies, the sun as well as the moon, originally pertained to the Goddess, before the male God claimed the sun, the larger and more luminous star, as his emblem, whereas the moon, the lesser body, whose light is derived from the sun, was appointed to the Goddess.

The rings in the hands of Lilith, with the staff tied to them, bear an extraordinary resemblance to the Egyptian *shen* ring, a symbol of eternity. In the staff wound by a cord we recognize the measuring rod and line used by the priestesses of Isis to establish the first geometrical data.[8] Thus, Lilith, with her royal headdress, her priestly insignia, surrounded by symbolical animals, was a truly divine figure, before she was degraded to the succubus, the satanic harlot or strumpet.

In Babylonian times, Lilith was considered the "hand of Inanna," who, on behalf of the Great Goddess, brought men from the street into the temple. Also Ishtar, revered as "sacred harlot," had command over hierodules called "Ishtaritûs," meaning "belonging to Ishtar." Even in

---

[8] *Der enteignete Mythos*, p. 135.

ancient Israel, the temple maids were called "saints" or "sacred women."[9] The orgiastic celebrations, which roused such horror in the biblical Wisdom Texts, have nothing to do with prostitution in our sense. Every young girl in Babylon, as Herodotus reports, submitted one time in her life to sexual congress with a stranger. This union was celebrated as the consummation of *hieros gamos*, the sacred wedding, in which the stranger represented God.[10]

Once the Goddess had been overthrown, and her cult vilified, it was easy in patriarchal understanding to turn the sacred harlot in the service of the Goddess into an abominable seductress. She suffered a split between the erotic-seductive aspect on the one hand, and the terrible aspect on the other. The people of Israel witnessed this transformation in their immediate environment. During the Babylonian captivity, Israel projected on Lilith the shadow of the Feminine, which it was no longer able to integrate. During this time, most of the legends about Lilith emerged. In the Bible she is mentioned only once, when the prophet Isaiah announced God's punishment of Edom. Every time God raves against heathens, he is talking about nations who worship the Goddess. In retribution for this heinous offense, Edom shall be destroyed with fire and sword. The text wallows in blood-curdling descriptions of a truly apocalyptic annihilation. After havoc has been wrought by the vengeful sword of the Lord, wild beasts and ghosts will take possession of the devastated land.

> Thorns shall sprout in its palaces;
> nettles and briars shall cover its walled towns.

---

[9] See also Barbara Black Koltuv, *The Book of Lilith* (York Beach, ME: Nicolas-Hays, 1986).
[10] Hurwitz, *Lilith: The First Eve*, p. 58.

It shall be rough land fit for wolves,
a haunt of desert owls.
Marmots shall consort with jackals . . .
There too the nightjar shall rest
and find herself a place for repose.

(Isaiah 34:13-14)

In the Hebrew original the "nightjar" is called Lilith. Martin Luther used *Kobold* ("hobgoblin") in his German translation. This goes to show how completely the erstwhile Goddess had transmuted into a creature of night, desert, and despair. She haunts a wasteland, devoid of human beings, and devoid of grace.

The more Jahve asserts his monopoly, the more satanic the image of Lilith becomes. Not only does she strangle men to death, but also pregnant women, and women in childbirth, and their new-born infants. Until today, orthodox Jewish families protect the lying-in chambers of young mothers with amulets and charms to guard against Lilith. In Aramaic spells handed down from ancient times there are representations of Lilith as a repulsive hag, with claw-like hands, her hands and feet bound with chains. The chains represent the spells that are to prevent her from doing harm.

Jewish tradition has it that Lilith is the real model of the Queen of Sheba, who bewitched Solomon. According to another tradition, she is the first Eve, before God created her from Adam's rib, as is suggested in *Faust*. One text, probably dating from the eighth century B.C., the Alphabet of Ben Sira, relates how Lilith was created and what happened afterward.

When the Almighty—may His name be praised—created
the first, solitary man, He said: "It is not good for man to be

alone." And He fashioned for man a woman from the earth, like him (Adam), and called her Lilith. Soon, they began to *quarrel* with each other. She said to him: "I will not *lie underneath*," and he said: "I will not *lie underneath* but above." She said to him: "We are both equal, because we are both (created) from the earth." But they did not listen to each other. When Lilith saw this, she pronounced God's *avowed* name and *flew* into the air. Adam stood in prayer before his Creator and said: "Lord of the world! The woman you have given me has gone away from me." Immediately, the Almighty—may His name be praised—sent three angels after her, to bring her back. The Almighty—may His name be praised—said to him (Adam): "If she decides to return, it is good, but if not, then she must take it upon herself to ensure that a hundred of her children die each day." They went to her and found her in the middle of the sea, in the raging waters in which one day the Egyptians would be drowned. And they told her the word of God. But she refused to return.[11]

What we have here is a power struggle between man and woman carried out on the most intimate level. Lilith rebels against the norm forcing her to "lie *below*" the man, which literally means to "sub-ject" herself to him. God created her equal to Adam and did not invest him with power over her. When Adam refuses to listen to her protest, she does the thing a good Jewish or Christian woman has learned never to do: She denies him and leaves her man. Even the angels, as God's messengers, cannot persuade her to return to him. Thus, the history of the curse

---

[11] *Lilith: The First Eve*, p. 120f.

takes its course. As punishment for her obstinate disobedience, she is condemned to murder children, unless they are protected by an amulet in the name of the angels.

As already mentioned, the legends around Lilith mainly arose during the Babylonian Exile (sixth century B.C.) and in the following centuries of the Diaspora, in other words, during times in which the Jewish people suffered extreme existential insecurity. Deported from their homeland, without their priesthood, without their sanctuary, the adaptation to foreign religions was a great danger. In this situation, there was all the more need to disparage the alien world—especially in the figure of Lilith—to set up boundaries to protect Jewish identity. Thus, Lilith became the negative female projection, whereas Eve, the submissive helpmate of Adam, became the model of a Jewish wife. Her primary duty consists in shielding her husband from the burden of a hostile environment, which threatens his manhood on all levels.[12] Hers, as Aviva Cantor puts it, is the "enabler role" to counteract the threat to Jewish survival. However, on no account must her strength undermine male authority and supremacy within the family.

A people, forced to lead a marginal existence amid foreign cultures, constantly suspected and persecuted by the rulers of the country, is prone to develop fears and a minority complex. As Aviva Cantor explains, exile was always somewhat less intolerable for women than for men, because their general condition of life was not changed as much by the disaster. The central fact of their lives, submission and obedience to men, was the same in exile as at home. It was the men who needed compensation for their sufferings. A woman who withholds herself in this situation releases potency fears in men, and endangers the physical sur-

---

[12] See Aviva Cantor, "The Lilith Question," in: *On Being A Jewish Feminist*, ed. by Susannah Heschel (New York: Schocken Books, 1983).

vival of the nation. A rebellious, independent woman aggravates man's insecurity. In a social context experienced as deeply humiliating, he had to retain the upper hand in his most intimate relationship. Therefore, male neuroses and fears were projected onto Lilith, who refused this service, the shadow woman, the flip side of Eve. Lilith is turned into a demon, a witch, split off by male consciousness as "evil anima" in Jungian terminology.

In the story of Ben Sira, Lilith commits the additional crime of pronouncing the ineffable name of God—a name so hidden and sacred that it is unknown to mankind, and in Holy Scripture it is but a chiffre, a symbolic sign. Lilith not only displays strength and self-assertion, courage, and firmness in action, but she is knowing beyond the knowledge of men, which is all the more offensive because she is a woman. For in the Jewish tradition, woman had no access to sacred learning and was not taught to study Scripture.

Today, Jewish women accept Lilith of the *Alphabet of Ben Sira* as a role model in their striving for ritual equality and personal independence. The story of Lilith may well have been handed down from mother to daughter by countless generations, as Cantor assumes, to keep alive the memory of female autonomy, which once upon a time was the birthright of every woman. Jewish women today, in America and elsewhere, look to Lilith to reclaim this right. The women of Israel embraced the cult of the Goddess longer than Israelite men did, and even in later times had an intuition of the divine origin of the demon Lilith.

In order to overthrow the Goddess completely, patriarchy had to make her revolting to women. It had to turn her into a destroyer of children, because the blessings of the Great Mother were naturally invoked by women during labor and childbirth. The wisdom of the Goddess inspired midwives and taught them the secret of plants. Thus, women, from time immemorial, were the natural healers and midwives. The Goddess, herself, called them to this service. Every new birth was proof of her love and creative power. The perversion of this divine function, an insatiable desire to murder children and pregnant women, can only be explained by the new patriarchal order, in which the supremacy of the Great Goddess had to be destroyed in the name of the Lord. To wrench her away from the souls of women, the jealous Fathergod had to turn her into women's greatest enemy. If nothing else availed, libel and slander achieved this purpose.

Lilith became the perversion of the all-embracing love of the Goddess. She is still beautiful and seductive, with her wild hair and swelling breasts, but she is frigid. She rouses men's desire without giving or finding fulfillment. A sterile female, she cannot have children in the natural way, but creates demons out of men's semen, stolen during the night.

In the *Kabbalah*, the Jewish mystical tradition, Lilith figures as the antipode of Shekhina, the "dwelling" of God in this world, and of Chokhma, divine wisdom, respectively. With Samael, her male companion, she forms the "unholy couple," and their union—a perversion of the sacred wedding—indicates the association of the feminine with evil. In the *Zohar*, the "Book of Splendor," the central part of the *Kabbalah*, Lilith appears several times. The following passage is particularly illuminating:

> She (Lilith) adorns herself with all kinds of decorations, like an amorous woman. She stands at the entrance to roads and paths, in order to seduce men. She seizes the fool who approaches her, kisses him and fills him with a wine whose dregs contain snake venom. As soon as he has drunk this, he starts to follow her. . . . Her adornments for seducing

men are her beautifully-dressed hair, red as a rose, her
cheeks, white and red, her ears hung with chains from
Egypt and her neck hung with all the jewels of the East.
Her mouth is (tiny) like a narrow doorway, a graceful orna-
ment, her tongue is sharp as a sword, her words soft as oil.
Her lips are red as a rose, sweet with all the sweetness of the
world. She is dressed in crimson, adorned with all the jewels of the world. . . . Those fools, who come to her and drink
this wine, commit fornication with her. And what does she
do then? She leaves the fool alone, sleeping in his bed, while
she ascends into the heights (heaven). There she gives a bad
report of him. Then, she obtains permission to descend
again. When the fool awakes, he assumes that he can take
his pleasure with her, as before. She, however, removes her
jewelry and turns into a powerful figure. She faces him,
clothed in a fiery dress of flames. She arouses terror and
causes body and soul to tremble. Her eyes are huge, in her
hand is a sharp sword, from which bitter drops fall. She
kills him (with this) and casts him into the very centre of
hell.[13]

This text, too, reveals that Lilith was not originally the debased harlot
and vile murderess, but the divine Feminine. She approaches man in
splendid attire and presents him the cup, as it was the custom of the
priestesses in the temple of the Great Goddess to welcome the man who
had come for the sacred wedding. The holy snake and the ritual potion
are converted by a later tradition into snake *poison*. Lilith wears
Egyptian ornaments, which again brings to mind the goddess Isis. The

---

[13] Hurwitz, *Lilith: The First Eve*, p. 141f.

color red is mentioned repeatedly. Lilith's hair, her cheeks, her mouth are red, and she is clad in crimson. Red, we remember, was always the color of the Goddess—the color of life, of blood, of energy, and love. The forceful figure in her fiery garment is a divine presence distorted to represent evil. Man's fear of this overpowering woman cannot be overlooked. Unable to dismiss her, he can only deal with her by turning her into a devil.

In different shapes and under different names, the myth of Lilith entered many cultures. There are Christian versions of Lilith legends in the Graeco-Byzantine, Syrian, Ethiopian, Southern Slavonic, and Rumanian traditions. In the folk tale of *Tannhäuser*, used by Richard Wagner for his opera of the same name, she makes her appearance as Lady Venus of the Hörselberg. In fairy tales we encounter her as witch, and she continues to flourish in the figure of the beautiful Lorelei, sitting on a rock high over the Rhine, luring men into death by her enchanting song. German poets, like Heinrich Heine and Joseph von Eichendorff among others, immortalized her in poetry.

Everywhere in patriarchy this disparagement of the Feminine as an expression of deep-seated male fear of the elemental female character took place. Analytical psychology has interpreted these implications, albeit in patriarchal fashion. The "evil anima," an alleged archetype of the soul, is in reality the distorted image of the former Great Feminine.[14] It is the expression of the disturbed primary relationship between man and woman. The archetype of the great Mother Goddess is not—and never was—"terrible," but the personification of divine creative power. Death and dying are contained within this concept, not as *evil*, but as part of life, as the eternal cycle of becoming and decaying. Not until the suppression of the Goddess that went hand in hand with

---

[14] Weiler, *Der enteignete Mythos*, pp. 178ff.

the subjection of women, was the seed of hatred between the sexes sown, and the Goddess of Heaven and Earth turned into the Terrible Mother. This is an expression of man's fear of her revenge, a fear only too justified. According to a universal law, every suppressed energy is driven underground and reemerges as a threatening "shadow."

The more Western civilization curbed free eros and forced it into narrow moral norms, the more suspicious woman had to become. Whatever set limits to male power and resists rational control, such as love as a basic human drive, or the nature of woman despite the process of taming and suppression for thousands of years—all this is experienced as dangerous. It releases fears, and is, therefore, relegated to the subconscious. In a world increasingly controlled and manipulated, all things mysterious, all things not accessible to Logos rouse suspicion. Woman appears to man as dangerous and mysterious.

A glance through the history of art and literature in the 19th century demonstrates clearly this mystification of the Feminine. It was the aestheticism of writers, like Walter Pater and Théophile Gautier, that invented the cult image of *La Gioconda* based on Leonardo's portrait of a bourgeois Florentine woman by the name of Mona Lisa. This picture has remained a cult image until today, as the crowds demonstrate who file past her in the Louvre, and who are prevented by a glass case and a cord from getting too close to what is perhaps the most famous painting in the history of art. Walter Pater, the influential British art critic and writer, endowed this plump, modestly dressed and by no means ideally beautiful woman, the wife of a local merchant, with features suggestive of Lilith.

> [T]he animalism of Greece, the lust of Rome, the mysticism
> of the middle age with its spiritual ambition and imagina-
> tive loves, the return of the Pagan world, the sins of the

> Borgias. She is older than the rocks among which she sits;
> like the vampire, she has been dead many times, and learned
> the secrets of the grave; and has been a diver in deep seas,
> and keeps their fallen day about her . . .[15]

At the turn of the century, when ritual impoverishment, the disenchantment of the world caused by a fanatical belief in science and the rise of crude materialism had reached a peak, the enigma of woman became a topos in painting as well as in literature, as a surrogate for religion, as it were. The mysterious lady, glamorized a century before by Romantic poetry as a creature of cosmic depth and wisdom, now became an obsession, a compulsive need to restore magic and glamor, if need be, the glamor of infamy, to the tamed and disenchanted Feminine. This was very different from the "Feminine Mystique" which, in this century, came to be exposed as the ultimate act of male manipulation in modern society and finally led to the outbreak of the women's liberation movement in the '60s.[16] The earlier phenomenon hovered between the sacred and the infamous, the human and the subhuman, desire and revulsion. Painters like Gustave Moreau, Fernand Khnopff, Franz von Stuck, and others, depicted woman often as a sphinx. These pictures, majestic animal bodies attached to trivial heads reflecting the fashion of the time, appear grotesque as we view them today. Artistic imagination obviously was no longer able to bring together the face of a woman and the body of an animal in a convincing symbolic entity. The sphinxes of ancient Egypt would mock these modern make-believes of the feminine mystique. All these attempts to present woman as a mythical being of animal instincts, ruthless and enigmatic,

---

[15] Walter Pater, *The Renaissance. Studies in Art and Poetry* (London: Macmillan, 1910), p. 125.
[16] Betty Friedan, *The Feminine Mystique* (New York: Dell, 1963).

appear contrived and neurotic. A culture which split off the Feminine loses the faculty to imagine the Feminine Divine and to give her authentic expression in works of art.

We get a similar impression from representations of the equally popular motive of Salome and Judith during the 19th century. Judith, in the painting of the Viennese artist Gustav Klimt, looks more like a frivolous lady of the *fin de siècle*. Where, it might be asked, is the Eternal Feminine in this period piece of refined decadence? Where is it, for that matter, in the *Salome* of Franz von Stuck, or in the well-known painting *The Sin* by the same artist? The contrived expression of infamy and mystery, the face half-hidden behind a curtain of raven hair, which has a silly rather than a seductive expression, seems almost ludicrous. No, this "sin" never tasted the fruit of the Tree of Knowledge. She has no knowledge, no wisdom. The dark side of womanhood, in these interpretations of 19th-century art, appears puppet-like, distorted, devoid of life and truth. It is plain and downright *Kitsch*.

There are countless literary treatments of the demonic and seductive Feminine toward the end of the 19th century. Lilith makes her reappearance even by name, as if the collective unconscious were driven to give her expression.

The French poet Victor Hugo, in *La Fin de Satan*—"The End of Satan"—the final part of his great verse epic *La légende des Siècles*, presents Lilith as *monstre femme*, the female monster. She is the origin of all evil, Satan's daughter. She reveals herself as the black soul of a dead world, an unknown, wicked, and infinite being, whom man calls "Disaster" with a shudder. Not until the end of time will she be vanquished by the Angel of Light.

Poets like Robert Browning, Dante Gabriel Rossetti, Arthur Symons, Gillaume Appollinaire, and, above all, Charles Baudelaire in *Les Fleurs du Mal*, drew on Lilith as the embodiment of the *femme fatale*. In Gustave Flaubert's tale *The Temptation of Saint Anthony*, Lilith appears as the Queen of Sheba, who harasses the saint with her seductive guiles, but fails in her wicked designs. With Heinrich Heine's verse epics as a model, Friedrich Christoph Johannes Wedde, a German poet all but forgotten today, wrote his *Lilith. Die Lösung des Welträtsels—ausgeplaudert von den Jünglingen zu Sais* ["Lilith. The Solution of the Mystery of the World—Revealed by the Youths of Sais"]. The ardently sought Goddess proves to be a terrible Lilith figure, a devil of lust.

Of special interest is the tale *La Fille de Lilith* ["The Daughter of Lilith"] by Anatole France, who found a device to blend skillfully the mythical level and actual reality, faith and science: a mysterious woman called Leila holds a man enthralled and burdens him with guilt. All the well-known requisites of the *femme fatale* are displayed: her beauty, her voluptuousness, her amorality and inscrutability.

> In all her glowing, scintillating presence there was something which seemed to contradict human nature; she appeared to me a lesser and at the same time a higher being than the woman God in his unfathomable kindness has given us as a companion in this earthly vale of tears.[17]

Leila says that she is "very old," and that her mother and sister are "the daughters of God." Elaborate evidence is produced to prove the fantastic thesis that Leila belongs to a pre-Adamitic race whose progenitress was Lilith, the first Eve. Since Lilith left Adam before the Fall, she was spared the divine curse and therefore has no soul to be redeemed. She knows neither pain nor death, neither sin nor guilt. Leila-Lilith, in this

---

[17] Anatole France, *La Fille de Lilith* ["The Daughter of Lilith"]. Translation mine.

case, is not an incarnation of evil, but an agonized creature longing for the joys and sorrows of human existence.

Also Frank Wedekind's tragedy, *Lulu,* is part of the literary Lilith tradition at the turn of the century. Wedekind called his work, which later was divided into two plays, *Erdgeist* ["Earth Spirit"] and *Die Büchse der Pandora* ["Pandora's Box"], a "monster tragedy." His aim was to expose the hypocrisy of bourgeois morals by confronting it with "the true animal, the wild and beautiful animal" in the shape of a woman. The name Lulu bears a faint resemblance to Lilith. She is meant to represent universal woman or the female prototype. Alternately, she is called "snake," "sweet innocence," angel and devil, harlot, beast, and "angel of death." But in reality, Lulu is a construct, a projection screen of masculine fantasies about women. She is neither the "earth spirit" as elemental being, nor Pandora, who, according to Greek mythology, is the cause of all the evil of the world. Lulu remains an artifact of peculiar unreality, expressive of the neurosis of the era. In an entry in his Paris diary, Wedekind called his drama *Astarte*, revealing his intention to set Lulu in parallel to the Babylonian goddess. He described his frequent visits of Parisian prostitutes as "offerings" at the altar of the Goddess.

The spirit of an entire epoch finds expression in this drama. It was prohibited by censorship and caused huge scandals, when the two parts were first performed between 1898 and 1904. *Lulu* was taken as an assault on bourgeois morality, whereas in truth it was but the shrill incantation of a bogus myth. An era in which the Feminine was split into the whore and the saint had no sense for what is really offensive in the *Lulu* tragedy. It is scandalous, not because Lulu allegedly reveals the "feminine prototype," but because her author, and the time he lived in, had no conception of the real prototype. In his posthumously published diary, the author revealed himself as a prisoner of that moral hypocrisy he had wanted to expose. When woman is degraded as a mere sex object, an amoral being of compulsive drives, the wisdom of the Goddess leaves the Earth. She goes away and hides where men cannot find and desecrate her. The Book of Job told that story.

Lilith is also an incarnation of evil in the novel *Lilith* by George MacDonald, published in London in 1895. Equipped with all the inventory of the English Gothic novel, this story takes place in a realm of spirits, where Lilith, Adam's first wife, is transformed to a ferocious leopardess and murderess of small children, conforming to the old stereotype of the female devil. Finally Lilith yields to the will of God and renounces her demonic nature. Behind this figure, too, looms Astarte, the Great Goddess, misunderstood and trivialized in this long-winded, moralizing tale, designed to give pleasurable shivers to the readers of this wild story of evil and divine justice—a genuine product of the Victorian Age.

In the meantime, a rehabilitation of Lilith is getting underway in the 20th century. In *Back to Methuselah*, a vast utopia of the evolution of the human race, George Bernard Shaw ventured to create a "modern Bible" and "metabiological Pentateuch."[18] Lilith appears right at the beginning of this colossal drama in five parts. In Shaw's arbitrary recasting of the myth, Lilith, by virtue of her immense will power, gives birth to a pair of humans, Adam and Eve, after which the fateful history of humanity takes its course. Birth and death, murder and manslaughter, cruelty and hypocrisy are "invented," as human beings refuse to become immortal. Not until Part Five do they repent their sins and acts of foolishness, and remember Lilith's legacy: an innate desire of higher development. In her long speech at the end of the drama, Shaw expounds his "religion of creative development": man will develop into a being of

---

[18] *Back to Methuselah* (1921), in: *The Complete Plays of Bernard Shaw* (London: Paul Hamlyn, 1965).

pure spirit and discard the body which always hampered spiritual flight. This development is brought about by woman, because it was she to whom Lilith bestowed the "greatest of gifts: curiosity." This divine quality, which Lilith shares, saved mankind from her wrath. She has unlimited power over human beings—like the God of the Old Testament turned female: "I am Lilith: I brought life into the whirlpool of force, and compelled my enemy, Matter, to obey a living soul." Already humans have attained longevity—a projection into the 32nd century—and are hatched from eggs. After a prolonged infancy, they mutate into the "ancients," who live purely in the mind.

This utopia of an evolved superhuman race is an intellectual fantasy in the true manner of G. B. Shaw: witty, satirical, iconoclastic, and yet for all its irreverent daring, it is immensely naive. Obviously, this Lilith came from the brain of an intellectual. There is nothing tangible or sensuous about her, and she is as tediously talkative as her author. The Goddess would not have dreamed to promote the fatal dualism between matter and spirit, or to imagine superhuman mental creatures as the future race of man, who knows neither love nor reproduces in the natural way.

The wisdom of matter as manifestation of the works of God is unknown to this Shavian Lilith. Shaw upgrades her by redeeming her from the stigma of iniquity, and practically puts her in place of God the Creator, but at the same time he reinvents her in a way that deprives her of all the qualities of the former Goddess. This Lilith is a *dea faber* without mystery, a technologist of human evolution with an irritating addiction to sententious utterance. Under the analytical gaze of the great British writer, who, as a true representative of his age, has no sense of the mystery of life, and a flawed relation to the Feminine, wisdom shrinks to intelligence, and the longing of the soul for transcendence is reduced to "curiosity." This rehabilitation of Lilith remains a mental experiment, a mere intellectual game.

The most charming and ingenious literary treatment of the Lilith theme was composed by a woman. The verse epic *Die Kinder der Lilith* ["The Children of Lilith"] by Isolde Kurz, published in 1907, caused a storm of indignation roused by male critics. The author was the first woman in this century who dared to give the Lilith myth a new interpretation. Let us take a closer look at this unusual work of poetic fiction.

The author turns the biblical tradition boldly upside down. Adam, the first man, has been created by God as a deficient being who needs the guidance and inspiration of a female companion. God gives him Lilith for his mate, "das lieblichste Wunderbild"[19] with golden hair and delicate wings.

> From Adam, this poor lump of clay,
> Through Lilith I built a passage-way
> Up to the highest seat of heaven . . .
> And so for him this mate did find,
> Half his and half of celestial kind,
> So that he may through love incur
> A rousing, kindling, bracing spur.
> Too heavy and too fine of bone,
> Powerless each, when on their own.
> I did not give her arms to kill,
> But spirit his mission to fulfil.
> He has the steady mind and frame,
> The muscle force that splits the rock,
> Hers is the ever-burning flame,
> The balance spring that moves the clock.[20]

---

[19] Or "Gnadenbild": an image of a saint with a miraculous healing power. Isolde Kurz, *Die Kinder der Lilith* ["The Children of Lilith"] (Stuttgart-Berlin: Cotta'sche Buchhandlung, 1908).

[20] Translation mine, as are the following passages.

Lilith's sweet hovering restlessness is intended to inspire man to great deeds, and to a higher life. It is God's design that humanity, as realized beings, shall re-enter the divine nature from which they came. But Adam grumbles. His mate, united to him in mutual love, is too strenuous for him. He wants his peace, and resents being constantly shaken out of his lethargy. Thus, the state of harmony between them is disturbed. This is the opportunity of Samael, the adversary. Again, the author gives an original twist to the story of Genesis. From the rib of sleeping Adam another woman, Eve, is created by Samael, not God. As the classical patriarchal female, Eve is the extreme opposite of Lilith. She worships Adam and only lives through him as his lesser half. She knows how to flatter him and to tie him to her by her helplessness. She drags him down by the torpid desire of the flesh and sets him against Lilith. At first, Lilith treats Adam's new companion lovingly, but soon she sees through Eve's stratagems and flies up to heaven. She returns one more time to tell Adam of the wonders of heaven, but in his life with Eve, he learned to rule and to command, and he demands of Lilith that she surrender to him. Indignantly, she rebukes him:

> How durst thou, Adam? Shame on thee!
> Thou shalt not lord it over me.
> There is but One to whom all bend,
> He bids me come, and here I stand.

To restore peace between them, she begs Adam to send Eve away, but he refuses, and Eve triumphs. In his rage, Adam causes a huge fire and destroys his workshop, where he wrought golden wings for himself, like Lilith's. By the side of the dull Earth-woman Eve, he has no need of them. Now also Lilith is overcome by anger:

> With dancing, red-hot sparks about,
> All of a sudden her wings spread out,

Dreadfully changed she seems to him,
Kin of the flaming Cherubim.

In her fiery robe, she reminds us of the overwhelming figure of Lilith from the *Zohar*. Now she disappears from the Earth irrevocably. Eve remains with Adam and brings him the forbidden fruit. God calls Adam to account:

This heavenly creature of noble birth,
whom I sent down to thee on Earth—
My only gift to her this dress
And for support thy faithfulness—
Thou cast her out who held this gem,
And lost the heritage of Man.

Adam's real Fall is not the consumption of a forbidden fruit, but his defection from Lilith:

Who from his first love went astray,
And Lilith's bounty cast away,
In order to gain Eva's grace,
Deserves the ruin of his race.

God drives Adam from Paradise, which he himself destroyed. But due to Lilith's supplication, God decrees that the toil and trouble of earthly life may be a path of repentance and reform. Lilith withdraws to the realms of heaven, but she leaves Adam a son. He and all beings born in his spirit will bring back the light into this world. However, they will be persecuted by men: "Denn Evas Kinder, die im Joch gebeugten,/ Hassen von Mutterleib den Lichtgezeugten." ["For Eve's children, bent in the yoke,/ Hate from their mother's womb those who are begot in light."] The epic concludes with the promise that whenever mankind is ready to evolve "a notch," God will send a messenger of light from the tribe of Lilith, until mankind has become perfect.

In this remarkable reinterpretation of the myth, Lilith is by no means the murderous seductress and killer of children, but Sophia, the feminine spirit of God driven away by Adam. She is the strength which inspires men und reminds them of their divine origin. At the same time, she is elementally bound to the Earth: "Wo sie erscheint, muß alles blühn,/ Was sie berührt, wird frisch und grün." ["Where she appears, all is abloom,/ Whatever she touches, turns fresh and green."] Only through union with her can man become godlike. Eve, on the other hand, is the typical woman of patriarchal society. Her self-image is dictated by the male. Whereas Lilith acts by divine empowerment, Eve can only use wiles and tricks, her petty treachery, the proverbial feminine stratagems. She drags man down, whereas Lilith raises him up to God. But in the end, Lilith will prevail.

Sixty years before the second women's movement started, Isolde Kurz divined that Lilith's hour would come round again. Today Lilith has returned as a mythical configuration of the Great Goddess. Lilith is the dark aspect of the feminine divine in opposition to Sophia, the light aspect. They belong together, and because the dark one has been suppressed and condemned for so long, it is coming back today consciously or subconsciously. The Goddess in both her aspects has become a need for the sake of the wholeness of life.[21] Significantly, the "Black Woman" makes a frequent appearance in the dreams of women in our time.[22] In the depth of the subconscious she leads to an integration of the lost

---

[21] See Gerda Weiler, *Ich brauche die Göttin* ["I Need the Goddess"] (Basel: Mond-Buch-Verlag, 1990); Edward C. Whitmont, *The Return of the Goddess* (New York: Crossroad,1984).
[22] Riedel, "Wandlungen der Schwarzen Frau."

wholeness, a loss experienced as painful particularly by women. The dark aspect suppressed in our culture—Earth, mystery, death and eros, magic and healing—belongs to the Feminine and was once the confirmation of her power.

Also, dreams of the Black Madonna emerge with remarkable frequency today. Many famous places of pilgrimage throughout the world are consecrated to the Black Madonna. She is considered full of grace and miracles, whether it is the Black Madonna of Montserrat in Spain, of Altötting in Upper Bavaria, of Einsiedeln in Switzerland, of Czestochowa in Poland (see illustration on page 116), or Guadelupe in Mexico and many other places in the world. Modern research has traced her back to the goddesses Ishtar and Isis.[23] From the Sumerian Ishtar she transmuted to Kybele and Artemis of Asia Minor, and from there she radiated through the entire Graeco-Roman empire. Also Hecate, the magic-working moon and death goddess, is associated with this line. All have a dark appearance, and represent the chthonic mysteries of life, as do some of the Hindu goddesses, whom we shall encounter in a later chapter. The Black Madonna preserved something which the light figure of the Virgin Mary lacks: the completeness of the Feminine Divine. The Jungian psychologist Dora Kalff considers her emergence in dreams as the "first impulse of the good feminine."[24]

> When she appears, then we can guess that the psyche is beginning to grow in a spiritual direction. . . . We are seeing a dawning of the feminine now. Women are beginning to realize that to follow the man's way is not working. We

---

[23] China Galland, *Longing for Darkness: Tara and the Black Madonna* (London: Penguin, 1990), pp. 144-147.

[24] Galland, *Longing for Darkness*, p. 142.

must develop our own capacities, not follow men. The Black Madonna is beginning to break through.[25]

Such a dream may cause confusion or even fear in women, when the Dark Goddess appears in a patriarchal disguise, or if her request of the dreamer seems overwhelmingly demanding and difficult. The liberating wisdom of the Goddess will not always be immediately recognized; the dark aspect may be shocking at first. To illustrate this kind of dream, inner experience and fantasy, I submit a dream report, in which this conflict becomes apparent, but finally is seen to heal and to turn into trust and confidence.

I am in a group of prisoners waiting for the warden, who has power over us. Then this person comes. It is a youngish, dark-skinned woman of about my age. She is wearing high boots up to her hips and a black leather jacket.

She takes us to another room, a kind of workshop, where everyone is supposed to select some work. I discover carved objects made of colored gems. "How beautiful," I think, "I should like to make things like that." I look for suitable tools and find a smaller and a bigger knife. Before I can reach for the smaller one, the Dark Woman comes over to me and says: "Take the bigger knife, it is better." Then the others leave the room, and I am alone with her. Suddenly she has a child with her, a little girl. She chats with me about her child in a familiar tone of voice. This creates a bond between us, and I sense that my fear is leaving me. Then the black woman touches my hair and says with a smile: "You have

[25] Galland, *Longing for Darkness*, p. 142.

fine hair."—"Oh no," I reply, "My hair is not fine at all, it is rather thick and coarse. *You* have fine hair." I stroke her head, and her hair is really soft as silk and very smooth. I am filled with a sense of joy. Suddenly I feel love for this woman welling up in me, and I wake up happy, as if I had grown in a mysterious way.[26]

The dreamer told me that normally she cannot remember dreams, but the memory of this dream accompanied her for years. Whenever her identity was threatened, when she had the feeling of losing ground, she was aware of this numinous female figure somewhere in her consciousness: dark, powerful, encouraging. As time passed, she became a kind of soul guide.

Let us take a closer look at this dream. The situation in the beginning is imprisonment. This might signify the imprisonment of woman and goddess wisdom in patriarchy, but strangely, it is not a male warden or overseer, not a threatening or intimidating figure, but a woman. Her gear reminds us of a female James Bond, a gangster or the "domina" type of woman, popular figures of high symbolic significance in the mass media. At first, we might recognize this woman as a female counterpart of Superman according to the patriarchal pattern. The color of her outfit is black, her skin is dark. This, too, evokes images with negative connotations—black as the color of evil, of night, danger, and crime. Gangsters wear black leather jackets. Black is also the color of Lilith, the "nightjar," the dark she-demon. The dreamer is also acquainted with the Hindu goddess Kali, who in her destructive aspect as "Terrible Mother" is represented black. Although the dreamer is not a Catholic, the image of the Black Madonna comes to her.

---

[26] From an unpublished monograph, translated by me.

Step by step the Dark Woman of the dream reveals her true nature behind the patriarchal mask. She is the director of a workshop of beautiful objects carved of precious stones. In patriarchal culture, gem carving is a masculine domain, but here women are expected to try their hands at it. The Woman encourages the dreamer to reach out for the bigger knife, the better tool. Like many women, the dreamer instinctively wants to take the lesser, being accustomed to modesty and never claiming the best. She does not think that she can handle the big knife. In their talk the Black Woman surprisingly identifies herself as a mother and adopts an easy, familiar tone, as women do when they talk about their children. She treats the dreamer as a friend. In their mutual caress there is a fearless tenderness, a delighted praise of the other woman's beauty. There is a magic charm and erotic attraction in the long hair of women. Also Lilith is always represented with long and beautiful hair. Significantly, the dreamer at first disparages her own hair, in accordance with her low self-esteem.

There is a fundamental change of her relationship to the black woman in the course of the dream. The initial figure of horror proves to be nothing but a cultural projection. She loses this ominous significance the moment when the dreamer enters into a direct relationship with her. She is no longer a warden or overseer, but a helpful and in the best sense of the word a powerful woman. She incites the dreamer to do something which she had no courage to do on her own and which the prevailing culture may never have permitted her to do: to get the proper tool for her proper task. The woman is called to shape, to create and to affirm by her own action the ancient wisdom of the Goddess. Many women are afraid of this, because they have been cut off from their sources for so long. The "Dark" was relegated to the realm of evil for too long. Today we are called to unite both aspects: Sophia and Lilith. They belong together and strengthen each other. If Sophia is celebrated at the expense of Lilith, we are likely to get a bloodless ideal, powerful only in a limited way as spiritual potential, but cut off from her polar opposite, and therefore out of balance. Lilith, at the expense of Sophia, evokes the danger of letting the dark get out of hand as magic attachment to the earth or eros without love. We need the healing of the dualisms of nature and spirit, body and soul, female and male.

The archetype of the Great Goddess is about to be liberated from patriarchal distortions to display her real self: as creative feminine potency, as power of being, which liberates in women and men their true natures; as love which does not cling, manipulate or degrade its object, which is not rooted in an abstract idea of God, but is the eternally streaming wellspring of life. The appropriate speech of goddess power still has to be learned, but we are holding in our hands again the sacred thread that leads us to her hidden reality.

We have tried to give some examples of the configurations of the Lilith myth in its patriarchal distortion. We saw that the myth adopted a demonic life of its own, because it was split off from the "good" Feminine, the "Wisdom-Sophia-Chokhma" and her more or less visible connection with the matriarchal Goddess. The overthrow of the Divine Mother led directly to the subjection of women with disastrous results for both sexes and for the image of God in our culture. For many centuries the negative Lilith myth determined the image of woman as the reverse of the idealized, pure image of womanhood, as represented by the Holy Virgin. In both extremes, wisdom is left behind, because the living connection with the powerful Goddess is cut off. Both are functions of the patriarchal shift, when the supreme value is no longer life, but power. The patriarchally biased God evaporates into an abstract realm of the spirit and confronts men mostly with the attitude of an omnipotent ruler. Wisdom, so much needed today, dissolves hierarchical power structures for the sake of life. She finds her resources in her

Lilith, *Sumerian terracotta relief, dated circa 2000 B.C. Collection of Colonel Norman Colville (reproduced in Erich Neumann,* The Great Mother, *Bollingen Series, Vol. 47, Princeton University Press, 1964, plate 126). The sovereign Goddess in her youthful beauty is shown here as mistress of the animal kingdom as well as of science and crafts, before she was perverted into a female demon. As we meditate on her in this early form, we restore her ancient dignity.*

experience of selfhood and overcomes the ancient battle of the sexes by feminine empowerment. The "return of the Goddess," and of her wisdom, is anticipated by many as a blessing to the Earth and to human beings in general, but it is especially dear to the hearts of women. It happens frequently that the demand of feminine autonomy on behalf of the Goddess emerges in the shape of a dream, in order to reclaim the values denied by our culture. Confronting Lady Wisdom in her dark aspect may be the condition on which Sophia is prepared to come back to Earth. They are the two faces of the one cosmic whole, in the macrocosm of the Earth as well as in the microcosm of the human soul.

It is difficult to part with Lilith as a symbol of evil. It was so convenient to project onto the distorted Goddess everything that is—in different ways for men and women—uncomfortable or threatening in the Feminine. Both men and women are called today to integrate her, and this act of integration must begin with a close look at her scintillating dynamic. We must meet her in the spirit of reverence that is due to an archetype, as a reality of our consciousness, which we were only partially or not at all aware of. We shall have to trace her, in order to hear her message and to face her. The dark aspect of the Goddess is in the process of changing our concept of God, as well as the image we have formed of ourselves and our gender role. Today we experience the Dark Woman in our inner lives. She challenges us to reach out for empowerment, so that we can speak and act from her experience.

Sophia

Meditation

OUR CONCEPT OF WISDOM is so limited that we are frightened when it appears in an unusual garb. All too often wisdom was considered mere *virtue, obedience,* and *submissiveness*—the "good" in a narrow moral sense. A figure of light, a high ideal, but bloodless; beautiful, but pale. In this reduced kind of wisdom, in her partial retirement from life, we have not been able to find Sophia. Where is her strength, her boundless capacity for love, the flame of her divine origin? For three centuries feminine wisdom was persecuted as witchcraft and black magic. The ancient wisdom was stamped out, when the wise women were burned at the stake. From then on, wisdom was cut off from goddess wisdom. She is returning today with the Dark Woman. The power of her presence and her strength are overwhelming. She becomes a threatening figure only when we turn away from her, as so many centuries have done. The Dark Woman has her own wisdom—the wisdom of the blood, the wisdom of death in life and life in death. We discover the mystery of natural transformation in the body of woman. The eternity rings in the hands of Lilith, fashioned by staff and cord, tied the measure of Earth to that of Heaven. Never should an earthly meter be the measure of all things, as the self-conceit and arrogance of the human mind presumed for so long.

Black Woman, rising from oblivion in the dreams of women and men, must not be confused with the masks of evil, which our culture attached to her. She desires to be heard and to lead our souls to wholeness. Give us the strength and wisdom to become what we are, what we are meant to be. Give us courage to rely on your wisdom, so that the intuition of poets, never that of philosophers or theologians, may come true:

> [S]omeday there will be girls and women whose name will
> no longer signify merely an opposite of the masculine, but

something in itself, something that makes one think not of any complement and limit, but only of life and existence: the feminine human being.[27]

Help us to fulfill and turn into tangible reality another, even bolder word of a poet:

> These poets will exist. When the endless servitude of woman is broken, when she lives for and by herself, man— heretofore abominable—having given her her release, she too will be a poet! Woman will find some of the unknown! Will her world of ideas differ from ours?—She will find strange, unfathomable, repulsive, delicious things; we will take them, we will understand them.[28]

[27] Rainer Maria Rilke, "Letter of May 14, 1904," in *Letters to a Young Poet*, M.D. Herter Norton, trans. (New York: W. W. Norton, 1934), p. 59.
[28] Arthur Rimbaud, *Rimbaud: Complete Works, Selected Letters*, Wallace Fowlie, trans. (Chicago: University of Chicago Pess, 1966), p. 309, Part 6: Selected Letters 1870–1891. This letter was dated 15 May, 1871, to Paul Demeny.

Chapter Three

THE PATRIARCHAL DILEMMA

A FTER THIS BRIEF EXCURSION INTO THE configurations of the dark aspect of the Goddess, which focused on only a few facets and branches of the development, we turn once more to biblical tradition. Also in the New Testament, wisdom plays a part, but a subdued and very different one compared to Lady Wisdom of the Old Testament and the Apocrypha. From now on, we shall call her Sophia consistently, as this was her name in the Gospels and the Letters of Saint Paul, all of which were originally composed in Greek. The close link between biblical Sophia and Greek philosophy now becomes apparent. Under the influence of Greek, or rather, Hellenistic thought, which spread throughout the entire Mediterranean world, the concept of divine wisdom changed. Sophia gained in stature, and at the same time she lost. Her independence was reduced, but on the other hand her identification with Jesus Christ gave her a new legitimacy.

Even moderate acquaintance with the research in this area reveals the complexity of thought under the Greek influence and an ambivalence of basic philosophical concepts. By comparison, the self-revelations of Sophia in the older texts were rich and many-faceted, yet clear and easy to grasp. Her imagery was diverse, but close to life and within the range of human experience. The ancient Goddess spoke with her own voice; she made herself known by her own utterance. She testified to the qualities of her power. In Greek philosophy, Sophia became an abstract concept, with its history of development and a new meaning attached by every school of thought. From the original meaning of wisdom as a sort of practical skill and know-how, Sophia was elevated to a transcendental realm and mutated into a lofty ideal beyond human reach. Pythagoras, Plato, the Stoics, the Gnostic School, the early Christian writers and church fathers each had their own understanding of Sophia. Early in the Christian era, wisdom basically meant three things: a faculty bestowed by the grace of God; a divine attribute or special quality of God; and thirdly a *hypostasis*, that is, a personification of God. Sophia became projected onto each person of the Holy Trinity in turn. In the interpretation of Clement of Alexandria, Gregory of Nazianz, Irenaeus, Augustine, or Thomas Aquinas, the image became more complex and more difficult to understand intellectually. More and more, the discourse on Sophia became one of erudite theology, an elaborate "system," which needed to be defined and set off against other patterns of thought, other "systems." There is no revelation at work any more, no evidence of divine truth, but speculation and conjecture, an attempt to penetrate divine mysteries with the human intellect.

The mind of the Greeks had provided an instrument for abstract thought, which no one with any claim to learning and wisdom in the Hellenic world could afford to ignore. The multiple interpretations and projections of central philosophical and theological concepts, like those of Sophia and Logos, seem rather confusing, but they respond to existent realities. They have a "seat in life," as it were. From the viewpoint of the individual author, they are consistent, even fascinating and beautiful, but each in their own way helped to wipe out Sophia as a divine person in her own right. When philosophers and theologians are at work, they invariably quarrel, and so Sophia got caught in the so-called Arian conflict over the question whether Jesus, as the Son of God, was of equal nature with the Divine Father.

There was also the struggle of the early church against Gnostic thought, with its own speculations about Sophia. Indeed, in the early Christian centuries, the image of God was far from established and accepted by all believers.[1] The "Gnostic heresy" worshipped Sophia as the feminine element of God, but was finally outlawed by Christian orthodoxy. As the revolutionary discovery of the Gnostic Gospels in the desert of Nag Hammadi showed, Christianity all but lost Sophia when the early Gnostics were condemned to silence and their scriptures were destroyed. Those texts which escaped destruction afford startling insights into *gnosis*, the Greek word for "knowledge." The Gnostics claimed to have intuitive insight into the nature of the divine, of which Sophia was a prominent part. But the spirit of the age was against Sophia; Logos carried the day.

The Greek concept of *logos* expanded at the same time as the decline of Sophia. The word denotes "logical" thought and speech, rational perception, but also signifies eternal truth and divine power, in which all things have their origin. The important fact is that *logos* became more and more the focus of philosophical thought, whereas *sophia*, wisdom, was left behind. Also, the two concepts partly over-lapped, when on the one hand *sophia* was interpreted as "world soul," but at the same time *logos*, via the Stoic tradition linked with Heraclitus, was understood as *pneuma*—spirit, world spirit, or world soul.

---

[1] See Elaine Pagels, *The Gnostic Gospels* (New York: Vintage Books, 1979). The significance of this impeccable piece of scholarship can hardly be overrated. Pagels is not a feminist theologian, but a historian of religion. Her findings, however, are grist on the mill for all who long to bring Sophia back to our image of God. Moreover, her analysis of gnostic beliefs affirms some basic attitudes of the spiritual quest of our time.

Sophia

When Philo of Alexandria (13 B.C.–A.D. 45), an influential Hellenistic philosopher of Jewish background, is held responsible for the suppression of Sophia by the concept of Logos, we have to take into account that this tendency already existed before his time. Philo simply built on it, and we may assume that his thinking had a considerable influence on the Gospel of John. The well-known opening words: "When all things began, the Word (*logos*) already was. The Word dwelt with God, and what God was, the Word was," remind us of the self-revelation of Lady Wisdom in the eighth chapter of Proverbs: "The Lord created (had) me at the beginning of his works..." Sophia is divine creative power, as the Gnostics affirmed. In the Gospel of John, this creative power becomes Logos. In Paul's first letter to the Corinthians we read (1:24): ". . . yet to those who have heard his (Jesus') call, Jews and Greeks alike, he is the power of God and the wisdom of God." In his letter to the Ephesians, Paul speaks of the "wisdom of God in all its varied forms" (3:10), which shall be made known through his church. Sophia is located in Jesus Christ, or the cosmic Christ, but also in the Virgin Mary as incarnated wisdom, as the origin and Mother of the Church, as well as in the Holy Spirit.

If we assemble all the passages about Sophia in the New Testament, we find counterparts in the Wisdom Texts of the Old Testament.[2] However, the references to Sophia in connection with Jesus are strangely subdued. One reason may be the need to define clear boundaries against the Gnostic movement, which also identified Sophia with Jesus,

---

[2] Such a comparison was made by Thomas Schipflinger, *Sophia-Maria: Eine ganzheitliche Vision der Schöpfung* (Munich-Zurich: Verlag Neue Stadt, 1988). This encyclopedia of sophianic texts compiled by the author during a lifetime has become an important sourcebook for the sophianic movement in Germany. An English Language edition is in preparation by Samuel Weiser (York Beach, ME, Nov. 1997). I owe much to this inspiring and inexhaustible work, as well as to the study of Susan Cady/Marian Ronan/Hal Taussig, *Sophia—The Future of Feminist Spirituality* (San Francisco: HarperSanFrancisco, 1986).

but did not accept his fully human status, his physical passion and res-urrection. The more Gnosis elevated Sophia, the greater was the danger for the early Church to be associated with the "Gnostic heresy." This may partly account for the fact that in the scriptures of the New Testament Sophia is given such low profile, although she is an indis-pensable factor in the legitimization of Jesus as the Son of God.[3]

The practice of identifying Sophia with Logos, and their joint pro-jection onto Jesus, was continued by the church fathers and in the theo-logical discourse of later times. An important element was lost in this process: Sophia's own identity and her closeness to nature. Today this loss is held responsible for the disastrous neglect of creation, the exploitation and destruction of nature. In subjecting her to his ends, man did not treat her wisely. Therefore, Wisdom withdrew from the world, as she always does when she is rejected.

The dilemma remains unsolved: The absorption of Sophia into the complex Christian concepts of God—her association with the persons of the Trinity and the church—has all but obliterated her stature, although it could not eradicate her altogether. Her viability is proved by the fact that, throughout the centuries, there have been single women and men who were moved by Sophia, the Wisdom of God, and bore witness to her, either in accordance with the prevailing theology or independently and even against orthodox teaching. There was never a question about the *femininity* of this figure, even though she became amalgamated with Jesus Christ. The sophianic side of Jesus Christ is his most feminine one. It appears that the mystically inclined person, be it man or woman, always longed for the feminine complement in the image of God. This deep longing for wholeness found ways of expression throughout histo-ry, in medieval *Minnesang* (courtly love poetry), in mystical Mariology,

---

[3] Compare Susan Cady et al, *Sophia—The Future of Feminist Spirituality*, pp. 50-52.

in the visions of Sophia and the sensuous, erotic language of the mystics of all times. It is a lamentable fact that in the wake of the Enlightenment, an increasingly materialistic worldview and the growing abstraction of rational theology, the Christian tradition lost the inspiration of *eros*.[4] Sophia was thoroughly co-opted by *logos*. The language of love—beyond *agape* and *caritas*—has no place any more in religious life. Yet, a religion lacking in *eros* loses its sap; it dries out and atrophies. The love of God and one's neighbor, the central message of Christianity, although of divine origin, has become pale and anemic. Eros, the passionate attraction to a polar opposite and the elemental drive for unity, has gone out of it. Modern Christianity lacks "Isis power," as Rudolf Steiner, a sharp-eyed diagnostician of the religious deficit in Christianity, called it.[5]

> We lost Isis, the Mother of the Saviour, Sophia, Divine Wisdom. . . . We do not lack Jesus, the perception of Christ, but the Isis of Christ, the Sophia of Christ.[6]

In other words: the Mother of the Savior is called for, not as the Virgin Mary, the humble and obedient servant of God, but as Isis, the creatress, the erotically charged Goddess of ancient times, who unites with Osiris for the sake of her divine wholeness, who searches for him among the dead and raises him up to new life. Isis is not an abstract principle of asexual love in superhuman remoteness—as the love of Mary is generally imagined—but she is passionately bound to the Earth and human affairs. From her divine womb all life comes forth. It is her special con-

---

[4] See Walter Schubart, *Religion und Eros* (Munich: H. C. Beck, 1966).
[5] Rudolf Steiner, *Die Suche nach der neuen Isis, der göttliche Sophia*. Four lectures, delivered in December 1920 (Dornach, 1980).
[6] Steiner, *Die Suche nach der neuen Isis*, pp. 30, 34 (translation mine).

cern that life is maintained within its organic order, its rhythm, its possibility to unfold and its natural decay. This is the "Isis of Christ," his Sophia, but she became submerged in a lopsided spiritualized Logos and a kind of wisdom inaccessible to human beings; in Holy Spirit descending in the shape of a dove from the dizzy heights of Godfather. Formerly, the dove was the symbol of the love of the Goddess, but this imagery was lost in the exclusive dialog of the Father with his "only begotten" Son. Like all the other attributes of the Goddess, the dove was transmuted into something else, in honor of a God who split himself off from feminine creative power. Sophia entered into the threefold conception of God in various ways, but she became invisible in the process. She is no longer perceived as an entity in her own right. She did not unite with the Holy Trinity to form a quaternity. Her origin in the Great Goddess became obliterated in orthodox Christianity. Whenever she appears in her own name, she does so by the back entrance, as it were, outside the religious mainstream. But whenever this happens, her speech is new, unheard-of, pronounced with images of stunning force.

Within our context, we can only point out a few examples and try to show the ways in which she raises her voice time and again, how she literally breaks through from the wellspring of the Divine. In the line of sophianic visionaries we find diverse personalities such as Hildegard, the German mystic of the Middle Ages, Jacob Boehme with his monumental, obscure utterance, Gottfried Arnold and others in his wake, as well as the Russian sophiologists of the 19th and 20th centuries. These individuals differ greatly, but they share the profound experience of Sophia as a divine presence. Through their works we get a glimpse of the radical authenticity of their visions. At the same time, Sophia is overshadowed by orthodox doctrine, a barrier which the visionaries were not quite able to overcome. Even a religious genius has to articulate her or his message in terms of the prevailing "paradigm" to some extent and cannot simply ignore the established tradition of thought.

We shall attempt to view this phenomenon with understanding and love, to appreciate the greatness of the revelation within the limits imposed, and at the same time we shall try to relate these sublime visions of Sophia to the burning needs of our age. It is not easy to get into the spirit of an older tradition, a religious *ambiente* of the past, to understanding it on its own terms, and then step back and view it from the vantage point of our time. It would be tempting to immerse oneself in the cosmos of Hildegard's visions and surrender to their wisdom, to roam through the tangle of Jacob Boehme's exuberant and highly idiosyncratic vision of God, to be entranced by the flights of Soloviev's sophianic poetry, rather than to detach ourselves from these enchantments and ask the question: What do they mean to *us?* Can we still draw nourishment from tradition? Can Sophia be re-awakened from these configurations, or do we have to find our own, to respond to our needs and our longings? However this may be, the tradition is worth knowing. It is so rich and varied that many years of study would not suffice to exhaust it. We can only acquire a fragmentary knowledge, but it is important to understand that the history of Sophia is a tree of many branches and that all of them mirror the development of human consciousness.

As we celebrate the return of Divine Wisdom in our day, we want to know where we are going. The intuition of the Feminine Divine is as old as mankind, but it went through multiple changes and deflections. Today we have a desire to heal the disruption that took place thousands of years ago, when the Goddess of many names was overthrown. In the crisis of our civilization we suffer the damages caused by this course of events. A change is imminent, and it is already partly taking place. As always in times of change, there is the temptation to throw overboard everything of the past and to start from scratch, but this can't be done.

Every new beginning has its source or origin. In other words, it would be most unwise to throw the baby out with the bathwater, thanks to the Goddess. All things that were once a driving force in the hearts and minds, in the heads and souls of human beings, have a wonderful way to survive. This is also true for the sophianic tradition. When all is said and done, Sophia never really died, but she went her own winding paths, drawing on ancient lore, gaining strength from the reservoir of archetypal images. Largely eliminated from the official discourse of God, she re-emerged powerfully in the visions of Hildegard, a nun from the Rhine Valley, in the 12th century of the Christian era.

Hildegard of Bingen
(1098–1179)

SO MUCH HAS BEEN WRITTEN about Hildegard in recent years that we shall limit our biographical notes to a few data.

The fact that her parents intended her for the church when she was still a small child is significant. This was the destiny of many sons and daughters well into modern times, and one never knew how it would turn out. In the case of Hildegard, this denial of "self-determination," as we would call it today, is to be counted as a blessing. The sensitive and delicate child was consigned to an anchoress, Jutta of Spanheim, for her religious education. She entered the convent of Benedictine nuns on the Disibodenberg in the Rhine Valley, before she was appointed abbess and founded her own convent on the Rupertsberg. As is well known, a medieval nun enjoyed liberties which were largely denied to aristocratic or lower-class women. For one, her calling protected her from an undesirable marriage. She was not subjected to any male domination except the church authorities, and therefore she was much less dependent than a daughter or a married woman. In addition, the monasteries were the only place in those days where a woman could educate her mind. In the position of an abbess she was able to shape the spiritual life of a community of women, as Teresa of Avila did in an outstanding way centuries later.

When both Hildegard and Teresa were literally overpowered by their visions, they felt inhibited to write them down, because as women they did not consider themselves worthy of this privilege. But whenever Hildegard disregarded the divine voice, she fell into a severe illness, and in fact she was ailing most of her life. Her achievements in the course of her long career, despite her physical weakness, are astonishing. She is acclaimed as a physician and healer with deep knowledge of the healing properties of herbs, as a poetess, a composer of music, an artist, but above all as a visionary, the *prophetissa teutonica*, the "German prophetess." In an era of great spiritual upheaval, when scholasticism began to establish a rational foundation for the perception of God, a flood of apocalyptic images broke loose upon this woman. She relates how it happened:

> In the year 1141 of the incarnation of Jesus Christ, the Word of God, when I was forty-two years and seven months old, a burning light coming from heaven poured into my mind. Like a flame which does not burn but rather enkindles, it inflamed my heart and my breast, just as the sun warms something with its rays. And I was able to understand books suddenly, the psaltery clearly, the evangelists and the volumes of the Old and New Testament. . . . I had felt within myself the gift of secret mysteries and wondrous visions from the time I was a little girl, certainly from the time I was five years old right up to the present time.[7]

[7] Hildegard von Bingen, *Scivias*. The English Translation from the Critical Latin Edition, trans. by Bruce Hozeski (Santa Fe, New Mexico: Bear & Company, 1986), p. 2.

In this great age of female mystics, some were overwhelmed by inner visions in their childhood. Mechthild of Magdeburg, who had lived for decades as a Beguine, until she entered the convent of Helfta, reports in her mystical work, *Das fließende Licht der Gottheit* ["The Flowing Light of the Divine"]: "In my twelfth year, one day when I was alone, I was greeted by the exceedingly blissful stream of the Holy Spirit. . . . This very sweet greeting came to me every day."[8] Thereupon she gave her soul up to the love of God (*Gottesminne*), and it is this quality of bridal tenderness which is so characteristic of feminine mysticism in the Middle Ages. Especially for the Beguines, who led a communal spiritual life outside the discipline of monastic rule, the mystical union of the soul with God was an intimate encounter with the divine lover. The soul is the bride, Jesus the bridegroom, and the idiom of this relationship is tender, poetic, and highly erotic. The feminine soul, longing for union, gives the most personal and individual expression to her love's desire. These testimonies are permeated with the spirit of the Song of Songs, the atmosphere of the ancient *hieros gamos*, the sacred wedding.[9]

By comparison, Hildegard's personality does not intrude into her visions. She does not view herself as the mystical bride of Jesus, but rather as a "trumpet of God," an instrument of the divine will. As a Benedictine nun, she abides by the teachings of the church, and yet she achieves an amazing freedom of spirit and boldness of expression. At times, the cosmic images she received seem to have a deeper significance

---

[8] Mechthild of Magdeburg (c. 1212-1290), *Das fließende Licht der Gottheit* ["The Flowing Light of the Godhead"], translated into modern German by Margot Schmidt (Zurich: Benziger, 1955), 4.2 (translation mine).

[9] The church did not always view this mystical exuberance with favor. In 1310, the Beguine Marguerite de Porete, the author of a handbook on mystical love, was burned at the stake for heresy. See Gerhard Wehr, *Die deutsche Mystik* (Berne-Munich-Vienna: Scherz, 1988), p. 135.

than her own reading suggests. From a modern point of view, we occasionally get an even more revolutionary message than she was able to communicate within the philosophical and theological framework of her time.

Her first great prophetic work, *Scivias* ["Know the Ways"], may seem strange, if not offensive, to the modern mind. It displays an obsession with the sinfulness of man, and there is a consistent warning to beware of the devil. The vices are castigated with a severity worthy of the prophets of the Old Testament. Every worldly desire, especially carnal lust, is of evil, and believers are told that they can only ascend to heavenly love by renouncing the world. They are admonished "to love those things which are of heaven and trample under foot those things which are of the earth."[10] In this great vision of God and humanity as part of creation seen against the background of time, the human being is an infant, a creature of weakness, forever struggling against the devil. Indeed, the devil rears his ugly head everywhere. Hildegard portrays him as a monster of obscene ugliness resembling a snake or a dragon. We constantly encounter dualisms: God and Satan, good and evil, virtue and vice, sin and innocence, spirit and the flesh, Heaven and Earth, the profane and the spiritual, the saved and the condemned. Here we have an inventory of irreconcilable opposites, which human beings at the end of the 20th century have learned to regard differently. Hildegard, as a child of her age, is seen to project the devil and everything evil outside, so as to be better able to castigate them.

Likewise, her image of man in this book follows the lines of biblical anthropology, as is to be expected. Woman is subject to man, and her purpose in life is to bear children. Hildegard justifies the exclusion of women from the ministry, because they are a "weak and fragile vessel"

---

[10] *Scivias*, p. 322f. (Vision 10:3).

and naturally inclined to yield to seduction. Hildegard's subconscious projection of sexuality onto woman as the epitome of evil is revealed with disturbing clarity in one of her last visions of *Scivias*. A female figure with a repulsive mask of the devil in the place of her genitals, is meant to represent the corruption of the church by vice and abuse, but what impresses the viewer today is not so much this pious intention, but the image of a woman with the devil between her legs. Hildegard clearly wishes to expose evil in the church and the immorality of the clergy, but by using this image as a symbol she unconsciously re-enforces the ancient misogyny of the church. In the age of the crusades, when Christian knights went forth to defend the true faith with the sword, no other than militant imagery was possible even to Hildegard's intuition. She calls men to take up arms against the Antichrist, the spawn of a depraved mother.

> This worthless deceiver will be cast forth into the world from a mother who had been nourished from girlhood until young womanhood with the crafts of the devil. She will be full of faults and full of despair and live among the most abominable people. . . . There she will secretly contrive the most wanton villainy of fornication, and she will pollute herself with several men of great baseness. She will act as if a holy angel has commanded her to accomplish this passion of depravity. And so in the most passionate burning of fornication, she will conceive the son of destruction, but she will not even know that she conceived him from the seed of these several men.[11]

---

[11] *Scivias*, p. 353 (Vision 11:25).

The devil's mother teaches her son witchcraft and brazenly calls her illicit sexual practices "sacred."

How can we not be reminded of Lilith in this instance, the "night-jar" banished to the desert, the promiscuous seductress of men, from whose sinfully spilled semen she derives her children? Without refer-ring directly to Lilith, Hildegard reveals the source of her imagery in the Old Testament. As we have seen, the Scriptures abound in invectives against the cult of the Goddess. We have to acknowledge that even Hildegard unwittingly contributed to the vilification of the feminine and helped prepare the ground for the persecution of the "witches" in later centuries. She also confirmed the anti-Judaism of the church in many of her statements, when she holds forth against "heathens, Jews and false Christians."

At first glance, *Scivias* presents a grim picture of man and the world. It is a book of exhortation and warning, reflecting the problems of her time, the threat to the church, the emerging conflict between spir-itual and worldly powers, and the decay of monastic discipline. Her greatest concern is the protection of the church as the body of Christ. Hence her stern warning to men to follow the path of righteousness, to "know the ways."

Where, in this irreconcilable opposition of Heaven and Earth, is any space for Sophia?

It is curious to observe that, on the one hand, Hildegard represents the teachings of the church, but on the other, her vision is far greater than her proclaimed belief. Already in this first book, the mysterious "power of green," is mentioned, *viriditas* in Latin, viridity or verdure, which signifies, above all, the power inherent in nature to make all things grow and blossom, but also the potential of the human soul in unity with God. Viridity, the green power, which animates and sustains the entire universe, is related to Sophia. It is rooted in love, the love of

God for humanity and the whole creation. It is the quality that keeps the world together, a divine creative power without which nothing can flourish or come into its own.

Where does this leave Sophia as a spiritual entity? Hildegard mentions her in her exhortations to men to embrace wisdom. This is the reduced biblical view, defining wisdom as the "fear of God," the correct administration of the sacraments and the word of God. Hildegard's Sophia seems absorbed by Logos according to the doctrine of the New Testament. However, her statements about Sophia differ to a great extent. There are visions in which divine wisdom appears in magnificent stature. As Queen of Virtues, she stands on top of her house with seven pillars, united with God, as Hildegard comments:

> She has been joined in God and to God in the sweetest embrace in a religious dance of burning love. . . . This beautiful image was looking into the world for people. This is because she loves people greatly. As a result, she always guides and protects with her own protection those who wish to follow her and to stand firm with her.[12]

This is Sophia as we know her from the wisdom texts, God's darling and the lover of men. As so often in the visions, an overpowering light is seen to radiate from her head like flashes of lightning, so that the visionary is unable to look into her face. Sophia appears as an even more monumental figure in another vision (II, 5): a majestic presence in silver and gold rising from mountain tops, holding to her breast a vast calyx. Embedded in this boat-like calyx are a number of human beings, including Mary as the incarnation of heavenly wisdom. This representation of Sophia

---

[12] *Scivias*, p. 312 (Vision III, 9:25).

shows a striking resemblance to the design of a gold signet ring of about 1500 B.C., from the palace of Knossos on the island of Crete. Here the Goddess stands in an equally majestic posture on a mountaintop of almost identical stylization, the "World Mountain." In her extended hand she holds the scepter of her authority.[13] Could it be that Hildegard's subconscious was flooded by images of an older deity, the Goddess on the sacred mountain, taking the visionary beyond her immediate mission? Hildegard repeatedly affirms that she never invented anything, that her visions were not dreams or hallucinations of an abnormal state of mind. She affirms that she only reported what she saw, when she was wide-awake and in full possession of her faculties. It was a formidable task to put into words those images by which she herself was overawed.

What do we make of the vision titled "The Universe" (I, 3) in the shape of an egg surrounded by flames? (See illustration on page 90.) From the outer sphere to the center, the cosmos is revealed layer by layer, adorned with twinkling stars, sun and moon in a configuration which reminds us of the Taoist symbol of Yin-and-Yang, topped by a fiery star with five additional stars of smaller size above and below. We recall that the number Five was sacred to the Goddess. What does the round shape in the middle signify, with a blue ring inside and a sort of horizontal wedge? Hildegard calls this wedge a "vast mountain," but refrains from interpreting it. To an unprejudiced eye, this shape in blue, surrounded and interlaced with green, is clearly a symbol of sexual union.

The ring, or circle, is an ancient symbol of the female principle, and the wedge penetrating it obviously resembles the male organ. Hildegard describes in detail the various "skins" of this cosmos, the wild elements in the interior, the hierarchy of the stars, but does not say a word about

---

[13] Reproduced in Sir Arthur Evans, *The Palace of Minos*, 4 vols. (1921-1936); also in: *In All Her Names*, ed. by Thomas Campbell and Charles Musès (San Francisco: HarperSanFrancisco, 1991), p. 65.

this highly significant imagery at the center. Would it have been too bold, too outrageous for a medieval nun to envision a *hieros gamos* at the heart of the universe, an act of sexual congress? She had condemned sexuality as sinful, permitted only for the sake of procreation, but never for pleasure or gratification. "Lust" according to narrow Christian morals was sinful.[14] The sexual act as physical expression of man's delight in woman and a woman's delight in her mate as a way of "knowing" the beloved, is outside her consideration. Hildegard conveys the received image, but she seems embarrassed to interpret it fully in words, because the imagery contradicts the idea of a patriarchal God as the sole creator of all things. Hildegard communicates great secrets, but this one remains veiled.

Her second prophetical work, *Liber de operatione Dei* (*The Book of Divine Works*), is a monumental vision of cosmological correspondences not easily accessible to modern readers. In this work of her ripe old age, the dualisms noted before are less conspicuous. In fact, they almost dissolve in the great design of God, in which everything has its place and which provides for correspondences on other planes of being. We human beings no longer represent the weak and sinful flesh, but are the divinely inspired crown of creation. With every part of the body, our physical and mental being, we are integrated into the cosmos. We are intended for wholeness, for the harmonious interaction of body and soul. The soul penetrates the body and works through it; it is the "green life force of the flesh." The sharp dichotomy of the earlier vision seems changed, because both body and soul exist, despite their different natures, as one single reality: ". . . it is the soul which brings the vital power of the body and the senses to us in full measure."[15]

---

[14] Incidentally, the German word *Lust* still carries this comprehensive meaning of pleasure, delight, and joy.

[15] Hildegard of Bingen, *The Book of Divine Works*, ed. and introd. by Matthew Fox (Santa Fe, New Mexico: Bear & Company, 1987), p. 158.

But the center of God's works is *love*. Love is the power in the heart of the universe. This is true Love, which is God:

> [C]onstantly circling, wonderful for human nature, and such that is not consumed by age and cannot be increased by anything new. It rather remains just as God has created it, everlasting until the end of time.[16]

With our physical and mental being, we are wholly dependent on cosmic forces. Our lives are sustained by the power of the elements and the assistance of all parts of the creation. Our actions inevitably influence the whole world, and therefore we carry a great responsibility. This is one of the thoughts which makes Hildegard, the medieval nun, appear as our contemporary. Her anticipation of natural catastrophes caused by human beings is truly prophetic:

> If the elements under the sun should be shaken by disasters, the fire of the sun will be darkened, as happens during a solar eclipse. Then it becomes an indication of errors and a proof that our hearts and heads have turned to error. They are no longer able to walk along the right path of the law, but fight each other in many conflicts.[17]

There are other passages, too, which express concern for the preservation of the world:

> And I heard a tremendous voice crying out from the elements of the world unto God: "We are unable to complete

---

[16] Hildegard of Bingen, *The Book of Divine Works*, p. 26 (Vision 2:2).
[17] *The Book of Divine Works*, p. 46 (Vision 2:32).

our course and cannot follow our orbit. For Man is turning us over and over by his evil deeds, and for his sake we give off pestilence because of the lack of any kind of justice."[18]

If Man does righteous deeds, the elements run their true course. If he does evil, then he calls up the elements for vengeful retribution on himself.[19]

The order of creation is sustained by wisdom, which is "mild and gentle."

Therefore, wisdom must be loved more than all the beauty of creation and is recognized as lovable by all saintly souls, since their desire of her loving sight is never satisfied.[20]

Not only God and Love are one, but in Hildegard's intuition Wisdom and Love are so closely linked that they can only be conceived as a unity. Divine Wisdom is permeated by Love, and vice versa. In a letter addressed to a religious community, she describes Love as a winged maiden of surpassing beauty, the "Mistress" of the world:

For creation issued from Love, because Love was foremost of all things.[21]

---

[18] *Liber Vitae Meritorum*, quoted in *Scivias*, ed. by Maura Böcker (Salzburg: Otto Müller, 1963), p. 389. Translation mine. To the best of my knowledge, there is no English translation of this work of Hildegard of Bingen.

[19] *Liber Vitae Meritorum*, translation mine.

[20] *Liber de operatione Dei* ["Book of Divine Works"], translation mine.

[21] Quoted in *Hildegard of Bingen*, ed. by Heinrich Schipperges (Olten-Freiburg: Walter, 1978), p. 159, translation mine.

Accordingly, there are two similar representations of Sophia and Love in the visions of *Liber de operatione Dei*. Both are female figures of regal appearance with flaming red countenance, clad in an underdress of white silk and a pale green tunic adorned with jewels. Viridity, the "greening power," has an important share in Love as well as Wisdom. Another figure identified as "Wisdom" by Hildegard is a spirit with six-fold wings in a praying posture. This entity, with the feet of a lion is wearing a tight-fitting garment of scales. Her head is flaming red, and in her womb she carries the head of an elderly bearded man. Hildegard interprets this figure as the "Omnipotence of God," but this person of feminine, or at least androgynous aspect, clearly suggests Sophia.

The countenance of all representations of Sophia in Hildegard's vision are red, the color of the Goddess. The lions' feet may remind us of the Goddess Lilith, her feet standing on the back of two lions. The strength of the lion symbolizes the power of the sun, which was associated with the Goddess before the patriarchal shift took over both sun and lion as symbols of the masculine principle. In the sixfold wings we see five luminous spheres, the magic number of feminine power that was sacred to the goddess Ishtar. The scaly garment may suggest water as the symbol of life and feminine creative power. Since ancient times water has been associated with the sphere of the feminine. Scales might also suggest the Age of Pisces, the sign under which Jesus Christ was born. Does the head of the old man in the womb in the figure stand for mankind in need of salvation, as Hildegard suggests? Or is it a symbol of Godfather, who is represented in a similar way in another of Hildegard's sophianic visions? In any case, the picture shows the Divine Feminine as *matrix*, the maternal womb that holds the masculine, according to the oldest intuition of mankind.

These are mysteries which defy definite explanation. Their meaning cannot be pinned down once and for all. They remain open to interpretation according to the intuition of a particular age, and this applies also to Hildegard's age. One of the differences between her time and ours is that in our time the distant past has been recovered and rehabilitated to an extent undreamed of in the Middle Ages. Whatever Hildegard may have divined about the Goddess, she was unable to put it into words, except in the context of biblical scripture and orthodox Christian belief. However, the symbolic content of the pictures, which were faithfully executed by a monastic helpmate according to her instructions, seems to waver between the Christian and an older conception of God. In her divinely inspired vision, Hildegard appears to have received more than she was able to articulate within her frame of reference.

The representations of Sophia in her second prophetical work are especially powerful. In one vision she appears as a red figure in a richly ornamented golden dress with fourfold wings, the head of Godfather elevated above her own, the sacred Lamb on her breast. Her feet tread on a black monster representing Evil. Hildegard calls this figure the Love of God, "the highest, fiery power" present in all life. Its pronouncement through the mouth of the visionary: "In wisdom I have ordered the universe," calls to mind the self-revelations of Sophia in the Wisdom Texts of the Old Testament and the Apocrypha. The same figure makes her appearance once again, her body a giant wheel to encompass the universe. In the center of this cosmos stands man, his limbs extended between Heaven and Earth, his whole being penetrated by the elements. This is a powerful image, which reminds Hildegard of her vision of the universe in the shape of the cosmic egg twenty-eight years before. This time, the cosmos is embedded in the womb of a figure resembling Sophia, her arms folded around it in a loving and protective gesture.

The range of Hildegard's imagery is inexhaustible. The more we meditate on it, the more insight we gain into her life's work, and the more does the initial impression of her as a dogmatic disciplinarian, as she appears in *Scivias*, fade away. With her prophetic gift, her practical concern for the world, her love of greening nature, of the arts, her knowledge of medicine, her healing capacity, and her untiring, active love of her fellow beings, she truly represents sophianic power.

It is no accident that Hildegard has been rediscovered in recent years, especially by women. Germany is being swept by a veritable Hildegard Renaissance. In any well-stocked bookstore one might easily find up to forty titles of her own works in various translations, commentaries, handbooks of "Hildegard Medicine," collections of her medical and cooking recipes. Medicines and ointments are prepared according to her prescription. Physicians and non-professionals alike find it rewarding to study Hildegard's views on natural healing. She knew about the interrelation of body and soul, the physical and spiritual nature. She was not concerned with curing symptoms, but with healing the person. She knew that true healing does not take place in the body, but in a transpersonal or transcendental dimension. The principles of psychosomatic medicine were self-evident to her. Hildegard, the medieval nun, became an inspiration to holistic medicine in our day.

On her advice, the common spelt (*Dinkel*), a grain of high nutritious value and resistance to pests, was brought back to German cooking. Natural food stores and most bakeries now carry spelt, and tasty breads and cakes made from this grain are widely sold. With Hildegard, the art of cooking is an issue of the greatest importance. As she uses the word, cooking stands for various processes of physical and spiritual preparation. She reports, for instance, that she was thoroughly "cooked" by her sufferings, in order to prepare her for the divine call. Similarly, the female and male juices are "cooked" in the act of sexual union, so that new life is engendered by the heat and the moisture. Cooking in Hildegard's understanding is an alchemical process of transformation, in which material elements as well as spiritual and divine forces have a share.

We are drawn to Hildegard's synoptic view of inside and outside, body and soul, nature and human being, human being and God. Despite the dualisms and the hierarchical order of the medieval world, this limitation gives way time and again to a more holistic vision. The opposition of the sexes at the expense of women and the condemnation of physical love appear in a different light when we meditate on her imagery or draw on her complete writings, including her book on healing and her letters. When man and woman become "one flesh," Hildegard no longer insists on woman's subservience or bondage to man. As she describes the act of sexual union in her plain and vivid language, what comes across is not the subjection of women, but the dignity of both sexes and their equality in the cosmic order. There is bliss and salvation in the unity of the male and the female. Despite her statements about the weakness and moral frailty of women, Hildegard has basically a very high opinion of her sex: "In woman there is the fountain of wisdom and a wellspring of complete joy . . .[22] Sophianic wisdom, which she herself embodies, is a charisma of woman in this fallen state of the world. Still greater and more powerful is divine Sophia as she appears in Hildegard's visions, in symbols the visionary herself is unable to fathom.

After centuries of oblivion, Hildegard of Bingen has returned, because our time and our damaged world are in need of Sophia. In an age when nature had not yet been destroyed in any degree comparable to our times, Hildegard appealed to humanity to take responsibility for nature. The cosmic order requires man to look after the creation of which he is part, and help to preserve it. She knew about the inner rela-

---

[22] From her correspondence, quoted in Schipperges, *Hildegard von Bingen*, p. 155, translation mine.

tionship and interdependence of all things, an outlook Western science came to adopt only recently. She considered herself a simple and uneducated woman, unworthy of the grace bestowed upon her as the transmitter of divine visions. Despite her scruples and her feminine sense of inferiority, she succeeded to convey in images and words a holistic cosmos pervaded by divine love. She bore witness to Sophia as a feminine entity, after she had practically disappeared in the teachings of Western Christianity. Indeed, Sophia cannot go under entirely. She will never be completely lost, but do we still know her?

As we rediscover Sophia in this time of emergency, when the protection of our habitat and a holistic approach to science and all areas of life are imperative, it is well to remember that Western civilization was offered advice and warning centuries ago through the inspired mind of a medieval nun. In some respects, the Middle Ages were indeed a dark age: patriarchal, militant, superstitious, full of religious prejudice and social injustice, but at the same time bursting with creativity. In the most turbulent times, a woman stood up who reminded humanity of the world order as it was designed by God. Eight centuries before the invention of "Greenpeace" and the foundation of Green Parties as a new ecologically-oriented force in politics, Hildegard of Bingen proclaimed the divine "greening power" in her prophetic vision.

If today there is mention of love as a cosmic force without which everything runs out of order, Hildegard provided a blueprint for this approach. Until a few years ago, it was considered bad taste, or downright absurd, to speak of love in politics, economics, or science, and to confess a love of trees seemed restricted to Native Americans and Zen Buddhists.[23] Today the insight is gaining ground that the universal net-

---

[23] When the American poet Gary Snyder was asked why he became a Zen Buddhist, he was reported to reply: "Because with Christians one cannot talk about trees."

work of relationships cannot exist without love, because life dies without it. This was Sophia's message from the beginning, as she allied herself with creation and dwelt among men. She is universally related and all-sustaining love, called *viriditas*, viridity, or "greenness" by Hildegard. It is this intuition of an original state of wholeness, symbolized by the power of green, which has the strongest appeal for us, as the natural viridity or verdure of our world is disappearing.

> Most noble Green,
> rooted in the Sun,
> shining in sparkling brightness,
> circulating in ways
> no human mind can grasp:
> Thou art enfolded
> in the embraces of God's secrets,
> gleaming in the first flush of dawn,
> glowing in the flames of the Sun![24]

---

[24] Hildegard of Bingen, *Carmina*, 39. Translation mine.

Hildegard of Bingen, The Universe. *From her book* Scivias, *Vision I,3: plate 4. Salzburg, Otto Müller Verlag 1987 (8th edition). This is one of her most famous and most mysterious visions. The core shows an act of sexual penetration. Clearly, the creation of the universe is not the work of a lonely Godfather, but of the loving interpenetration of male and female energy.*

Meditation

HOW CAN WE UNDERSTAND what our senses fail to grasp? How is it that viridity is rooted in the sun? What makes Green bright and luminous in the cycle of being?

We took the natural verdure for granted. To our way of thinking, greenness was so ordinary, inexhaustible, and permanently available, we gave no thought to the consequences when we started to destroy it. Today, viridity, the Green of nature, has become most precious to us. It refreshes our eyes, it composes the air we breathe, it keeps the moisture in the ground, so that the soil does not dry out and is not blown away by the wind. Life-enhancing Green, so agreeable to the heart and the imagination. Heart meditations are based on the color of Green, to relieve sorrow, to take away pressure, to translate heaviness and oppression into a livable quality, some small greening hope. What else is hope but a certainty deep down in the heart that there will be an answer, that there will be ways and means, that life is stronger than death? There is a power hidden in viridity, the indefatigable, inexhaustible force of life pulsating in all things. It preserves the world, it maintains the planets in their orbits, it makes the electrons dance around the nucleus. It makes the blood circulate in our veins and turns every day into a new beginning. With every sunrise life, light and hope return. This is how Green is rooted in the sun, because nature requires the light of the sun to put on greenness, just as we need the warmth of the sun to overcome the dark, to think vibrant thoughts, to feel joy.

It is the power of Green that surrounds us tenderly, that opens the door to love. The power of Green is the power that does not violate, but convince; the gentle force that splits the rock, because the living growth is stronger than insensible matter. In everyday life, we often neglect the power of Green, because our hearts are not in our daily pursuits. In our everyday life we are often insensitive to the divine mysteries, even in hours of joy and celebration, hours which have become rare and often do not deserve the name of a feast. And yet—when I look at the green leaflets unfolding in a glazed pot on the window sill, the power of Green is just as tangible as on a green meadow or in the fragrant woods. It is always there, even if I cannot feel it, when my heart is numb and my eyes are dull. God's mysteries surround me at all times, in every leaf and blade of grass, in a laughing eye, in a word of love or a silent gesture of tenderness. There is no end to it, when I think about it. One mystery is woven into another, one spark of Green kindles another. I have a part in everything, and everything is part of me.

I often think that I am lonely, yet I am not. The love which I do not feel, the greening power which I cannot grasp still sustain me. It shaped my body and mind, it gave me the strength to pursue the work I am meant to do, so that love may be increased in the world. If I grow strong in the power of Green, I know that I can never be lonely. The sluggish heart, the paralyzed will, the broken courage, the fear of love—all these evaporate in the sign of Green, absorbed as by the rays of the sun. I was not daring enough—as a woman, as a man. I was stingy with my viridity, until I realized that the treasure cannot increase unless it is given away.

Descend on us, greening power of all life, pervade our whole being. Make us ready to receive your abundance, here in this world, in our everyday lives, as the nun Hildegard received it in the cell of a convent and wherever she went.

J a c o b   B o e h m e
(1 5 7 5 - 1 6 2 4)

SOPHIANIC MYSTICISM RUNS THROUGH the Middle Ages like a deep subterranean stream. It finds expression in the mysterious visions of Hildegard of Bingen, in the personal, highly internalized love relationship between the human soul and Sophia in the testimony of Mechthild of Magdeburg (*Das fließende Licht der Gottheit*) or Heinrich Seuse (*Büchlein der ewigen Weisheit*—"Booklet of Eternal Wisdom"). It enters into the worship of Mary, the religiously inspired poetry of courtly love (*Minnesang*), as well as countless works of art. She makes her appearance as a regal figure in illuminated manuscripts and codices, as one who shares God's throne or as the divine mother at whose breasts bearded men suck the milk of wisdom, or as spiritual *Ecclesia*, personified Church, from whose heart flow the seven rivers of wisdom.[25] On the one hand, she embodies the maternal love of the Virgin Mary, as in the Madonnas of the Protective Cloak; on the other hand, she becomes a spiritual figure lifted high above the usual image of Mary. In Germany, the popular representations of Saint Anne with Mary and the Christ child display a Trinity which is more reminiscent of the ancient myth of Demeter, Kore, and the divine child than the male-dominated Christian Trinity. Even more striking are those wooden sculptures of Mary, the "Vièrges ouvrantes," with doors in their bodies that can be folded out. The wombs of these virgins not only contain Jesus Christ, but also the head of Godfather.[26] Here the Feminine, the Great Mother, shelters the divine Masculine according to the ancient conception. Mary figures, not only as the obedient servant of God and Mater dolorosa, but

---

[25] See Erich Neumann, *The Great Mother*, Bollingen Series, vol. 47, plates 174, 175 (Princeton: Princeton University Press, 1964).

[26] Neumann, *The Great Mother*, see plates 176, 177.

---

as the Queen of Heaven of ancient memory. Potentially at least, Sophia in her full majesty also entered the Virgin Mary. Sophia, the feminine spirit of God, while receding more and more as an independent figure, is projected onto Jesus Christ, Mary and even the Church as the "body of Christ" or the "bride of God." The more the original figure of Divine Wisdom is disappearing out of sight and her feminine-divine primacy is waning, the more she finds ways and means to express herself through other channels. As a divine entity, she cannot be totally erased from human consciousness. She may be obliterated and persecuted— down to the horror of the witch trials; she may be tortured and physically annihilated, she will withdraw from the mainstream of culture, yet she will find ways to survive. She will bide her time, until the world is ready for her return. In extremely unsophianic times, she will occasionally speak through an outsider who is in touch with her when others no longer are.

The period after the Reformation, when dogmatic dispute reached a point of stagnation and threatened to obliterate the living word of God, can hardly be called a sophianically inspired age. Orthodox belief and adherence to exoteric rites had become more important than the true Christian spirit. The discourse of God was controlled by academic theologians, and the fact that a simple tradesman from the province like Jacob Boehme, who had not studied at any university, dared to interfere with learned theology, was a thorn in the flesh of the authorities. Boehme was born in the Silesian town of Görlitz and was a shoemaker by trade. In his time religion had become a pawn in the game of power, and the imminent Thirty Years' War was at least as much a struggle for political dominance among European nations as a religious war.

At this time, the young shoemaker had a mystical experience in his workshop. In the sunrays falling on a pewter vessel he suddenly saw in a flash the inner core of nature as the heart of God. He was deeply shaken and decided to test his experience out of doors. In the fields and meadows the vision returned, and now he was certain that what he had seen was real. He kept his silence for twelve years to contemplate his vision, and after that he described the secrets revealed to him in his first book, *Aurora*. The manuscript circulated among his friends and acquaintances, before the church authorities got wind of it. *Aurora* immediately incited the violent hatred of the chief pastor of Görlitz. Boehme was promptly accused of heresy, thrown into jail and forbidden to write.

For a long time Boehme obeyed this injunction, until the voice of vision could no longer be kept down. While his social position deteriorated, and he had to take to the road as an ambulant peddler, his reputation among the landed aristocracy and the educated in the Silesian countryside was increasing steadily. Many of his contemporaries longed for the testimony of a man who truly had experienced God. His utterance is mysterious, but stirring and sincere and full of unmistakable signs of divine authority. His fame spread within the German Empire and abroad and continued to grow after his death. Across the boundaries of nationality, language and time, he inspired generations of poets, philosophers and religious thinkers. He could always be depended on for an original approach to matters divine, when the life of the mind and the spirit of the age got into a rut. His deep introspection into the mysteries of nature brings him close to our generation, which is concerned about the destruction of nature.

He thought in terms of qualities, not quantities, and in fact, the word "quality" is a key concept of his speculative theosophy. Most of the time, he uses a quaint word of his own coining: "Qual" or "Quall," which suggests a combination of "quality" and German *quellen*, "to spring, well or surge," to describe the dynamic quality of Being, as it is forever welling up, forever changing, replacing the old with the new. If in this process things are out of balance, then the "quality" literally turns into "Qual," a word which in ordinary German usage means "pain" and "suffering," even "agony."

This takes us right to the center of Boehme's dynamic thought. It was mainly fueled by his perplexity over the state of the world: the disturbing fact that good and evil, light and darkness, are continuously mixed. He was troubled by the question how in this medley of qualities God could be conceived as good and unified. In Boehme's spiritual perception, God was the source of glaring opposites and contradictions. He saw that all things in their polarity came from the same *Ungrund*, "non-ground," the Nothing of God. All of Boehme's writings deal with the unfoldment of the relationship between God and the natural world, the nature of God and the position of Man in creation. Even in his most daring speculations, he always tried to remain a straight Lutheran whose desire it was to penetrate the word of God with his vision. He knew that enlightenment by the Holy Spirit was needed for this task, and in proud modesty he claimed that by the grace of God he had received this illumination. He warns the reader that only a person thus enlightened will be able to follow his discourse. This is indeed true, and his readers at all times must have wondered whether they really understood what he was trying to get across in his innovative, idiosyncratic and highly obscure language. The difficulty is obviously not only the subject matter, the speculations on the deepest mysteries of Being, but they are expressed in an idiom which is extremely taxing even for German readers.

What separates us from Boehme is more than the passage of three-and-a-half centuries. Here is a person who cannot fall back on any traditional language. He is unfamiliar with the discourse of philosophy and theology, because he is not a learned man. He did some reading in the field of natural philosophy, astrology, and mysticism, but he cannot rely on any precursor for the expression of his insights. Thus, he is obliged to create a language of his own to fit his perceptions. He must dive into the creative center of language itself and there find the means to make his vision explicit. The fact that the German language lends itself to this deep mining in the magma of prelingual perception is one of the reasons why Jacob Boehme entered history as the "Philosophus teutonicus," a truly German philosopher. He struggled hard to express himself, and for the sake of truth, risked obscurity, complexity, and even crudeness. This quality makes his writings "dark" and difficult to read, but also extremely authentic. His idiom is never abstract, but full of images and metaphors from nature. This sensuous approach is typical for his way of thinking. In his travels across the country, nature was always in front of his eyes, and it was inseparably linked with his experience of God. In nature, in the eternally welling source of polar qualities, God is forever manifest. Here he is present, because his qualities or "well spirits" (*Quellgeister*) are the same that form nature and man.

Similar to Hildegard, Jacob Boehme applies viridity, the greening and growing of nature, to spiritual processes, as for instance, when the spirit is "greening" in the soul. His use of language demonstrates the close interrelation of inner and outer phenomena, the rootedness of all things in *one* source. This is sophianic thinking. In his first work, *Aurora*, Sophia is not yet explicitly mentioned, but in various places, he calls nature "the mother of life" and "a mother, from whom everything wells." In his passionate desire to get to the origin of the Divine, the "being of all beings," Jacob Boehme views Godfather within the Trinity as "giving birth" to his Son. He keeps coming back to this birthing capacity of the Father, and Father and Son together bring forth the Holy Spirit. However, in his exposition of the sevenfold "well spirits" of divine potency the fifth, Love, suggests Wisdom, and the seventh "well spirit" is Nature, which is seen as the mother giving birth to all things. The Divine Mother is present in nature, and her loving relationship with all living things is an authentic aspect of Sophia. However, in this work she does not yet have a share in the Divine Being. Boehme describes his vision of the dynamic Godhead.

> But here thou must know that the *Deity* doth not stand still, but worketh and riseth up without *intermission*, as a pleasant wrestling, moving or struggling. Like two creatures which in great love play together, embracing, struggling and wrestling one with the other; now one is above, by and by the other, and when *one* hath overcome it yieldeth or giveth over, and letteth the *other* rise up again.[27]

The image that comes to mind is Sophia playing before God as his "darling and delight," as suggested by Proverbs 8:22. Boehme is overawed by God's imprint on the entire creation. Everything, the movement of the stars, the weaving of nature, the physical and spiritual disposition of man, are all made from the same divine material.

Fascinated by the eternal struggle of opposite qualities, Boehme never tires of lashing out against the devil, the adversary, as Martin Luther did. This medieval obsession with the devil is one of the things a modern reader will not adjust to easily. Also, the arrogance of referring to "blind Jews, Turks and heathens" can hardly be called sophianic and touches a sensitive point of modern consciousness. Even the most narrow-minded defender of the Christian faith would hardly pronounce blithely: "O thou blind Jew, Turk and Heathen, desist from thy *calumniating*, and submit thyself in obedience to God, and walk in the light . . . .[28] In another passage, however, Boehme has a more liberal out-

---

[27] Jacob Boehme, *The Aurora*, trans. by John Sparrow, ed. by C. J. Barker and D. S. Hehner (Edmonds, WA: Sure Fire Press, 1922), 11:97, 98, pp. 155f.
[28] *Aurora*, p. 247.

look. He acknowledges that the heathens have their share in God and refers to them as "Brethren." He goes even beyond that:

> Or dost thou think that God is the God of the *Christians* only? Do not the *Heathens* also live in God, *whomsoever doth* right or *righteousness* God loveth and *accepteth him*.[29]

In fact, he is saying that the heathen often leads a more godly life than the Christian. Then, indirectly, he is seen to retract these words. Religious tolerance was not a virtue of the 16th and 17th centuries, and Boehme generally strove to remain within the frame of orthodox teaching.

The Age of the Reformation, the Counter-Reformation and the Post-Reformation period were anything but sophianically inclined. It was the culmination of the persecution of witches. The chasm between the immaculate, spiritualized Virgin Mary and the ordinary, earthly woman was not to be bridged, and in this intolerable division the Feminine Divine all but perished. In the Lutheran faith, God became even more masculine. The worship of Mary and the saints, many of whom were women, everything feminine or sensuous in the church and in the procedure of religious service was suppressed for the sake of the "pure Word." And yet, in these most adverse times, a prophet stood up within the Lutheran faith who looked straight into the Divine Being and interpreted in his rugged, sensuous language what he saw. As Jacob Boehme perceived *that which really exists*, namely God in all his works from the beginning of time, he had to envision Sophia, too, for she also *exists*.

---

[29] *Aurora*, p. 248.

In Jacob Boehme's later writings, Sophia gains more and more importance, but his references to her are not without contradictions. We have to admit the possibility that Boehme, although he would have known the Wisdom Texts of the Old Testament (perhaps without the Apocrypha, which were not included in the Lutheran Bible), may not have responded to them, as the spirit of his age was heavily set against the Feminine Divine. At any rate, he refers little to these parts of scripture and relies wholly on his own vision. It differs from the Christian concept of God, the Trinity of Godfather, Son and Holy Spirit, from which Sophia disappeared as a divine person. She was absorbed by Jesus, Mary, and the Church. On the other hand, she is close to the Holy Spirit as his attribute, because the Spirit can only derive from the wisdom of God. But where is she herself? Perhaps we are adding to Boehme's speculations yet another, if we assume that he might have given clearer expression to Sophia, had he not felt obliged to relate her to the orthodox Trinity. It is obvious that he would see her as the "Mother of Nature," because this view results from every deeper contemplation of nature. But how does this "Mother" relate to God, if Divine Wisdom, the "noble Maiden Sophia," cannot give birth, as Godfather of the Holy Trinity claimed this privilege all for himself? In this respect, the *Six Theosophic Points*, a work from Boehme's most creative period, appears to be quite obscure. Wisdom is accorded a place in the Godhead, but only as a mirror, in which God reveals himself:

> For it (Wisdom) is that which is uttered, which the Father utters out of the centre of the Heart by the Holy Spirit, and stands in divine forms and images, in the ocular view of the Holy Tri-unity of God; but as a virgin *without bringing forth*. It generates not the colours and figures which shine forth in it, and are revealed in the ground and essence; but all is together an eternal *Magia*, and dwells with the centre of the

---

heart in itself, and by the spirit goes forth from the centre out of itself, and manifests itself in the eye of the virgin wisdom endlessly.[30]

Curiously, in Boehme's vision, pregnancy and giving birth is the prerogative of the masculine principle. The desire for creation "impregnates" the Father and gives birth to creation from his divine will. Thus, Sophia acquires a relationship with God which is difficult to understand. She *mirrors* the will of God, but has no generating power. Wisdom is the medium through which God makes himself manifest, and in this reflection is perfect joy and fulfillment in God. The image of the mirror, however, which Boehme uses time and again in this text, is ambivalent.

Another startling point is the emergence of a "hard, bitter and great" fear or anguish (*Angst*) in the process of creation. The wheel of this fear is observed to turn round and round in a frenzy. It is the nameless fear of nature, because it can only be natural life, not *principium*. How different is this condition from a feminine concept of creation, for example, of the Egyptian goddess Isis. In her universe, all polarities, as life and death, are resolved in the maternal matrix. Could this fear have anything to do with the perverse claim that the male principle gives birth to creation, excluding the female? Boehme is not speaking about fear inherent in creation after the Fall, but about a primordial fear within the process of creation itself. It is relieved by the "other will" of the Father, his loving heart, which he drew from the "mirror of wisdom." This other will of God is "the force of gentleness and love." It is ruled by the Holy Spirit, which is primeval wisdom or the wisdom of the virgin. She herself, however, does not create anything.

---

[30] Jacob Boehme, *Six Theosophic Points and Other Writings*. Translated into English by John Rolleston Earle (New York: Alfred A. Knopf, 1920), I:17, p. 17. Italics mine.

> And this is called virgin Wisdom; for it is not a genetrix, nei-
> ther itself reveals anything, but the Holy Spirit is the reveal-
> er of its wonders. It is his vesture and fair adornment, and
> has in it the wonders, colours and virtues of the divine
> world: it is the house of the Holy Trinity, and the ornament
> of the divine and angelic world.[31]

Sophia appears to be a great and noble concept, but her greatness is difficult to apprehend. On the one hand, she is associated with the "wellspring of love and compassion" of the divine heart, but on the other
hand, Boehme states that the wisdom of God *has* being (*Wesen*), but *is* no
being or entity. Therefore, she does not have the status of a person like
the divine Trinity.

In reading and interpreting Boehme, we may wonder if it is per-
missible to try to pin down a visionary, who after all only saw "as
through a glass darkly"? In other passages, divine Sophia is seen to be
radiant and full of glory. In Wisdom, God beholds his own being as in a
parable. She is the "utterance" of the word of God.

> This wisdom of God (which is the virgin of glory and beau-
> teous ornament, and an image of the Number Three) is (in
> her figure) an image, like angels and men . . . like the blos-
> som of a branch, out of the spirit of God. For she is the *sub-
> stantiality* of the spirit, which the spirit of God putteth on as
> a garment, whereby he manifesteth himself, or else his form
> would not be known; for she is the spirit's corporeity . . .[32]

---

[31] *Six Theosophic Points...*, I:62, p. 27.
[32] Jacob Boehme, *The Threefold Life of Man*, translated by John Sparrow (London: John
M. Watkins, 1909), 3:49, p. 135.

God himself is invisible; he can only be experienced in the radiance of his majesty. We feel Sophia, his glorious power, within us, for she is our life and guides us. She is "the matrix of the earth, so that it was a visible, *palpable* image in substance, wherein heaven, earth, stars, and elements stood in substance, and all whatsoever liveth and moveth was in this one image."[33]

Although Sophia, in this view, has no form of her own, she is embodied in the Virgin Mary as the mother of incarnated Logos. Sophia enters or "lets herself into" Mary. Boehme speaks so tenderly and positively about this intimate relationship between the earthly Virgin Mary and the heavenly Virgin Sophia as only someone who has experienced her is able to.

Sophia approaches mankind with the greatest tenderness and passion in the spirit of Jesus Christ. In the dialog between the Soul and Sophia in Boehme's *Christosophia (The Way to Christ)*, the Virgin Sophia enters into a bond of love as the heavenly bride of the soul of man, her bridegroom. Here, she speaks with her own voice as the beloved of heaven, who would dwell within the soul always, as long as man is faithful to her. Her speech is gentle and pleading, inspired by the fire of love, which is of heaven, but can only articulate itself through words and parables.

> O noble Bridegroom! Let your countenance remain before me! Give me your fire-rays! Lead your desire into me, and enkindle me so that then, by my Meekness, I shall change your fire-rays into white-light and lead my Love through your fire-rays into your fire's essence. Then I shall kiss you forever!

---

[33] *The Threefold Life of Man*, 11:12, p. 308.

> O my noble Bridegroom! How good is my union with you!
> Just kiss me with the desires of your strength and might!
> Then will I show you my beauty and rejoice with you in
> your fire-life's sweet love and bright light.[34]

Sophia has to withhold her highest treasure, her "little pearl," because the soul is prone to disloyalty, as long as it dwells in an earthly body. But Sophia will always remain with her bridegroom and imbue him with the rays of her love. However, "I am not wedded to your earthly flesh, for I am a heavenly queen, and my realm is not of this world."[35]

Nowhere does the synthesis of the ancient Queen of Heaven and the spirit of Jesus become so clear and imperative as in this love dialog. It still has the power to move, if we are willing to enter into the spirit of this erotic language and imagery. It is hard not to sympathize with the lofty spirituality of this Christianized Sophia, as she speaks to the human soul with such loving-kindness. If we approach this testimony of Sophia with Boehme's understanding, we may be content to silence for the time being our desire for a Sophia greater than this, more powerful as a creative agent, a Sophia who is not only the "mirror" of divinity, but has her full share in the Divine.

Reading Jacob Boehme is not easy, but the reward is considerable. His thinking in categories of quality instead of quantity; the polarity of Being; the holistic view, in which everything is intrinsically linked to all other things; God in his eternal, dynamic unfoldment; the sacredness of nature as vestment of the divine spirit; the responsibility of the human being toward creation and his or her own divine being—all of these are important issues today. Our world is in such a predicament, because

---

[34] *Christosophia*, I:47, published in English as *The Way to Christ*, by Jacob Boehme, translated by John Joseph Stoudt (New York and London: Harper & Brothers, 1947), pp. 34-35.
[35] Jacob Boehme, *The Way to Christ*, p. 36.

Western tradition neglected them. If Jacob Boehme could have foreseen the extent of the present destruction of the world, he would have blamed it on the "devil" or on "evil." But what is "evil"? According to Boehme, so-called evil is caused by an imbalance of polar qualities. Today we realize that the flawed relationship between Masculine and Feminine is the cause of many other incongruities so harmful to our lives. Boehme does not explicitly draw this conclusion, but he implies it. He, himself, did not marginalize the Feminine. He honored it by placing Sophia highly within the cosmos, in heaven as on earth. As "Mother of all things" she is present in the most remote corner and vibrates in all of life. However, she has only an indirect share in the Trinity of Father, Son and Holy Spirit. She is like a vapor, as it were, hovering above the threefold godhead. God depends on her for his revelation, but she "does not give birth." She *has* being, but *is* none. These are hopeless contradictions which Boehme is not aware of. He merits our gratitude for a concept of God that is not static, narrowly defined or abstract. God, forever creating himself from the welling source or *Ungrund*, will be transformed when the time is ripe for a new vision of the Divine.

In the Wake of Jacob Boehme

WHENEVER THE NEED BECOMES URGENT, divine abundance has a way to break through and fill the need. Where the territory is most arid, the desert most bleak and burned by a relentless sun, hidden wells start to flow. It is conspicuous that during the time after the Reformation, when the Protestant awakening was nearly smothered by narrow-minded, doctrinarian theology, sophianic mysticism found new channels. Protestant Christianity had stripped itself even more of the Feminine as compared with Roman Catholicism. It had turned into a religion which, according to C. G. Jung, "had lost any metaphysical representation of woman." Martin Luther, and the reformed Protestant churches of Zwingli and Calvin, banished even more radically mysticism of any sort. Since the Virgin Mary and the saints no longer played a part in religious life, the Feminine abdicated as a theological reality. Whatever remained of the feminine potency, was the god-fearing, chaste, and subordinate housewife according to the role model of the Protestant family. Ideally, she is the embodiment of all those wifely virtues we encountered in Proverbs (31:26). Her *sophia* is worldly prudence, untiring industry, fear of God and willing subordination. Her place is at the feet of God, not by his side as co-creator.

In this stagnant situation of the early Protestant Church, Jacob Boehme stands out like an erratic block. He was met with hostility, and suffered from the unabated hatred of the orthodox clergy till the end of his life. Some, who were inspired by him and carried on the light of Sophia after him, fared no better. The influence of Jacob Boehme was immense, not within the Church, but with philosophers and poets, with mystics of his own kind, or within the sophianically inclined Russian church. Yet this dry and hostile soil continued to bring forth sophianic individuals who bore witness to Divine Wisdom under the most adverse circumstances. It was mostly men who, in those times, spoke up for Sophia. After the secularization of Catholic monasteries, the well of female mysticism dried out, and inside the Church women were sentenced to silence. Had they dared to report any unorthodox vision, they would have run the risk of being condemned as witches. The flames of the stakes blazed high from the 16th well into the 18th century. Only men could afford to be religious outsiders, and even for them it was dangerous, as the life of Jacob Boehme shows.

Whenever the mystery was revealed in a personal vision, Sophia appeared as a real and incarnate figure, as complement and "mirror" of God according to the wisdom tradition of Solomon: "She is the brightness that streams from everlasting light, the flawless mirror of the active power of God and the image of his goodness" (Wisdom 7:26). The visionary was always prompted by his own experience. Sometimes he was overwhelmed by it after an inner struggle. It changed his life and compelled him to tell of his experience in words too weak and ambiguous to do justice to the mystical reality he had seen. When the true feeling comes through, the statement generally has a freshness and charm even today, whereas the luster of the original experience faded when a theological vindication was attempted.

One example is *Gottfried Arnold* (1666-1714), the most important sophianic visionary, after Boehme, in the post-reformative era. Disgusted with the sterile erudition of Protestant scholasticism, he turned to the emerging pietistic counter-movement and immersed himself in the writings of the early church. A fully-fledged theologian, he was appointed Professor of Ecclesiastical History, but resigned from his chair only a year later, when he found that he was unable to live in the spiritually barren climate and empty reasoning of academic theology. His statement, that it is impossible to be a Christian and a professor of theology at the same time, created a scandal in the whole country. He finally ruined his reputation with his great work *Unparteiische Kirchen– und Ketzerhistorie* ["Unprejudiced History of the Church and Its Heretics"], published in 1699, in which he attempted to prove that the true spirit of the gospel could be found more often with so-called heretics than in the orthodox church. This denunciation of ecclesiastical history, his critique of the petrifaction, vanity, and verbosity of theology, was considered an offense without precedence. From then on he was an outcast, but he went on to take his "heresy" even one step further.

In *Das Geheimnis der göttlichen Sophia* ["The Secret of the Divine Sophia"], published in 1700, Arnold undertakes a comprehensive vindication of sophianic doctrine as he found it in the Wisdom Books of the

Old Testament and the church fathers. The first part of the work consists of a large collection of passages with references to Sophia, with his own commentary. This compendium is undoubtedly intended to align his own view of Sophia with tradition. This purpose gives this part of his work a somewhat anxious, timid and pedantic quality. The second, lyrical part speaks quite another language. In these confessional poems the author expresses an ardent mysticism of love without patriarchal inhibition. In a long poem he describes how Sophia came to him bodily and exchanged vows of love with him:

> And thereupon she sweetly bent to me,
> And rested her left arm against my right,
> She pressed me to her heart (so kind was She to me)
> And kissed me. I see her rosy face
> Before me still, her purple lips so bright,
> Studded with drops of pearl and full of grace . . .
> Her brow's serenity, her eyes so light.[36]

Not all of the poems have the same poetical quality or power of expression, but some of them carry a glow which is enchanting even today:

> Thou mistress of my youth so kind
> And playmate of my marriage,
> The sovereign ruler of my mind,
> My angel and my carriage.
> I travel and I walk with thee,
> I never will forsaken be,
> Though no one else I see.[37]

---

[36] Gottfried Arnold, *Das Geheimnis der göttlichen Sophia*. Facsimile reprint of the edition of Leipzig, 1700 (Stuttgart: Frommann, 1973), II, p. 293. Translation mine.
[37] Arnold, p. 49, translation mine.

Thou art, oh, sister, my sweetest wife,
A well in a garden, a fountain of joy,
A pond overflowing with waters of life.[38]

Arnold had been profoundly stirred, and found it difficult to adapt the truth of his inward experience to current theology. Even the lyrics cannot quite make up for the apologetic clumsiness which so obviously mars the prose part.

His sophianic doctrine is linked to the familiar Christian positions. Arnold, too, identifies Divine Wisdom with Jesus, as heavenly bride. She is "the most beauteous loving nature of God," which has to be sought after and may indeed be found. "Therefore, attend to yourselves, and turn the whole force of your love . . . to your inner being and to Sophia as she appears therein."[39] This is the heart of his message: Sophia dwells inside of each human being. It is here where she has to be awakened and sought. One may search all the records from one end to the other, but without any real experience of Sophia, she will not come alive. All the testimonies and speculations of the fathers can only be a precarious affirmation of her existence. Arnold makes the most varied use of Wisdom, according to the sources referred to. Whereas in the wisdom tradition of the Old Testament Sophia is still an independent person, Christian thought projected her onto Jesus and the Virgin Mary, thereby redeeming the fateful separation from God which Adam had brought upon humanity. By desiring a human wife, Adam had lost Wisdom, his "secret bride." As a consequence, he deprived himself of the feminine part of his nature and retained only the masculine one.

This is a profound thought, which recalls the ancient myth of the original human as androgynous, though Arnold does not explicitly refer

---

[38] Arnold, p. 53, translation mine.
[39] Arnold, Preface, par. 19, translation mine.

to it. He describes the union of his soul with Sophia in a richly sensuous language, as all lovers of Sophia have done since the Song of Solomon, but this eroticism has only a symbolic function, and has nothing to do with earthly love. From this central dualism basically all others derive. There is a rift between Sophia, the sweet, heavenly bride, and Sophia, "the disciplinary rod," who metes out "harsh punishment" in case of disobedience. Here the internalized image of God as the punishing judge is projected onto Sophia. The intimate, and often very simple, style of Arnold's sophianic poetry differs conspicuously from the baroque pathos of the apologetic part and the invectives against "atheists, sneerers, the worldwise, libertines, Stoics and Epicureans," whose "treacherous minds" are hardened against Divine Wisdom.

Gottfried Arnold displays the whole dilemma of sophianic prophesy in patriarchal times. His immediate experience is powerful and beyond suspicion, but when it is made to fit in with the traditional frame of reference, the picture is curiously ambiguous. Sophia is divine, but not a Goddess; she *has* being, but *is* none (the familiar, mind-boggling distinction). She is somehow present in the Trinity, but at the same time also in Mary. She approaches human beings as a female figure, and leads the soul to an encounter of love which can only be expressed in erotic language, but at the same time she is removed from all earthly desire. The mystery of these opposites is not always resolved in a higher truth. There is a wide gulf between the opposites, no matter how hard the authors try to integrate them. After all, patriarchy eliminated the feminine from the idea of God and declared the human woman as basically deficient and morally deformed. All sophianic visions, even those of the darkest epochs, are a blazing signal that the patriarchal concept of God does not fit divine reality. Sophia interfered time and again and corrected this bias, but her noble stature remained ambiguous and is always subject to interpretation. The Feminine Divine, which she represented, was reduced by subtle theological stratagems and made to serve the patriarchal God.

Nevertheless, the sophianic undercurrent was never entirely cut off. Time and again it broke through with elemental force. Sophia, as the archetype of the Feminine Divine, might appear dormant for some time; it may disappear from the mainstream of religion, but it cannot be extinguished altogether. The soul of man needs her as much as the soul of woman, and if women are forbidden to speak out, men will give expression to her. They have borne witness to Sophia despite patriarchal dualisms and distortions. They risked persecution and became martyrs of Sophia, yet remained true to their sophianic perception. In times when the sophianic spirit was extremely weak, those who experienced the truth of Sophia were breaking new ground. They were helpless in the beginning, as they had no adequate language, no epistemological equipment and could only refer to traditional metaphors. These venerable testimonies, themselves, are in part obscured by the patriarchal paradigm. Besides, they are removed from the actual present by long stretches of time. Every epoch produces its own images. Every vision is incommensurable and requires its own forms of expression. This is what every visionary struggled to achieve: Hildegard of Bingen, Jacob Boehme, Gottfried Arnold, and even the elemental power of the Silesian Master, is full of obscurity and contradiction.

Others, like *Johann Georg Gichtel* (1638-1710), renounced any attempt to describe this experience. Gichtel is worth mentioning as the third great sophianic visionary after the Reformation. He was also Lutheran, and in some respects suffered a similar fate as Boehme and Arnold. He, too, felt repelled by the dry abstractions of academic theology, was persecuted for his criticism and even imprisoned for some time. Of all his visionary experiences, the most overpowering was the appearance of divine Sophia, when he was 35 years of age. He celebrated the sacred wedding with her, and henceforth aspired to lead a life of ascetic poverty and chastity worthy of this union. He only wished to *live out* his experience, not to describe it. Yet with his letters, collected in *Theosophia practica*, he left to the world a significant work of sophianic mysticism.

Sophia appeared to him in a most differentiated way. On the one hand, she revealed herself as a person of overwhelming reality, visiting him in physical shape and blessing him with her caresses, so that human love no longer held any attraction for him. On the other hand, he believed that Sophia was Adam's helpmate before the creation of Eve. Because Adam craved a mate for his animal nature, he fell from grace, and Sophia was lost to him. These thoughts recall the myth of Lilith of the cabbalistic tradition, or rather, Gichtel anticipated the modern interpretations of Lilith by Isolde Kurz or G. B. Shaw.[40] She figures as "the heavenly virgin of the inner being . . . who is a light blown from our fiery soul."[41] According to his understanding, she entered into Jesus Christ, and only through Christ may the soul receive Sophia.

> We are unable to conceive of heavenly Sophia outside Jesus. She is not God, but his mirror; she is not Jesus, but his heavenly flesh and blood, and if we draw Jesus to us, we likewise attract Sophia.[42]

> If we draw Jesus to us, we shall regain in him our virgin, whom we lost in Adam, and at the same time we shall receive the strength of Jesus in our inner being, in order to control the outer nature and to do God's will.[43]

---

[40] See above, pp. 49-54.

[41] Johann Georg Gichtel, *Theosophia practica* (1722), vol. II. p. 1030; quoted in Walter Nigg, *Heimliche Weisheit* (Zürich-Stuttgart: Artemis, 1959), p. 245, translation mine.

[42] *Theosophia practica*, vol. I, p. 395, translation mine.

[43] *Theosophia practica*, vol. II, p. 1030-1031, translation mine.

In his youth, Gichtel was a man of brilliant gifts, who could have commanded a place of distinction in the world. However, his experiences of God, especially his vision of Sophia, changed him so thoroughly that he found any form of worldly employment incompatible with his spiritual life. He lived by himself in comparative poverty, and later he founded the community of the *Engelbrüder* ["Angelic Brethren"], whom he bound to a life of celibacy and strict sexual abstinence. He denounced marriage as a place of "bestial lust," and carried his fanaticism to a point of hysterical hatred of the flesh. His uncompromising purity, however, was most attractive to women, and when a young girl confessed that she had fallen in love with him, he had a fit. According to the record, his teeth were chattering, and his body was shaking with an attack of high fever. He rejected the very idea of marriage with a woman as a temptation of the devil, and prayed to his heavenly bride for protection.

Thus, Gichtel widened the gulf between Sophia, the Divine Feminine, and human womanhood. Cut off from human love, his ardent sophianic eroticism evaporated into an aseptic realm of the spirit. The glorification of the Feminine Divine fostered the degradation of the concrete woman here and now. In this division, the patriarchal bind is brought to the point. The more Sophia and Mary are elevated to heaven, the more woman on Earth is devalued. She remains "sinful" and "fallen," the "gateway of hell" (Tertullian). The sacred wedding, which in the old goddess religion was rooted in the loving union of man and woman, is now possible only in the spirit, the inner space of the soul, not in communion with one's polar opposite in the flesh. Therefore, the veneration of Sophia, despite her sublimity and her loving personal expression, led to a peculiar remoteness from Earth and a devaluation of human love.

Among the circle of sophiologists in the wake of Jacob Boehme, we may also mention *Johann Jakob Wirz* (1778-1858) as a representative of the period just after the Enlightenment, at the beginning of the industrial revolution. The times in general were hostile to Sophia, and yet even now the light of Divine Wisdom was not totally obliterated. In the sober environment of the reformed Protestant Church of Switzerland, Johann Jakob Wirz stood up, a weaver from Basel, who founded the "Community of the Nazarenes." He beheld incarnate Sophia in the shape of the Virgin Mary and distinguished three degrees of Divine Wisdom: In the first degree, she is the friend and travel companion of the seeker; in the second, she is a mother, the true Mother of God, of higher rank than Mary.

> In the third degree, the holy wisdom of the soul is a woman, by whom man steps out of his separation and becomes whole again. Not until this union with Divine Wisdom has resolved the separation of man and regained what was lost, can man call himself a complete human being.[44]

The thought of man suffering from a fatal division within himself is of urgent concern, but the idea that the desired wholeness is linked to a true sophianic completion of the image of God has not been fully understood. In Wirz' view, the motherly aspect of Sophia, her caring love, and his duty to serve her are predominant. He, too, has a close personal relationship to Sophia, but apparently no vision of his own like his precursors. He was inspired by sacred wisdom, but not stirred in his inmost being. Although he held a position of authority among his followers, and was considered a prophet, his doctrine of Sophia did not become the leaven it might have been. She must become a burning desire, until the soul cries out: "I will not let you go, unless you bless me!"[45] Anything

---

[44] *Zeugnisse und Eröffnungen des Geistes durch Johann Jakob Wirz*. Heilige Urkunden der Nazarener-Gemeine (Barmen, 1863). Vol.I, p. 492. Quoted in: Schipflinger, *Sophia-Maria*, p. 157, translation mine.

[45] As Jacob cried out when he wrestled "with God and with men, and prevailed" (Genesis 32:26).

merely edifying or palliatory, any disguise of the root of the disease must fall away, if a revelation is to take place.

With Johann Jakob Wirz, the sophianic stream in central Europe dried out for some time. Jacob Boehme had kept it alive, and his influence reached Goethe, the poet Novalis, the Romantic School, and the philosophy of German Idealism, starting with Friedrich Schlegel and Schelling and leading up to Hegel. With Franz von Baader, who died a few years before Wirz, another theosophical thinker arose who touched the mystery of Sophia. Also, the Anthroposophical School of Rudolf Steiner had sophianic perceptions, but in modern times no one was overwhelmed in body and soul by Sophia, as the older visionaries had been.

The Black Madonna *of Czestochowa, Poland. This Byzantine image, by an unknown artist, has been revered in the monastery of Jasa Gora since 1382. The streaks on her right cheek, as if she were weeping, were caused by slashes from the sword of a soldier. The damage could not be repaired, and the disfigurement became accepted as part of her charisma. The Madonna of Czestochowa is all-merciful and kind, and is said to have worked many miracles. The contemplation of her gentle features has been a healing experience for many believers.*

Meditation

Ich sehe dich in tausend Bildern,
Maria, lieblich ausgedrückt,
Doch keins von allen kann dich schildern,
wie meine Seele dich erblickt.

Portrayed in glory, Mary, I see you,
In images a thousandfold,
But none of them can truly show you
As I beheld you in my soul.

—NOVALIS[46]

WE DO NOT SEEK SOPHIA TODAY in the traditional image of Mary, the humble servant of God, virtuous, transfigured by sacrifice, accepting her destiny without asking a question, blessed among women, raised high above the life of women on this Earth. The contradiction is insoluble: to aspire to the heavenly virgin, and yet to love, conceive and give birth in the human way. In her mild countenance we did not find Sophia. We found a submissive, humble, self-effacing woman—not the sovereign, not the sharer of God's throne, his lover and confidant, his darling playmate on the face of the Earth.

Playfulness—under the spell of the cross and the sorrows of the *mater dolorosa* we forgot what playfulness means. We confuse it with idleness, with childish stuff, and need to learn again that the world is rejuvenated in playfulness. In play, the hidden soul forces are renewed. In play, there are no hostile projections, as all children know, who do not even need a common language to communicate with each other. In play,

---

[46] This, and the following poetry, from Novalis, a German romantic poet (Friedrich von Hardenberg), whose work we could not find in English. The German poem is published in *Werke im einem Band*, "Geistlione Lieder," xv (Munich-Vienna: Carl Hauser, 1984), p. 198. Translation is mine.

lovers find ineffable happiness. Play is the language of love, an inexhaustible wellspring from which fresh water flows. In play, fixed role models are changed. In playfulness, one assumes the coloring or flavor of another, his or her "tincture," as Jacob Boehme would say, his or her humanity, masculinity or femininity. Both maleness and femaleness become a garment we throw off when we are in the heart of love, playfully transported by Sophia. She leads us on paths of wisdom unknown to us. She is resurrected in every individual soul. As Novalis, the wisest, most profound and most childlike of the early Romantics, tried to put the ineffable into words in the second stanza of his poem:

> *Ich weiß nur, daß der Welt Getümmel*
> *Seitdem mir wie ein Traum verweht,*
> *Und ein unnennbar süßer Himmel*
> *Mir ewig im Gemüte steht.*

> *Since then, the turmoil of the world*
> *Dispersèd like a dream I find,*
> *whereas a nameless bliss unfurled*
> *Forever sweetly in my mind.*

We are told of many a mystic who renounced the world for the sake of a life dedicated to God, and some were rewarded with an undisturbed enjoyment of "nameless bliss." But—Sophia desires to dwell on Earth, among human beings, in the midst of "the turmoil of the world." It is here where she wants us to work, to experience joy, to play and foster love between all beings. As we encounter Sophia today, be it as an intuition or a longing of our hearts, we cannot lock the door behind us and leave the world to itself. Mystics are needed today who are wide awake and concerned about the world, empowered women and men, who carry Sophia within them like the sap that rises in a tree and brings forth leaves and fruit when the time is ripe.

The Russian Sophiologists: Vladimir Soloviev (1853-1900)

IN RUSSIA, THE TEACHING OF SOPHIA, the feminine wisdom of God, met with a receptivity as nowhere else. The oldest Russian churches had been named after her, like the cathedrals of Kiev and Novgorod, and it might aptly be said that the "Rus of Kiev," the heartland of Old Russia, crystallized around the image of Sophia. Kyrill, the "Apostle of the Slavs" and the father of Russian culture, experienced a mystical revelation of Sophia when still a child. She became the "first representative figure of juvenile Russia."[47] As the earliest subject of Russian icons, Sophia, the Wisdom of God, appears as a majestic female figure with wings and fiery countenance, as in the famous icon of Novgorod. Russian Orthodox Christians have always been familiar with Sophia from liturgy and iconography.

The Russian icon has a very special significance. It is not simply a representation or likeness of a saint or a person of the Holy Trinity, but it is intended to actualize the Divine, to make it visible and palpable as a living presence. In the icon, the kingdom of God is actually present. For this reason Russian believers are extremely attached to their icons. In the old days, every house had its family icon, and often more than one. It was the most precious possession of the household, and held in even greater reverence than the crucifix in the corners of German peasant homes. When an icon was old and faded or broken, it was not thrown away or burned, but buried in the ground like a body. The painting of icons was, and still is, the privilege of monks, who undergo a period of fasting and meditation before they start their work in strict

---

[47] "...die erste Wesensgestalt des kindlichen Rußland." These are the words of Pavel Florensky in *An den Wasserscheiden des Denkens* [A Florensky Reader], ed. by Sieglinde and Fritz Mierau (Berlin: Kontext Verlag, 1991), p. 100f.

accordance with a set of time-hallowed rules. In icon-painting there is no place for individual artistic expression. It is a pure offering to the Divine and should have an appearance as if it were "not fashioned by human hand," as the Russian saying goes.

Russian folk belief, with the worship of saints and icons, has a particularly feminine flavor. Anyone who experiences a religious ceremony in a Russian church cannot fail to be impressed by this femininity. It is felt in the magnificent vocal music, in ritual, in the texts of the liturgy, in the emotional participation of the people, expressed in frequent bowing and crossing, and in the devotion mirrored in the faces of the congregation. The charisma of the Russian church is definitely feminine, although the Russian Orthodox clergy, like its Roman Catholic counterpart, clings tenaciously to the traditional male hierarchy. Russian churches, the walls covered with frescoes and icons, lit by innumerable candles, resounding with a music of unearthly beauty, resemble a divine cave, a great female womb, just as Russia, as a country, was always considered feminine. The people call her "Mother Russia," not Fatherland, *patria*. The *startzy*, the saintly hermits who have been immortalized in Russian literature, as in the works of Dostoevsky, are motherly in their loving guidance of seekers and supplicants. They always were a special feature of religious life in Russia, even during the long period of Soviet oppression. The *startzy* are wise spiritual guides. They are known for their empathy with the suffering, and minister to their spiritual needs with tender compassion.

This spiritual climate of the Russian church may explain why Russian women always felt at home in the church. Contrary to their Western sisters, they never felt suppressed or marginalized by the church. They do not question a concept of God which is represented by a masculine hierarchy, because it is imbued with a feminine spirit—the spirit of Sophia. Plato and Neoplatonic thought, in which the Greek concept of wisdom plays a central part, has been a greater influence on Eastern Christianity. For this reason, Sophia of the Orthodox Church differs significantly from that of the West, who became absorbed by Logos. Eastern theology never subscribed to Logos to the extent of the West, and therefore Sophia was never marginalized in the same way, but always maintained a high status in the realm of the Divine. In addition, the feminine character of the pre-Christian religion of ancient Russia, centered in the worship of Mother Earth, may still play a subliminal role, especially as Russia was christianized fairly late, at the end of the tenth century. The Eastern mentality, as has often been observed, is more feminine compared with the rationally-oriented, masculine Western type.

However, a "sophiology," a religious philosophy focused on Sophia, only emerged toward the end of the 19th century with the impressive figure of *Vladimir Soloviev*. He was a truly universal spirit. Having studied Western philosophy, especially the theosophy of Jacob Boehme, he attempted to reconcile philosophy, theology, and science in a great synthesis. All of his visions, developed in the years of his youth, might have revolutionized the world, if the time had been more receptive to them. He experienced the split within Christianity with deep personal anguish, and one of his greatest concerns was the reunion of the Eastern and Western churches. If God is *one*—the premise of all his thinking— there can be only *one* church. He believed that the Russian people had a special mission to lead mankind back to the unity of one faith. In his view, the Russian church was to accept the supremacy of the pope in Rome, an impossible proposition to the Russian clergy. Soloviev, the daring philosopher, the passionate believer, the universal scholar of genius, a character of childlike innocence and purity, antagonized many authorities. Even his teachings of Sophia, nurtured on the sophianically fertile Russian soil, offended the church. Nevertheless, it had the greatest influence on all Russian sophiologists after him—Pavel Florensky, Sergei Bulgakov, Nikolai Berdyaev, to mention only a few names familiar in the West. Russian sophiology remains focused on Soloviev. He started a line of thought that had been dormant in the Russian character and in Russian Orthodox faith for a long time. Today, Soloviev's teachings on Sophia are being rediscovered with enthusiasm by the Christian revival in post-Soviet Russia.

Like Hildegard of Bingen, Jacob Boehme, and Gottfried Arnold, Soloviev had personal visions, which inspired him for the rest of his life. His first vision of Sophia overwhelmed him at the age of 9, during a Pentecost service. She appeared to him as a lady of unearthly beauty and benevolence. When he was 20, he encountered her again in the Reading Room of the British Museum in London, where he devoured all the books on Sophia he could find. But this time she only revealed her face to him, and he was overcome by the desire to behold her once more in full stature. An inner voice directed him to go to Egypt, and he set sail for Cairo at once. One night, he was prompted to rush out into the desert in full evening clothes. Sophia had called him. He fell unconscious and might have perished in the desert, but on the second day, at sunrise, he was blessed by a complete vision of Sophia in all her glory. She revealed to him the abundance of the Godhead, the eternal One. The bliss of this vision was never to leave him again. Many years later, Soloviev described his three encounters with Sophia in a long poem.[48]

After this third experience, Sophia, the "eternal friend," became the key figure of young Soloviev's theological thought. From now on, she was "forever in his mind," as Novalis had said of his own experience of

---

[48] "Three Encounters." I was unable to locate an English translation of this poem, or any of Soloviev's poetry. His name, incidentally, is transcribed in various ways: Soloviev, Solovyov (phonetically the most approximate) and Solov'ev. I opted for Soloviev, as a number of his works in English translation were published with this spelling of the author's name..

the Virgin. The Russian mystic had seen her incarnated as a female figure of divine radiance. Now we shall observe how she changed into a complex theological entity in Soloviev's analysis. The challenge was to fit his immediate, sensuous experience into the framework of an Orthodox image of God, which necessarily reflected patriarchal anthropology. Soloviev did not mean to be heretical, but wanted to define the position of Sophia within the Orthodox frame of reference, a position she had basically always had in folk piety, in liturgy, and iconography. His most consistent statements about Sophia are contained in *Russia and the Universal Church*, a work originally written in French and published in Paris, as it became increasingly difficult for him to publish anything in Russia.[49]

As Sophia can only be understood in the context of the Trinity, we shall look first at Soloviev's concept of God. Whenever called for, his ideas will be stated in his own words.

His basic idea is quite orthodox: God represents the Absolute as unfolded in a three-partite person. This triad is indispensable to the Divine, because God can only maintain his personhood by establishing himself as an opposite to another, and by observing and enjoying himself in the third aspect of his being. In the unity of his absolute being, three interrelated subjects or hypostases have to be postulated, corresponding to the names of the Holy Trinity: Father, Son, and Holy Spirit. The unified substance of the divine Trinity (the "universal essence") is the All in One. It is the abundance and the absolute wholeness of being. Here, Sophia makes her appearance as "this universal essence, this absolute unity of the universe is the inherent wisdom of God (*Hokhma, Sophia*)."[50] She carries within her the hidden potency of all things, and

[49] W. Soloviev, *Russia and the Universal Church*, trans. Herbert Rees (London: Geoffrey Bles, 1948).

[50] As Soloviev's works in English were not available to me, I quote from the standard German edition of his works.

is herself subject to God, according to Proverbs 8:22: "The Lord created me the beginning of his works . . . ."

Soloviev's speculations explicitly refer to the Wisdom Texts of the Old Testament. The antithesis of the Divine consists in the multiplicity of the creation, to which God in his love has given the freedom to choose between good and evil. Multiplicity, however, is always in danger of falling into the emptiness of chaos, but with Power, Truth, and Grace, the divine principle is able to defeat chaos. This act is the eternal expression of God's absolute essence, which is his inherent wisdom. The *indissoluble bond* between the three persons of the divine is Wisdom. She "plays" in God's presence (Proverbs 8:30,31) by calling forth the innumerable possibilities of existence outside God, and in this play God becomes aware of himself and proves himself powerful.

In these reflections, Sophia appears as an element—she can hardly be called a "person"—which is indispensable for God's self-awareness. She belongs "intrinsically" to the Father, the Son, and the Holy Spirit, but has no existence in herself. The argument is highly sophisticated, and readers not quite at ease on this level of abstraction may find that they have to go through these passages several times to grasp their meaning. The argument is stringent, and the logical brilliance will not fail to impress even a reluctant mind, yet this whole intellectual fabric has a glittering unreality we have learned to identify (and reject) in our quest for a new image of God.

In his theosophy, Soloviev introduces a second feminine concept, the *World Soul*. She is not to be confused with Sophia, although she may come close to her.

> Just as this world is the opposite or the reversal of divine
> wholeness, the World Soul is the opposite or the antitype of
> the intrinsic wisdom of God. This World Soul is a created

entity, the first of all created beings, the *prima materia* and the true substratum of our created world.[51]

The World Soul is the principle of creation. It has existed from eternity as a pure essence in God, the "hidden foundation of eternal wisdom."

> This potential and future Mother of the world outside the Divine corresponds to the actual and present Father of the Deity as his ideal complement.[52]

This is an important point. The Feminine is projected into created matter, according to the conception of Greek philosophy. As a "potential" Mother, the feminine principle is relegated to the mundane world, which Soloviev explicitly calls the "lower," to complement the Father. *His* is the reality as Absolute Being. *Hers* is the potentiality, the possible or future being. With this precise gradation and limitation the Feminine as *materia prima* acquires a dubious existence. She is real and indispensable to God as his "completion," but only in the sense of the potentiality of a vague future. Soloviev carries the argument even further. As the World Soul is but a potentiality, it is of changeable nature. It may oppose God, or it may work with him, and only in the latter case will it become identical with eternal wisdom.

The immediate reality of the World Soul is chaos, but it is capable of changing position. The torn and divided World Soul has a deep desire for simplicity and oneness, and by grace of the Word of God, which is Sophia incarnated in Jesus, it may reach unity at last. Divine Wisdom not only represents the oneness of the Absolute Being, but also

---

[51] V. Soloviev, *Schriften zur Philosophie, Theologie und Politik* (Munich: Erich Wewel, 1991), p. 78, translation into English mine.
[52] Soloviev, *Schriften*, p. 79, translation mine.

contains the power to unify and heal the torn existence of the world. Thus, Sophia is not only the principle of One-in-All, but by her own wholeness she is, at the same time, the unity of opposites. Within man and through human beings, she may be realized completely. Therefore, her "delight" is in mankind (Proverbs 8:31). She is the true source of all being and the purpose of creation, the essence of the Holy Spirit that swept over the surface of the waters. Thereby Sophia is not the fickle "soul," but the guardian angel of the world.

Soloviev may not be aware that he is introducing a feminine ontology with his interpretation of the Hebrew word *reshit*, "beginning." This word is of feminine gender, and this gives a special significance to Sophia's statement: "The Lord created me the beginning of his works" (Proverbs 8:22). *Reshit* not only refers to time, but to a quality of the divine being. If God made Wisdom the feminine beginning of creation, we may conclude that she is the feminine head of all beings, and this is in fact what Soloviev is arguing. He might have drawn conclusions from this idea that would have given the Feminine a very different place within the divine being, but even this inspired thinker fails to do this. He never questions the patriarchal system, and so this internalized attitude does not allow him to take this step. He clearly supports the biblical anthropology: The "primary" human being is man, and woman is "only the completion of man." The "perfect female" is deified nature; the "perfect man" is the God-Man incarnated in Jesus Christ. Soloviev also differentiates between "masculine reason and consciousness" and "feminine heart and instinct."[53] These are the classical definitions of masculine and feminine nature and their relative position within the hierarchy of creation. The Holy Virgin, as female incarnation of Sophia—opposite Jesus Christ as male incarnation—Soloviev regards as

---

[53] *Schriften*, p. 81.

"united with God in a purely recipient, passive union. . . . No mutuality is at work here, no divine co-action on her part."[54]

Soloviev, who personally had such a high appreciation of the Feminine, who loved Sophia more than anything, and had meditated profoundly on the meaning of love between the sexes, seems to be saying that woman has no charisma other than the passive subordination under the will of God. From a feminist point of view, Soloviev is caught in the patriarchal bind, despite his life-long worship of Sophia and his extraordinary intellectual and spiritual powers. Yet, how could he have thought differently? He went as far as he could to secure Sophia a place of distinction in the trinitarian supremacy, and even this was too audacious for the Orthodox authorities. He was accused of Gnostic and cabbalistic speculation, whereas in his own understanding he had only tried to interpret Sophia from the biblical sources and to assign to her the greatest possible significance as the intrinsic wisdom of God.

Orthodox theology preferred to leave her where she was and where she had always been: embedded in the piety of the people, associated with the mild Virgin Mary, encapsulated in golden icons, shrouded in mystery, which the human spirit shall not attempt to penetrate. Soloviev, fired by his ardent soul and the unforgettable impression of his visions of Sophia, attempted to reflect her relationship with the divine, with creation and with humanity, and to investigate her charisma with the power of his intellect.

Soloviev's image of Sophia is exalted indeed: closely linked to the divine being, indispensable for the unity of God's threefold personhood, and the salvation of the world. Yet, though fueled with intellectual passion, this concept remains an abstraction. The point is that even in the inspired theosophy of Vladimir Soloviev, the feminine principle cannot

---

[54] *Schriften*, p. 91, translation mine.

be a divine person in her own right. As long as intellect and consciousness are relegated exclusively to the male, heart and instinct exclusively to the female, the Feminine *cannot* be a spiritually creative potency. The sophisticated, even sublime speculations of Soloviev, a display of brilliant intellectual acrobatics, basically exhibit the same dichotomy even within the frame of the sophianically inclined Christianity of the East. On the one hand, there is the longing of man for the redeeming quality of woman, Goethe's "Eternal Feminine," and so the Sophia principle is given uneasy space in the vicinity of the holy triad, but it must on no account infringe on masculine primacy. Therefore, Sophia appears as an entity hovering somewhere between and above the divine persons, a certain "aura" or fluid which, contrary to the self-revelations of Sophia in the old Wisdom Texts, and contrary to Soloviev's own experience, never coagulates into the stature of a person.

Soloviev's Sophia serves as the mysterious link between the divine persons as their "essence." In a subtle way she is instrumental to the process of creation and to the unity of God and human in Soloviev's vision of a future theocracy. She is permitted to bestow her blessings in every possible way and to assist in the salvation of mankind, but she is not entitled to pronounce the Word of creation from the empowerment of her own feminine-divine being.[55] When all is said and done, Soloviev, an ardent lover of Sophia if ever there was one, is seen to waver between his loyalty to her and to his congenital patriarchal prejudice. From a feminist viewpoint, Soloviev remains an embarrassment.

Perhaps Russian Orthodox women and men will have to cross this

---

[55] This contradiction is particularly conspicuous in the work of Russian Orthodox theologians, despite their revaluation of the Feminine in their understanding of Sophia. See especially Paul Evdokimov, *Woman & the Salvation of the World: A Christian Anthropology on the Charisms of Women* (Crestwood, NY: St. Vladimirs, 1994). I discussed this well-known book at length in my earlier book, *Wandel des Weiblichen* ["Transformation of the Feminine"] (Freiburg: Herder, 1988), pp. 121-125.

Rubicon one day, as other Christians did. It is conceivable that Sophia, as she is represented in the great Russian tradition, will undergo a change in the future. Russian spirituality never suffered from the burden of an exaggerated rationality as Western Christianity did. The great sophianic thinkers—Soloviev, Florensky, Bulgakov, and others—got caught in the patriarchal bind like the rest, but all the same their appreciation of Sophia led them to a more sophianic concept of God. All of them were familiar with the writings of Boehme, this vast quarry of an unorthodox vision of God's polarity. Soloviev, in his later years, came to believe in a "religion of the spirit," a kind of interconfessional church. The sophianic features of such a spiritual community without dogmatic limitations might become more salient, for example in the concept of the Divine Androgyny. The idea is not new, and there are signs that Soloviev was in sympathy with it. This concept, however, would amount to a complete re-interpretation and transformation of the patriarchal Trinity. This cannot be done simply by representing the Holy Spirit as a woman, as the anonymous artist of the ninth century so happily did in a Bavarian country church. Especially in Russian sophiology, all persons of the Trinity, particularly Jesus and the Holy Spirit, but also the Virgin Mary, are permeated by Sophia, however in such a complicated and abstract way that she seems hardly real. She remains a concept, a theory. She cannot capture the heart or the imagination. Maybe the best sophianic message is still contained within the icon or in the personal confession of a lyrical poem.

Soloviev left to us the most beautiful and moving testimonies of Sophia in his poems.[56] In the German translation they convey something of the charm and a radiance which, in his own day, was a power-

---

[56] See *Soloviev's Leben in Briefen und Gedichten* ["S's Life in Letters and Poems"]. The poems found a congenial German translator in Ludolf Müller. The poems explicitly about Sophia are nos. 2, 3, 13, 23, 48, 100, and 102.

ful influence on his contemporaries and on Symbolist poetry. At the turn of the 19th century, Russia was in mental and spiritual turmoil foreshadowing the events to come. It was the eve of the violent upheavals symbolized by the coming of the Antichrist. Yet Soloviev and his generation also felt the presence of a divine guardian spirit in female shape. The poet Soloviev pays homage to her as his eternal friend, the Mistress of the Earth, the Woman of the Apocalypse and Queen of Heaven, the haunting, beautiful image of his dreams, a savior, the embodiment of his own soul. The tone is rapturous, and the images flow in profusion. Sophia is vested with all the loveliness of the Earth, but her home is the eternal light. With metaphor and rhythm, abstract theology dissolves into palpable images, allegory and parable.

Pavel Florensky (1882-1937) and Sergei Bulgakov (1871-1944)

THESE INDIVIDUALS CAN ONLY be mentioned briefly, but they do need to be mentioned. Florensky is such a towering spirit that any cursory treatment must do him injustice. He was a Russian Orthodox priest, a scientist of genius in various fields, a theologian, philosopher, poet, and is considered the Russian Pascal, or Leonardo da Vinci. A man of stalwart faith and outstanding human qualities, he was persecuted and finally murdered in a Stalinist prison camp. By many of his countrymen he is revered as a martyr and a saint. From early youth he experienced the wholeness and the interrelationship of all being, which must lead to God at last. Like Soloviev, he saw no contradiction between science and religious faith. On the contrary, he maintained that scientific phenomena can be truly understood only in the context of the Christian faith, the Church and her teachings. Like Jacob Boehme, he had a mystical experience which revealed to him the mysterious forces of nature.[57]

One chapter of his main theological work is devoted to the concept of Sophia.[58] He is aware of the difficulty in describing her as a spiritual entity, since she is neither God, nor the Son of God, nor an angel, or a saint. The soul of the Russian people has always regarded Sophia as "an independent and mysterious being," and the theologian cannot hope to penetrate her. How true! Florensky recognizes in Sophia "genuine humanity" and "the living soul of nature and the universe." As a monad integrating all creation in a unified whole, she is viewed by Florensky as a religious axiom. She is *there* as a reality, not as a construct of the human mind. She represents the divine being most intimately related to creation, "the eternal bride of Logos" and the guardian of the world, whose personal ideal and final cause she is. "She is the bridge and point of contact between God and creation, the very center and the peak of creation." She is embodied in the virginal power of Mary on the one hand, and in the Church on the other. It is the function of the icon, as an authentic work of divine inspiration, to make Sophia visible as a celestial being, as Virgin Mary or the mystical Church. In the icon, the symbol *is* what it symbolizes.

Only when the collected works of Florensky are published and available in translation, will it be possible to assess his ideas on Sophia within the context of his scientific thought. From the beginning, he

---

[57] See "Meinen Kindern. Erinnerungen" ["To My Children. Memoirs"], in Pavel Florensky, *An den Wasserscheiden des Denkens* [A Florensky Reader], ed. by Sieglinde and Fritz Mierau (Berlin: Kontext Verlag, 1991), p. 13. As far as I know, there is no English translation available of this text as of this writing.

[58] *Die Säule und Grundfeste der Wahrheit* ["The Pillar and Foundation of Truth"]. All the following quotations from Florensky can be found in Schipflinger, *Sophia-Maria*, pp. 180-187. While I am aware that a second-hand translation must remain unsatisfactory, the passages quoted are so explicit that they cannot differ much from the Russian original.

firmly believed science to be related to transcendental values, a notion that emerged in the West only recently. In his holistic world view, which integrates science and religion, Sophia holds a key position.[59]

Sergei Bulgakov, a close friend of Florensky's, who was able to escape to Paris in the '20s, based his thought on the work of Boehme and Soloviev, but he also developed some original and controversial thoughts of his own.[60] To his understanding, Sophia represents universal being, which integrates the divine and the creation. She *is* the Holy Trinity. This concept goes one step beyond Soloviev, who saw Sophia as the "essence" of the Trinity. It seems as if Bulgakov were trying to add a fourth person to the threefold godhead. Yet he takes precaution against such a supposition by differentiations which are difficult to follow. On the one hand, the intrinsic nature of God within the Trinity is identical with Sophia; however, she is not a hypostasis herself nor an independent divine entity. The real offense to Orthodox thought was Bulgakov's view of the divine *and* creaturely being of Sophia in unity and diversity, thus approaching a pantheistic attitude. This dual nature, he says, is her mystery, which theological intellect cannot hope to fathom. Sophia cannot be understood from biblical sources alone, but must be seen in a wider ontological context.

Bulgakov's revaluation of Mary, however, is in the true Russian tradition. He rejects the exclusively christological interpretation of Sophia according to the Byzantine dogma and views Mary as hypostasized

---

[59] It would be fascinating to compare P. Florensky and Pierre Teilhard de Chardin, who was also a scientist and a religious philosopher. His hymn to *The Eternal Feminine* is directly addressed to Divine Wisdom, and it shows many parallels to the conceptions of the Russian sophiologist. Also, the Gaia hypothesis of James Lovelock and Lynne Margulin is related to the idea of Sophia as a "monad of creation" and guardian angel of the world (see Schipflinger, *Sophia-Maria*, chapters 18 and 19).

[60] See Schipflinger, chapter 16.

Sophia in the realm of creation. Thus, he bestows on her a cosmological dignity, which corresponds to the Russian sensibility. For this reason, Russian churches dedicated to Sophia are generally consecrated to Mary, contrary to Byzantine churches, which are consecrated to Jesus, like the famous Haghia Sophia of Istanbul, the former Constantinople. Mary, as Sophia, is the "ground of the world" and at the same time the "power of its transfiguration."

These few remarks will have to suffice for our purposes. Certainly, Bulgakov's appeal to Western Christians to learn more about and appreciate Russian spirituality is fully justified, but speculative sophiology in particular can't be separated from the piety of the Russian people and Russian iconography. This is the native soil that nurtured it and makes transplantation difficult. Furthermore, philosophical speculation in the East and the West took Sophia to such heights of abstraction that it is hard to follow her. True, the Russian sophiologists developed a noble concept of Sophia, but they, too, intellectualized her to an extent which lay thinking and feeling can hardly appreciate.

However, we owe to Russian sophiology three great gifts. For one, it sanctified the created world by placing Sophia as a mediator between God and the world in the divine plan of redemption. This sophianic quality of nature counterbalances the terrible failure of the West in this respect. Russian Sophia restores to our profaned, exploited and desecrated world a divine dignity. Nature is the body of Sophia; she protects it from chaos and leads it to unity with God. This is her mission and her intrinsic being.

Secondly, Russian sophiology—especially the work of Bulgakov—revalued the Virgin Mary, who has become a comparatively pale figure in the West. Even in Russian thought she is not a Goddess, but her proximity to Sophia, Divine Wisdom, or her identity with her, confers on her a stature which only the most hair-splitting theological definitions can distinguish from explicit divinity. She is Divine Wisdom, Compassion, and Love. Her charisma is cosmic. Without her neither the Earth nor the Trinity of Father, Son, and Spirit would have existence. This sophianic intuition of Mary elevates her beyond the pure and humble servant of God in Western Christianity. Especially Protestants, who may find it difficult to relate to Mary at all, will be grateful for this concept.

Thirdly, Russian sophiology introduces us to the icon as a source of sophianic wisdom.[61] Where theology gets lost in abstractions, the image of the icon, cleansed of all contingency and any personal ambition of an individual artist, leads the viewer straight into contemplation. Sophia is experienced as a truly divine being, as one can see in the famous icon of Novgorod, among others. Perhaps we understand her better when we immerse ourselves in an inspired image of her than by trying to follow mind-boggling definitions. In the icon, an intuition is at work that transcends any discourse. It is more direct and more daring than words can be. What else do we behold in the icon of the "Mother of God who makes the corn grow" but a Christian renaissance of the "Mother of Corn," the Greek goddess Demeter? The visual image fills the symbol with life. It gives concreteness to an abstraction, and turns an idea into reality.

We tune into the world of the Russian Sophia with admiration and reverence, but we also have to ask the question which this whole discussion, regrettably brief, has been leading to. Can she be made relevant for our time, for the world in crisis? We specified her gifts, but will they be able to effect a vital change? Or is her natural environment, the Russian Orthodox Church, an insurmountable barrier? Persons who are not rooted in this tradition and a religious spirit which

---

[61] See Pavel Florensky, *Iconostasis*, Donald Sheehan and Olga Andrejev, trans. (Crestwood, NY: St. Vladimir's Seminary Press, 1996).

subjects all areas of life to the Church, may find it difficult to accept her. In addition, like any other Christian sophianic theory, the Russian Sophia cannot be separated from the dogma of the Trinity. This is the central focus. Sophia is defined by her relationship to the divine persons, and outside this premise she does not exist. It appears that the Russians, from their deep intuition of Sophia, stretched this dogma to the utmost limit, but were unable to transcend it. Sophia remains *created* Wisdom. Godfather, the Creator, whom she mysteriously permeates, was there before her, and stands above her. As long as the Feminine is not located in the godhead itself, as long as it is subservient to God the Creator, as long as it is his "complementation" (in the same sense as woman in patriarchy is considered subservient and complementary to man), Sophia cannot act from divine empowerment in her own right. The sacred wedding has to take place within the deity—as Hildegard saw, but dared not say. If the revelation of a new time were to reinterpret the universal principle of the Trinity, would we still speak of Sophia? She was a Hebrew and a Greek intuition, reverberating distantly, though often very clearly, the ancient Goddess. Her wisdom consists of a whole range of supreme qualities: love, kindness, bounty, justice, compassion, the ordering power, the life force—the "power to make grow"—among others. But then, these qualities approach divine authority and creatorship, which all our spokesmen of Sophia, from Solomon and Sirach down to her prophets in our century, anxiously seek to avoid. Within the patriarchal system there is no place for the Feminine as an independent, creative principle, and this applies to Divine Wisdom, too. She may be elevated to a high spiritual rank; she may hover around God in intimate association with Him and lead an ambiguous, precarious and often suspect existence between essence, hypostasis and personhood, but she definitely may not act from any divine authority of her own.

What prevented her protecting the natural world from violation, forestalling the aggressiveness of an arrogant and brutalized *logos*? The answer clearly is that in this world she had no legitimacy. Her spiritualization cut her off from the earth and condemned her to passivity. Her loving kindness—the hallowed "Eternal Feminine"—forbade her anger, and last not least, she was robbed of her vibrant erotic power. If she is to become an active force again, a redemptress in this time of history, she will have to regain the "Isis power" of the Goddess of Heaven, the sovereign eroticism of Astarte, the maternal anger of Demeter. Her maternal *love* alone was not able to prevent disaster, the coming of the Antichrist. She desires to be reborn as a new collective symbol of the Feminine Divine. For this end, no new system of philosophy is required. The age of theosophic or philosophic ideologies is definitely over. Jesus himself was no theologian and had no theology. He referred to the "Father" because in his time, a thousand years after Moses brought down the decalog from the mountain, it was no longer possible to refer to the Divine Mother. Sophia will return on different premises—in a spirit no longer embarrassed by the patriarchal paradigm inherent in Christian dogma.

Chapter Four

RADICAL SOPHIA

T HROUGHOUT HUMAN HISTORY SOPHIA can be traced like a red thread. Rarely was she able to reveal herself in her full stature as in times immemorial, but she was always there, a broad subterranean stream at one time, a small trickle or a faint rumor of some lost knowledge of the wholeness of the Divine at another. She erupted in visions of individual human beings, or, as with the Russian sophiologists of the 19th and 20th centuries, as a subtle theology, which left the question of her divinity unresolved. The time had not come yet for a new apotheosis of Divine Sophia.

Our time hardly noticed that there was one radical prophet of Sophia before Women's Liberation who recognized her divine potency and reconstructed her step by step from the sources of mythology. Some of us might wish that this prophet of Sophia had been a woman, but the fact is that this remarkable person was a man. *Otfried Eberz* (1878-1958) is not even widely known among German feminists, although a new edition of his most important book with chapters from his other writings came out a few years ago.

Reading Eberz is an experience of a special kind. A reader gets the impression that he wrote from a great intellectual and spiritual tension, like one who knows that his theses run counter to the conceptions of centuries, even millennia, concerning God, Man, and human history. He concentrated on one essential fact: the violent paradigm shift in prehistoric times, and he commanded the whole range of classical mythology and drew from all available sources to support his thesis. His stance is that of a passionate philosopher circling around his subject with an intensity close to obsession. The one subject to which he devoted his life's work was the restoration of Sophia.[1]

For a woman, the discovery of the writings of Otfried Eberz can be profoundly stirring. How is it, she may ask, that this classical scholar, a student of mythology and biblical history, a universal historian, knew so much about the sufferings of women in patriarchy, understood so well the "problem that had no name"? His analysis goes straight to the heart of the matter. Some of his observations are so poignant, so painfully true, that they may be experienced as a shock. How can a man who had spent most of his life in monastic solitude, buried in archives, the very image of a German professor, define so well the pains which overshadow and confuse the lives of women, at a time when women themselves generally did not understand the predicament? He saw the connection between the degradation of women in patriarchal society and the suppression of Sophia by male *logos*. Women, whose thinking and feeling differs from men, are homeless in a male-dominated world.

> Women had to suffer the suppression of much that was most precious and essential to their souls, and to assume the character masculine absolutism forced upon them.[2]

---

[1] Otfried Eberz, *Vom Aufgang und Niedergang des männlichen Weltalters* ["The Rise and Fall of Male Supremacy"], henceforth abbreviated *AuN*, ed. by Annemarie Taeger and Lucia Eberz (Bonn: Bouvier, 1990). As Otfried Eberz' works are not available in English, I have translated the text.

[2] Eberz, *AuN*, p. 59.

He knew intuitively, when he was a young student, that so-called progress was a misconception of patriarchal thinking. This was the reason why feminine wisdom had been disinherited in prehistoric times. He collected evidence to prove his thesis in the great libraries of Europe, and was able to corroborate it more and more. To him, it was an indisputable fact that the present masculine or "hoministic" age had been preceded by a feminine age of high sophistication and culture. Modern research came to the same conclusion, but when Otfried Eberz published his theses in three essays about the "Rise and Fall of the Masculine Age" between 1929 and 1931, he was a solitary prophet in the desert. The early '30s were the beginning of a particularly brutal "hoministic age," the Nazi era, and when Hitler seized power in Germany, Eberz was promptly forbidden to publish. His theses were considered "undesirable" by the Nazi authorities.[3]

Even today, after so many feminists, scholars, and writers have critically questioned the patriarchal image of God, the most tenacious stronghold of the male-dominated order, Eberz' daring seems extraordinary. His approach is more radical than that of all the other sophiologists. He is not only convinced of the existence of a prehistoric "gynecocratic" age, but also pleads for a return to this original, woman-oriented social order. The reason is that in Eberz' opinion only this society is ontologically justified.[4] This is to say, the cosmic order, itself, is evidence

---

[3] His widow, Lucia Eberz, told me that Hitler had met Eberz before 1933, and was so fascinated by him that he requested his services for Nazi propaganda. Eberz flatly refused. Being forbidden to publish, Eberz barely survived the Nazi era as a private scholar.

[4] The term "gynecocratic" is somewhat misleading, as it was not an age in which women "ruled" (from Greek *kratein*, "to rule") over men, but when feminine values were dominant. Eberz had in mind what Riane Eisler in *The Chalice and the Blade* (San Francisco: HarperSanFrancisco, 1988) more aptly calls the "gylanic" age (from *gyne*, "woman," and *andros*, "man"), when women and men lived harmoniously together in a partnership-oriented society.

of the divine feminine principle, and as the primary ontological principle it takes precedence over the masculine. This idea represents a true quantum leap in sophianic thinking.

The starting point of Eberz' studies was mythology. Whether of Sumerian-Babylonian, Egyptian, Greek, Germanic, Hebrew, Aztec, Indian, Chinese, or African origin, all mythologies give evidence, openly or in coded form, of a gigantic battle in prehistory between an original female Deity and a male adversary. The original Goddess is inconceivable without her male counterpart, the son-lover, who is torn to pieces, killed, castrated, and cursed with magic spells by an evil enemy, the representative of the incipient patriarchal age. The passion and resurrection of the male consort of the Goddess, reported in all mythologies, is interpreted by Eberz as the great feminine Apocalypse, which could only be expressed in symbol and myth. The memory of this tremendous happening could only be preserved in the guise of historically irrelevant and ambivalent metaphors, which often became distorted in patriarchal interpretation. The great Goddess mourns her son-lover who was sacrificed to the new masculine ideal, and she follows dangerous paths to seek his body and restore it to life. Thus, the Babylonian goddess Ishtar seeks Tammuz in the underworld, the Egyptian Isis gathers the dead limbs of Osiris and joins them together. In similar fashion, the male part of the androgynous divine pair is killed and has to be resurrected by the female. Likewise, Mirjam (Mary) of the Hebrew myth seeks Jeshua (Jesus) and, as Mary Magdalen, stands weeping at the empty tomb of the historical Jesus.

In Eberz' view, in the beginning there was the divine androgyne, Sophia and Logos. Sophia is to be considered the primary, Logos the secondary principle, because Logos is derived from Sophia, and not vice versa. Their bipolar unity was torn apart by brute force at the beginning of the second or patriarchal eon. This tragic event, marked by unimaginable violence, took place over several millennia and is the beginning of the eon which is drawing to a close today. The stories of the myths about gods and goddesses mirror real events in human history, no matter how distorted they appear in mythology. As above, so below. Gods and mythologies arise as reflections of actual conditions on Earth. So-called "divine revelations," Eberz argues, are conditioned by the state of consciousness of mankind at a certain time. Man's image of himself will necessarily be transferred to his image of God. The basic assumptions that shaped human conditions on Earth are projected into supernatural reality. Human beings create the kind of God they are prepared for at a given period of time. What was the original state of consciousness of the prehistoric human as reflected by the fragments, often distorted, of mythology as it was handed down to us?

In classical Greek and Roman literature, as well as in Genesis, we find reports about a legendary paradise or "Golden Age." All sources agree that this was a peaceful age, in which humans and the whole creation lived in harmony, when wars and bloody sacrifice were unknown. As Empedocles writes in his *Hymns of Purification*:

> They did not have Ares as god or Kydoimos, nor king Zeus nor Kronos nor Poseidon, but queen Kypris. Her they propitiated with holy images and painted animal figures, with perfumes of subtle fragrance and offerings of distilled myrrh and sweet-smelling frankincense, and pouring on the earth libations of golden honey. Their altar was not drenched by the . . . slaughter of bulls, but this was the greatest defilement among men—to bereave of life and eat noble limbs. All creatures, both animals and birds, were tame and gentle to men, and bright was the flame of their friendship.[5]

---

[5] Empedocles, *The Extant Fragments*, ed. by M. R. Wright (New Haven, CT: Yale University Press, 1981), pp. 282f. Quoted in a German verse translation by O. Eberz in *AuN*, p. 130.

Such a condition of universal peace and love is only conceivable when unity is a general state of consciousness. It is not the result of self-conscious virtue or morals, but of all-embracing unity as a law of existence. Love was dominant over Strife, because no other condition was known. Only when difference, otherness, dualism, the split between subject and object break this norm, can the "will to power" and as a consequence, the war of all against all, replace the "will to unity." The fact that the female body gives birth to both sexes, just as Mother Earth brings forth the variety of plants every year, must have been a numinous experience for early humans. Human beings experienced themselves in their dual sexuality, issuing from one maternal womb, and this appeared to them divine and corresponding to the laws of the universe.

The idea that both genders were once united in an androgyne half male and half female is an ancient intuition of mankind. The desire of the sexes to merge in loving union gave rise to this universal image of a bisexual entity, as Plato, among others, described (and caricatured) it in the *Symposium*. When this dual entity threatened the power of the gods, it was split in two halves, which henceforth were destined to seek each other. This myth reflects the "division of the world's parental pair," the fall into duality with disastrous consequences. This rent can only be healed by love.

> Love alone is that primal force by which two individuals of opposite sex merge . . . to form a single, indissoluble dual entity. Thus, two human halves, transcending the conflict of their polarity, become one whole, integrated and complete human being.[6]

---

[6] Eberz, *AuN*, p. 81.

Accordingly, early mankind could not but imagine God as a Divine Androgyne issued by a female *Urgrund* (primordial ground or matrix).

> It is not surprising, therefore, that the original human monad, bisexual and anthropomorphically projecting its own likeness on all things, also symbolized the unity of the divine monad as love and absolute unity of both potencies. What other image could have occurred to man to express the creative power of God? . . . All acts of creation on the divine and the human level were conceived by the bisexual monad as ways of engendering and giving birth to life.[7]

Eberz argues that the natural religion of early humanity was bound to be an androgynous monotheism. God represented Mother and Father at the same time, or, more specifically, a male-female Universal Mother, who was often given the characteristic features of both sexes. This androgynous deity, Sophia, symbolizes the unity of subject and object, the merging of both poles to form a higher wholeness. This is *philosophia perennis*, eternal wisdom, the only philosophy with an axiom based on an irrefutable universal law. Eberz calls the intuitive perception of the unity of the gender dualism "gnosis" or *visio intellectualis*, intuitive insight by "intellect" as a means of holistic perception. It is a kind of *Wesensschau*, a view of the essence of reality. Here, "the One recognizes itself in identity with subject and object."[8] This insight cannot be gained by the rational mind or logical reason, but by the "perception of the heart," which is more germane to the inner nature of the female than the male sex,

---

[7] *AuN*, p. 118.

[8] Otfried Eberz, *Sophia-Logos und der Widersacher* ["Sophia-Logos and the Adversary"], henceforth abbreviated *S-L* (Munich: reprint by Lucia Eberz, 1978), p. 8.

---

because women are capable of bringing forth life. The first eon, therefore, was a "gnostic gynecocracy." In Eberz' understanding, gynecocracy does not mean a rule or predominance of women, which would be nothing but the reversal of patriarchy, but the primacy of the universal law of life, to which women have a closer affinity than men. Therefore, the female sex is the true vehicle of the gnostic *philosophia perennis*.

> The reason is that feminine perception is an instinctive and intuitive vision of the intrinsic nature of things, rather than a rational grasp of their functional relations, an experience of inward growing and becoming, rather than a tying together of the mechanical succession of phenomena. Therefore, the feminine is the pole of metaphysical knowledge.[9]

This "gnosis" (not to be confused with historical Gnosticism) is primarily the wisdom of woman. Man, too, may share it, but it is woman who takes the lead, and he will have to learn from her.

> All deeper spiritual life beyond the merely intellectual man owes to his awakening by woman. In this respect man has the receptive and issuing (*gebärende*) part, woman the generating or engendering part.[10]

Sophia is knowledge of the metaphysics of love, consummated in *unio gnostica* as opposed to *unio zoologica*, the mere sexual and procreative instinct. Sophia desires love for its own sake, for that higher union which makes human beings co-creators of God. The hoministic or agnostic order of life prevailing in the second eon supplanted the sophianic will to union by unipolar ego consciousness, thereby driving

---

[9] Eberz, *AuN*, p. 109.
[10] *AuN*, p. 110.

woman into a profound inner loneliness. It is the tragedy of woman in the patriarchal age and the deepest cause of the so-called battle of the sexes that she is not allowed to live according to her law of life. The conflict of the sexes is neither destined to last forever, nor is it a natural condition, but the result of that reversal of values which occurred in the Neolithic Age, roughly between 9000 and 2000 before the Christian era. The originally feminine Trinity, Sophia containing Logos and their offspring, the Androgyne, had to transmute under pressure of a changed reality on Earth into a monotheistic Fathergod and subsequently into the all-male Trinity of the Father, the Son and that mysterious entity which in Christianity is called the Holy Spirit. With the precise and deliberately pedantic words of Otfried Eberz:

> The One, as absolute potentiality, contains within itself the feminine potency, including her gnostic capacities, as well as the male potency, including his gnostic capacities. The feminine potency of the One, which is Sophia, the spiritual Mother, is the primary potency of the One, on account of her gnostic receptivity; and by her longing she brings forth her spiritual son, Logos, the secondary potency of the One. By drawing this "Son" into herself, they become a new, third person, the Androgyne. The gnostic feminine potency of the One, Sophia, is therefore the "first person," whereas the male potency of the One, delivered into gnosis by Sophia, is the second, and the gnostic Androgyne, issued from both in the One and by the One, is the "third person" in this gnostic Trinity.[11]

---

[11] Otfried Eberz, *Sophia und Logos oder die Philosophie der Wiederherstellung* ["Sophia and Logos, or the Philosophy of Restitution"], henceforth abbreviated *SuL*, published posthumously by Lucia Eberz (Munich, 1983), p. 280f.

She is a "universal formula because she contains both potencies of being in their relation to each other," whereas the patriarchal Trinity of later times only has a formula "for the male potency of the One setting itself up as absolute."[12]

From this approach, it is obvious why even the Russian sophiologists failed to integrate Sophia in the Trinity. There is simply no space for her as a divine person, even though theologians bent over backward to achieve the impossible. There is no way out. Sophia must remain a hybrid, circling around God on the periphery, but banished from the center of his being. The fact that she commanded her true stature in the heart and the intuitive perception of many a sophianic visionary is more proof of her ineradicable ontological power than of the ability of patriarchal theology to integrate her in the image of God.

The universal formula Sophia-Logos-Androgyne is simple and yet difficult to realize, because it turns the accustomed way of thinking and the deeply entrenched concept of God upside down. The feminine Trinity containing the masculine within herself, a veritable *Vièrge ouvrante*, amounts to a theological quantum leap. The whole cosmos is based on bipolarity. It exists in the sexuality of creatures, within the atomic nucleus, as well as in the macrocosmos of the planets.

> Yet only in Man the cosmic contradiction of sexually different individuals is dissolved by the experience of unity in duality, and this appeasement of opposites is called Love, meaning a kind of recognition, volition and feeling on a level of metaphysical significance.[13]

---

[12] Eberz, *SuL*, p. 281.
[13] Eberz, *AuN*, p. 45.

We have to probe deeply into our interior to salvage Love—the sentimentalized, trivialized, misguided and generally abused love between the sexes—as a metaphysical and cosmic power. Only in this urge to achieve a loving union of polarities can the battle of the sexes and other dualisms be overcome. This is "the Work of Love," as Soloviev calls it, whose understanding of the metaphysical significance of love is closely related to Eberz' views.[14] The meaning of sexual love consists neither in the gratification of instincts nor in procreation alone, but in the creation of *one* absolute personality by two finite polarities. Love in this form, perfect Sophia, restores human wholeness by the free union of the feminine and the masculine principle.

When divine Sophia is spiritualized to an extent where she is totally removed from Earth, as it happened in the Christian tradition, she stands in danger of losing touch with human life. Sophia is rooted in all-embracing eros, including human love. Because Sophia was lost in our culture, co-opted by Logos, love, itself, became degraded, religion lost the spirit of eros, and our houses of worship are devoid of love. It seems ironical that the popular church traditionally depends on women for support, although it conceded only with certain reservations that women, too, were created in the likeness of God, and although it stigmatized women as the source of all sin and subjected them to the rule of men. The longing of woman for *religio*, love-in-relationship, is so great that she accepted her devaluation and still sought the union of her heart with the divine inside the church. The *Jesuazusen* of the Middle Ages, as Eberz calls them, devoted female worshippers of Jesus, religious women

---

[14] Compare Soloviev's profound treatise *The Meaning of Love*, trans. by Jane Marshall (London: Geoffrey Bles, 1946). Central to Soloviev's metaphysical view of heterosexual love is the union of polar opposites based on the gender difference. Therefore, Soloviev regards homosexuality as a "metaphysical disease," precisely because this union of polarities cannot take place between two persons of the same sex.

in the convents and the Beguines, always found ways and means to revere Jesus as the sacrificed feminist God and to unite in mystical love with the resurrected Christ, despite the sanctions of the patriarchal Church. The superior religious genius of women comes from this innate desire for loving union. While women leave the church in masses today, others are trying to instill into the Christian religion a new sophianic spirit. Nobody has been more affirmative than Otfried Eberz that this is indeed the task and the privilege of women.

> The world is now waiting for women of feminine genius who are called upon as prophetesses, priestesses, and teachers of their sex to restore the bipolar cosmic balance, which was destroyed by masculine unipolarity. However, this balance cannot be fully restored unless the feminine polarity . . . is ready to utter its own Word complementing the masculine . . . .[15]

> The decay of the masculine primacy cannot be denied, nor the rise of the feminine pole. There are no signs whatsoever that this development can be obstructed in the long run. As a consequence, the tension and opposition between the sexes will be aggravated and deepened for some time. A state of transition, a renewed hostility between the sexes, is threatening humanity, but historical analogy makes the final victory of the feminine pole seem not improbable. The sex which is capable of experiencing and rehabilitating the metaphysical meaning of love, rightfully deserves it.[16]

[15] Eberz, *AuN*, p. 106f.
[16] *AuN*, p. 80.

Perhaps we shall witness at the end of history, as in its beginning, a Feminine World Age; perhaps woman will once more redeem herself and man from his mania of destruction. In any case, the secret of love belongs to her. When she was forced to surrender her mysteries to the male, they were exposed to profanation and devaluation, and finally to that obscene "sexual enlightenment" through the male single-gender-being (*Eingeschlechterwesen*). It has become all the more clear that only woman can be the guardian of the meaning, i.e., the metaphysics, of love. . . . Everything she can learn from man is of secondary importance to life; but that which man will have to learn from her again is the very condition of life, is life itself, the double-gender-being (*Zweigeschlechterwesen*).[17]

These words, written at the end of the '20s, were prophetic. We must remember that Otfried Eberz' theses were not backed by modern research or the sensational discovery of the Gnostic Scriptures of Nag Hammadi. He gained his insight into the condition of the world exclusively from his superior knowledge of mythology and his intuition. This most uncompromising of all sophianics worked and wrote in complete isolation. There was no network, no support for his thought. Between 1931 and 1958, the year of his death, he was able to publish hardly anything. It takes a very sturdy mind and robust spirit to keep going under such circumstances and to pronounce views that went completely against the grain of his time. Today, half a century later, his conclusions are fully corroborated by feminist research, by archeology, studies in religion, and even by science. The monumental work of Marija

[17] *AuN*, p. 140.

Gimbutas, the vision of a partnership-oriented society by Riane Eisler, the research and the visions of many women and men like Joseph Campbell, the doyen of mythological scholarship, were all preceded by Otfried Eberz, an unknown German scholar. Now the "old paradigm," the patriarchal world order of Logos, is clearly seen to collapse. Today, sophianic wisdom is evoked for the salvation of the planet, and women and men in many walks of life focus their work on the concrete implementation of the spirit of Sophia. Their confidence, like Eberz', that Sophia will prevail at last is based on the necessity of her victory, because without it there is no chance of survival.

The core area, however, where Sophia has to be recovered, is the relation between the sexes. As Eberz predicted, the feminist movement unleashed a new battle of the sexes.[18] There is definitely a conservative backlash against women all over the world, but at the same time a consensus is growing that the female-male balance has to be restored. As long as the relation between the sexes is out of joint, that is, patriarchally deformed, there can be no peaceful world order. Innumerable small and greater steps will have to be taken by individual women and men to change their consciousness, before we can approach world peace.

The problem of God will then partly solve itself, and partly it will be determined by evolution, the sophianic process, as we may call it. This requires the lifting of the veil that shrouded the origin of religion in darkness; the investigation of myths and fairy tales, the oral traditions which disguised and passed on the secrets of the past; the abolition of patriarchal taboos. At a time when women generally were not empowered to investigate their past, Otfried Eberz took up the thread of

---

[18] See Susan Faludi, *Backlash: The Undeclared War Against American Women* (New York: Crown, 1991), an investigation of the repression of women in public life during the 1980's, as patriarchal resistance against the emancipation of women.

Ariadne and followed Divine Wisdom straight into the source. Today numerous feminist theologians are working to rehabilitate Sophia. In many publications and public events Divine Wisdom is brought back into our consciousness.[19] In the present emergency, sophianic thinking is evoked in studies in the fields of theology, archeology, mythology, and history, in intuitive ways by meditation and feminine self-awareness. We may speak of a sophianic network today, which is woven in many places and in the consciousness of many women and men.

When Otfried Eberz formulated his historical-philosophical theses, this resurgence of Sophia did not exist. Step by step he uncovered what happened in the prehistoric time shift and analyzed the reasons for this apocalyptic upheaval. Precise details as to the time, character and condition of the patriarchal change as it occurred all over the world will never be reconstructed. There can be no final proof of what really happened, but there is evidence which an inspired and informed vision may bring to light. Otfried Eberz had that kind of vision. He pieced together fragments distorted by patriarchal bias, reconstructed the historical context, and found the truth. In a second step, we shall now take a closer look at various strands of his thought. We shall first review his point of departure.

To Otfried Eberz it was an indisputable fact that "gnostic gynecocracy" was at the beginning of human society. Only the creative potency of the Feminine could have been the model of divine creativity, and this conclusion would naturally have led to the primacy of the Feminine. Eberz had no doubt that women had created this social order. They were predestined to be the priestesses of the ancient Goddess sanctuar-

---

[19] As in America, Goddess lore was revived in Germany (see the work of Heide Göttner-Abendroth, Gerda Weiler, Christa Mulack, Verena Kast, Ingrid Riedel, Hildegunde Wöller, Jutta Voss).

ies. The female elite was organized in a House of Women, the male elite in a House of Men. Of the two, it was the House of Women which naturally transmitted the cosmic law of the unity-in-polarity and therefore occupied a higher rank. The uncontested primary authority was Sophia. But since the Feminine contained the Masculine as in the female womb, there was no hostile opposition of the sexes. As far as the conditions of the reversal of the relation between the sexes are concerned, Eberz essentially agrees with the discoveries of modern research.[20] The external cause of the paradigm shift he considers to be the invasion of militant tribes (Aryans) into the matriarchal or Goddess-centered cultures of the Eastern Mediterranean. They came on horses and carried weapons, whereas the conquered peoples were organized in peaceful agrarian societies. The hoministic overthrow, which ousted the Goddess and forced women under the domination of men, must have taken place with unspeakable cruelty over a long period of time. The Goddess was replaced by a pantheon dominated by male gods and finally, in the case of the Semitic tribes, by a monotheistic Fathergod.

Originally, even the Aryans must have lived in a gnostic-gynecoratic society for the simple reason that no other origin is conceivable. Whatever may have caused the conquest, the fact is that in the transition from a nomadic society of hunters and gatherers in the Paleolithic and Mesolithic Age to a more sedentary agrarian society in the Neolithic, women by and by were deprived of important fields of activity and had to concede to men their high social position. For Eberz, the most important change is the shift in human consciousness:

----

[20] Among other works, see especially *Weib und Macht* ["Woman and Power"], ed. by Richard Fester; Margaret Ehrenberg, *Women in Prehistory* (Norman, OK: University of Oklahoma Press, 1989); Riane Eisler, *The Chalice and the Blade* (San Francisco: HarperSanFrancisco, 1988); and the works of Gerda Weiler.

> The feminist aeon of humanity came to an end when the
> ego-consciousness of the masculine element developed in
> hypertrophical, titanic fashion at the expense of gnostic self-
> awareness. Gradually it suppressed and forgot the earlier
> state and finally waged war against it as a disturbance and
> infringement of the agnostic ego-consciousness.[21]

At one time, the masculine will must have rebelled against feminine primacy, possibly as a consequence of the discovery of the causal relation between intercourse and procreation, and posited its male individualism against the feminine-masculine synthesis. The will to power was born, the principle of "having" over the principle of "being," greed against sufficiency, competition and violence against harmonious cooperation. The source of all violence is the prehistoric rape of the female sex. The violation of nature and every weaker opposite is but the consequence of this original rape. By transference, the new God had to be jealous and vengeful, and he had to fight with unrelenting violence whatever was left of the Goddess culture. In order to break her power, gnostic Sophia had to be attacked in her masculine pole, the "feminist God." The passion and resurrection myths of antiquity derive from the persecution of the gnostic House of Men. Eberz penetrates the confusingly complex and contradictory story of mythology, especially the Greek, where the Goddess and her Son-Lover were treated with unparalleled cruelty. Hesiod has the story of a creature of dual gender, Gaia-Uranos, whom the Titans tore apart, castrating Uranos. The new hoministic God is Zeus, an inveterate seducer and rapist, who usurped the birth-giving capacity of the old Goddess. A closer look at Dionysos shows that he is actually a "feminist God," who was torn to pieces by the terrorist priest-

---

[21] Eberz, *SuL*, p. 591.

hood of the Titans, and was resurrected in the Mysteries. Only in the secret societies associated with the mystery cults was the lore of the Golden Age of gnostic gynecocracy transmitted, as well as the prophecy of a resurrection of the divine androgyne in the future. Also the Mysteries of Eleusis represent, as previously mentioned,[22] the resurrection of the Great Goddess, Demeter-Kore, in her twofold aspect. Pandora, whose name suggests the all-bestowing and all-kind, is reversed into her opposite in Greek mythology. She now becomes the source of all evil, just like Eve in the biblical story.

It is difficult to tune into a time when such myths were forming as a response to actual events. According to Eberz, the transition from the gnostic-gynecocratic, or feminine, age to the hoministic, or male-dominated, age took many millennia. No human being experienced within a lifetime the overthrow of Sophia and her "Double Order," but in the course of many generations the violent shift must have been inscribed in the human subconscious and crystallized in symbolic stories in the myths. The knowledge of the old social order and its religion was preserved in patriarchal distortion even in later religious scripture. Thus, the prophet Ezekiel of the Old Testament is transported to Jerusalem in a dream, right to the gate of the temple of Jahve, where he witnesses the "atrocity" committed by women, who mourn Tammuz, the feminist God of Ishtar (Ezekiel 8:14). Not even the authors of the Scriptures could prevent memories and documents of the sophianic age from entering the canon of the Old Testament.

Otfried Eberz points out that the text of the Song of Songs, for example, was handed down in fragmented form. This happened probably by intention, in order to disguise its real provenance, but a closer look reveals that this is unmistakably a collection of bridal hymns, which the

---

[22] See previous discussion on page 14f.

divine couple, Mirjam and Jeshua, were offering each other under the symbolic names of Shulamit and Solomon.[23] Shulamit is an independent woman, who confesses her love to the man of her choice, and praises his beauty, as he praises hers. All of nature, the whole creation, is summoned to celebrate the bride and her groom. The couple is removed to a realm of absolute and indissoluble love, which is stronger than death. Sick with love, Shulamit goes out into the streets to seek her lost lover. She suffers herself to be beaten and dishonored: "The watchmen on the walls took away my cloak" (SoS 5:7). She seeks him, as the Goddess of old sought her divine lover. Eberz suggests that this desperate search and public humiliation symbolizes the passion of Sophia and Logos.

Significantly, Shulamit takes her beloved not into her father's house, but to "my mother's house, to the room of her who conceived me" (SoS 3:4). And the groom comes to her "wearing the crown with which his mother has crowned him, on his wedding day, on his day of joy" (SoS 3:11). The context is clearly a woman-oriented social order, which preceded the patriarchal order of the Old Testament.

Eberz interprets the passion and resurrection of Jesus of Nazareth as the historical manifestation of an ancient Hebrew myth, the story of Mirjam and Jeshua, following the pattern of the sacrificed feminist God and the *dea dolorosa*. Jeshua-Jesus, the "anointed," is sacrificed by Jahve to atone for the "original sin" of mankind. This original sin consists of man's defection from the law of God, of which woman is even more guilty. Just as the Goddess offered the sacrament to her lover, Eve, inspired by the snake, the symbol of goddess wisdom, offers to Adam the apple from the tree of knowledge. The apple or pomegranate, as we know, is an ancient symbol of love. Shulamit sings:

---

23 Eberz, *S-L*, pp. 101-103.

Come, my beloved, let us go out into the fields to lie
    among the henna-bushes;
let us go early to the vineyards
and see if the vine has budded or its blossom opened,
    if the pomegranates are in flower.
There will I give you my love,
when the mandrakes give their perfume,
and all rare fruits are ready at our door,
fruits new and old
which I have in store for you, my love.

(Song of Songs 7:10-13)

The "original sin" was Eve's gnostic act, the initiation of her mate into higher wisdom. Jahve takes revenge by driving the human couple out of Paradise, but this punishment does not expiate the crime of regression into the order of the Goddess. Time and again, the order of the Goddess was revived and threatened the new patriarchal God. In the Christian myth, the Messiah is sacrificed vicariously for mankind and takes Jahve's revenge upon himself.

Thus, the blood of the feminist God is spilled once more in the sacrificial death of Jeshua. In this reading, the story of the passion of Christ appears as the old myth clothed in a new form.[24] No doubt, the historical Jesus was a liberator of women, as Otfried Eberz pointed out several decades before modern feminism.

---

[24] In her book *Ein Traum von Christus* ["A Dream of Christ"] (Stuttgart: Kreuz Verlag, 1987), Hildegunde Wöller comes close to Eberz' interpretation from her own Jungian perspective. Significantly, this well-researched, persuasive, and beautifully written book by a feminist Lutheran theologian was received with hostility by mainstream Protestant theology.

By declaring the female sex capable of contemplative perception and gnostic love, and by elevating the unmarried, contemplative woman above the active and married one, he restored to women their spiritual dignity. The hoministic cult of Jahve had robbed them of this dignity and confined the whole sex to a mere biological and material existence.[25]

The women showed their gratitude when they stood by him under the cross and by being first at the tomb. Mary of Magdala, who was favored by Jesus as his most intimate friend and companion, was the first who saw the resurrected Christ. Eberz has a daring thesis that Mary Magdalen may have become the founder of a new mystery religion.

> Supported by the devotees of Jesus among her associates, it was Mary Magdalen who saved Christianity from extinction by establishing the doctrine of the resurrected Christ. Easter is the resurrection of crucified Jesus by the love of a woman.[26]

Subsequently, the apostolic takeover by Paul and his successors turned the church into a male-dominated institution. The charisma of Mary Magdalen, this "passionate woman of spiritual genius," who "had recovered in ecstasy the feminist God of the first aeon,"[27] was then transferred to Mary, the mother of Jesus. In the Virgin Mary, the humble *Ancilla domini*, this charisma could now be safely "hominized" without any danger to the patriarchal order. In the course of Christian history,

---

[25] Eberz, *S-L*, p. 123.
[26] *S-L*, p. 126.
[27] *S-L*, p. 131f.

Mary was elevated more and more, up to the dogma of her Ascension, especially in Russian Orthodox doctrine, without trespassing on the all-male Trinity. Eberz agrees that in the Holy Trinity there is no place for the feminine principle, a subject we discussed at length in the previous chapter.[28] Sophia as extolled in 17th- and 18th-century theosophy, as well as the Sophia of Soloviev and his followers, is not the real Sophia, the feminine-divine principle.[29] In Eberz' view, the true Sophia can only be recovered from the secret tradition of the mysteries and the *Jesuazusen*, the female devotees of Jesus who preserved the mystery of the divine androgyne, as well as by the powerful sophianic spirit of the present.

So much for the prophetic insights of Otfried Eberz. As he said, it is time that we expand the understanding of Christ to include the dimension of Sophia. The cosmic Christ, as envisioned by Christians in Asia and by progressive Western theologians like Matthew Fox, is inconceivable without Sophia.[30] The cosmic Christ is not a *pre-Christian* concept, but the wisdom in all religions which needs to be revived for the healing of the crucified Earth. Matthew Fox envisions a sophianic or cosmic culture, in which new personal arts will be cultivated.

> They include the art of friendship, the art of making beauty where we dwell, the art of conversation, of massage, of laughter, of preparing food, of hospitality, of the sharing of ideas, of growing food and flowers, of singing songs, of making love, of telling stories, of uniting generations. . . . The personal arts include the arts of listening and of heal-

[28] *S-L*, p. 135.
[29] *S-L*, p. 136.
[30] See Matthew Fox, *The Coming of the Cosmic Christ* (San Francisco: HarperSanFrancisco, 1988).

ing, of enjoying oneself with others in simple ways; the art of creating our lifestyles and our communities; the art of conviviality; the art of parenting and of forgiving.[31]

All of these sophianic arts are based on a loving relationship with other human beings, with our environment and the Earth at large; they seek wholeness and unification within the whole.

The pioneering spirit of Otfried Eberz rescued Sophia from the rubble of millennia, and proclaimed a sophianic revelation in the future. At his time, he was not yet able to show feasible ways to put the sophianic principle into action. All his prodigious intellectual energy went into the rehabilitation of Sophia and to predict her return. In the most obscure writing of the New Testament, The Revelation of John, he found conclusive evidence that she will indeed return.

The Revelation is truly a book "sealed up with seven seals," which is still a puzzle for exegesis. The obscurity may lift, Eberz suggests, if we read the twelfth chapter about the coming of the apocalyptic woman as a prophesy of the victory of Sophia in a new aeon. This episode stands in the center of the book like an erratic block amidst a scenery of titanic battles of God waged against the powers of evil, the "whore of Babylon" and the idolaters who are still seduced by the ancient Goddess. We are familiar with this battle from the Books of Moses and the Wisdom Texts, but the wrath of God was never before displayed in such formidable imagery. The apocalyptic Judgment wreaks awful destruction. The Earth is visited by plagues and natural disasters surpassing all imagination. Almost two thousand years after John, the "servant of God," was overwhelmed by these images on the island of Patmos and received the order to record what was revealed to him, we have to

---

[31] Fox, *The Coming of the Cosmic Christ*, p. 200.

acknowledge that some of the predicted disasters have indeed come true. Does the description of the violent earthquake at the breaking of the sixth seal, when the sun turned black and the moon became red as blood, when the stars fell to the Earth, the sky vanished, and every mountain and island was removed from its place (Revelation 6:12-14), not evoke the threat of an atomic holocaust? Does the mind's eye not see burning oil fields when we read that the abyss was opened and "smoke rose like smoke from a great furnace, and the sun and the air were darkened by the smoke from the shaft" (Revelation 9:2)? Even more disturbing is the image of a great star shooting from the sky, flaming like a torch, as it fell on a third of the rivers and springs.

> The name of the star was Wormwood . . . and men in great numbers died of the water because it had been poisoned (Revelation 8:11).

This is the destruction of the natural environment of our day, the pollution of water, air and earth. The parallel becomes haunting when we learn that the Russian word for wormwood is *chernobylnik*!—It is hard not to believe in an apocalyptic Judgment visited on mankind at the end of this century, with polluted waters, burning atomic power plants and oil wells, carpets of oil spilled in the oceans, and all the rest of the destruction of our planet.

Two "beasts" make their appearance in the Revelation. One of them is horned and crowned and full of blasphemy. The second has "two horns like a lamb's, but spoke like a dragon" (Revelation 13:11). They are obviously intended to represent the powers of evil, but what does the confusing combination of lamb (the symbol of Christ) and dragon (the symbol of the Devil) in the second beast mean? There is an ambivalence here, more precisely: a hearkening back to the gnostic age, when the

Great Goddess was still the patroness of animals. As we know, the snake was sacred to her. Time and again, the "dragon, the snake of old" appears in Revelation, as the adversary waging war on God and the angels. But the apocalyptic beast remains a mystery. On the one hand, it is allowed to utter "great things,"[32] as befits its royal ascendancy, symbolized by the crowns on its ten horns. On the other hand, it "opened its mouth in blasphemy against God" (Revelation 13:6). The wicked beast has power over men. It seduces them to idolatry and keeps them in thrall. Then, abruptly: "Here is wisdom!"[33] Defeated by God, the beast will return before the final damnation, but it needs "wisdom" to understand it: Its "seven heads are seven hills on which the woman sits" (Revelation 17:9). This is a clear reminiscence of the Goddess enthroned on mountaintops, and it takes wisdom indeed to understand the ancient symbolism. At the time of the Revelation, men generally did not understand it any more. It would have been lost on John, the pious servant of God exiled on the Isle of Patmos, as on subsequent generations of bewildered readers, who wrestled with the hidden meaning of this imagery. Thus the beast, relegated to the realm of evil, still retains features of Sophia, the old Goddess.

In the middle of these mysterious and staggering apocalyptic events a woman appears "robed with the sun, beneath her feet the moon, and on her head a crown of twelve stars" (Revelation 12:1). She is pregnant and cries out in the anguish of her labor. She is delivered of a male child

---

[32] Greek *megala*, Latin *magna* (Revelation 13:5), literally means "great things." The Cambridge Bible I am using translates "bombast," which carries a negative connotation, whereas the Greek original leaves the meaning open, so that the ambivalence of the beast can be appreciated.

[33] In both cases (Rev 13:8 and 17:9) the Greek original says *sophia*. In the first instance, the Cambridge Bible translates "key"; in the second, "cue," thus obliterating the deeper meaning of these passages as related to wisdom.

"who is destined to rule all nations with an iron rod" (Revelation 12:5), but his birth is threatened by a great red dragon waiting to devour the child. In a story of stunning similarity, Kronos in the Greek myth is waiting for Rhea to give birth, and devours her children as soon as they are born, because according to a prophesy they threaten his power. Only Zeus escapes, and he, in fact, overthrows Kronos. The apocalyptic woman "fled into the wilds, where she had a place prepared for her by God" (Revelation 12:6). Here she lives protected by God, until the danger is over. We cannot miss the reminiscence of Lilith, the "nightjar," who dwells in the desert with the wild beasts (Isaiah 34:14).

Eberz is convinced that the apocalyptic woman represents "Sophia, the feminine potency emerging throughout the cosmos."[34]

> [She is] Sophia triumphant, the gnostic feminist Church which, at the end of the hominist aeon, will overcome the Antichrist, the dragon of jahvistic hominism, and will give birth once more to the gnostic-gynecocratic Messiah.[35]

In Eberz' interpretation, the essential message of Revelation is that the return of Sophia is imminent. She will come between the Beast and the Lamb, between the persecution of the dragon and the trumpet blasts of the divine Judgment, between the cosmic woman robed with the sun and the great whore of Babylon clothed in purple and scarlet. God is still jealous, fierce and vengeful—or does he simply allow cosmic justice to take its course? The crimes of men against the creation invite their pun-

---

[34] Eberz, *S-L*, p. 150. This view is shared by C. G. Jung; see "Answer to Job," in *The Collected Works*, Vol. II, Psychology and Religion: East and West, trans. R. F. C. Hull, Bollingen Series No. 20 (Princeton: Princeton University Press, 1958.)
[35] Eberz, *SuL*, p. 297.

ishment, as Hildegard of Bingen predicted, and as we have witnessed in this century.

If the vision of Sophia in all the splendor of the stars should prove too dazzling for comfort, let us take a look at her antipode, the "great whore" of Babylon, the condemned, but still great and strong city. She faces the vengefulness of Jahve with scornful pride:

> I am a queen on my throne! No mourning for me, no widow's weeds! (Revelation 18:7)

What is really behind her alleged "fornication"? Is it that she kindled in men the desire for beauty, for powerful eros, glamour and abundance, the very zest of life and the ability to enjoy the good things of the world? "Babylon" stands for all of this. Contrary to the cosmic woman, she has a sensuous appreciation of the Earth and derives pleasure from it. It is obvious why the new hominist God would have accused her of fornication and magic, the blood of the saints and the prophets: it was done to justify his wrath. We remember that the unipolar masculine God has to do his utmost to vilify the Goddess, in order to legitimize his relentless persecution of her. Perhaps the world would be a different place, if Christian asceticism had not so much disparaged eros and the sensuous enjoyment of creation. For the sake of life's wholeness, let us not be so hard on Babylon![36]

Otfried Eberz' argumentation is of remarkable stringency, but his aphoristic conciseness does not make for easy reading. He scanned the mythologies of many cultures and a vast amount of religious sources in

---

[36] See also C. G. Jung, "Answer to Job," ¶ 721, where he says that the destruction of Babylon means "the utter eradication of all life's joys and pleasures," with disastrous consequences for the Christian Age.

his quest for Sophia, and his search was rewarded. Eberz does not subscribe to the Western view of history as a linear progression from the unconscious "primordial slough" of the beginning up to the highest levels of masculine Logos. This straight line of development never existed in his view. The price of "progress" in the current sense was the loss of Sophia, and this definitely was too high a price to pay, as we realize today. The straight line must be changed into a circle again, or rather, a spiral, which maintains always the link with the source, as it ascends to higher levels. With every new turn, it revolves around the eternal, immovable center. The sophianic law of life, which is the One identified with itself in variety, is this ontological center. Jesus' commandment, "Love your neighbor as yourself," because the next person *is* yourself, means precisely this, and it does not sound one bit less revolutionary today than it did at the time of Jesus. Because of the dire need of the planet Earth, an emergency far greater than Eberz could have foreseen, humanity has reached a certain consciousness of oneness, but only Love will lead to the unity and wholeness required. The *Unio mystica* of man and woman, in which woman is the natural teacher and guide, is the great healing force in the relation of the sexes. This, according to Eberz, shows the way to a comprehensive healing of our time. When this primary relationship was upset in favor of male dominance, every sort of violence and exploitation was sanctioned in the name of masculine power. It is only consistent that the violation of Sophia in the relation of the sexes created a masculine image of God, which even the sophianic break-through at various times in the course of centuries was not able to balance.

With rare independence of mind and spirit, Otfried Eberz helped to prepare the ground for the sophianic paradigm shift. His analysis of the "hoministic age" is more pertinent than he could have guessed at the time. Even his critique of the early movement for the emancipation of women has a point, if that emancipation is only concerned with the question of equal rights. He observed the emergence of a *femme machine*, who is bound to suffer more than *homme machine* from the hoministic world order, its dehumanizing technology and spiritual emptiness. He had women in capitalist industrial society in mind the same as women in the "hoministic ochlocracies" (mob rule) of totalitarian Communism. He could not have foreseen the collapse of the Communist system, and he did not live to see the new feminist movement and the search for wisdom in many parts of the world and many areas of modern life.

The miracle of this man, who legitimized Sophia as an eternal law of life, is even more astonishing for this reason, and he deserves to be better known. Today women who have never heard of Otfried Eberz embrace his ideas: women in the USA, in Europe, in Asia, and Africa. They evoke the Feminine Divine and contribute to the current sophianic stream the tradition of indigenous peoples, who, in some measure, preserved wisdom as a principle of life. To all of them, the teachings of Otfried Eberz, an unknown German sophiologist, might serve as a welcome tributary to their own welling source.

If we want Sophia, we have to return to Love. This is her basis and her foundation. We can no longer exclude her from any area of life. She is needed in politics and in economy. She is needed in our dealings with minorities and the disenfranchised, with millions of starving, brutalized children, with our exhausted, violated Earth. We need her, the Goddess may help us, in our "religion of love," which is as empty of love as our ordinary lives. Religion sided with Logos at the expense of Sophia, but when it suppressed Sophia, it threw out Love, too. We have to learn again that Sophia is at the heart of all religion. We have no choice but to nurture this root, so that one day it may grow into a blossoming tree.

"Sojourner Truth Plate." The design shows the plight of the black slave and a brave woman's rebellious spirit. The middle images seem hieratical, lifted out of the realm of human misery, aspiring to the stars and moutain peaks. The "Sojourner Truth Plate" is one of the plates in The Dinner Party *by Judy Chicago © 1979 (china paint on porcelain, 14" diameter). Photo by Donald Woodman. Used by permission.*

Meditation

(The following ritual, "A Journey into the Bible with Music, Dance and Meditation," was created by the Korean liberation theologist Chung Hyun-Kyun. It was performed by her with the assistance of the Asian Institute of Liturgy and Music from Manila on June 11, 1993, during the Protestant Convention in Munich, Germany.)

IN THE NAME OF SOPHIA we call today for the intuition of all peoples. Philippine dancers and singers in native dress, carrying birch trees with a luminous flower among green leaves, draw near in rhythmic steps, accompanied by the sound of drums. The audience, a crowd of about two thousand people, join in a simple song with the words:

> *Be quiet, my heart,*
> *the trees are praying.*
> *I said to the tree:*
> *Tell me about God—*
> *and it blossomed.*

In the "Village of Silence," the first stop on the journey, the trees lay down their testimony of God. They blossom like the roses, simply because it is their nature to do so. The tree silently unfolds its blossoms in our hearts. Only in silence do we become aware of it—its shape, its beauty, its needs, its inner being—without asking "Why?" It is what it is. Trees are not created for the purpose of serving us. They have their own being and their own end bestowed by God, and we have no right to subject them to our arbitrary causes and to exploit them.

In the "Village of Breath" we become aware that we are all indissolubly woven together in one great fabric by our breath. In the vast context of being, we are all neighbors to one another. The outbreath of one species in the world is the inbreath of the other. The oxygen we inhale to sustain our lives is exhaled by the plants, and they draw nutriment from the moisture which the water releases into the air. In the great cycle of being no one can say: "I don't know you; you are a stranger to me." The texture of life, itself, brings home the words of Jesus: "Anything you did for one of my brothers here, however humble, you did for me"; and: "Anything you did not do for one of these, however humble, you did not do for me" (Matthew 25:40,45).

In the "Village of Creation," the woman—*ruah*, the feminine Spirit—vested in the robes of a priestess, calls Adam into life. Powerfully brought into the world by her, accompanied and nurtured by her strong maternal breath, he enters his own body, learns to use his limbs, responds to her gestures, as a child responds to his mother. He tries his freedom and finds it, supported by her loving care. She releases him into life, but he stands behind her, uniting with her, first as her son, then as her lover and husband, her masculine half. The two halves have become *one*. They move their arms like *one* pair of wings, they are wrapped in *one* garment covering both of them. This is the sacred couple, eternal and inviolable, Sophia and Logos, whom she loves as her own soul, her flesh and blood. In the sacred wedding, the *hieros logos* is born, the sacred Word of creation. The longing for union is the origin of speech. Human beings learned to speak and respond, to share and to listen, in a movement of giving and receiving, which is as responsive and mutual as inbreath and outbreath. Speech which is not heard evaporates into nothingness. Speech without response has no substance. Only in loving relationship does the word flourish. Only in mutual utterance, where hierarchy and dominance have no place, can love grow.

In the "Village of Division" human beings are separated from each other. There is a rift between man and nature, man and woman. The opposite is no longer half of one's own self, but the *other*, the enemy.

Power and violence are born. Woman and along with her, nature, are turned into a property owned by man. In this primal conflict, the battle of the sexes flares up, harm is done to creation, which threatens our livelihood. If you do not "convert swords into plows." . . . If you do not turn back at the last hour . . . so that men and women may walk side by side, till the soil together, and nurse the Earth back to health. Men and women look at each other and dance a roundelay, for their own pleasure, to celebrate creation.

With arms spread out the dancers sweep through the hall and invite everyone to join their merry procession. The great hall is breathing, talking, laughing. *Ruah* has entered. This liturgy of living images and enacted scenes, dancing and singing, turned a crowd of two thousand people into a friendly, happy community. Strangers join hands, move closer to each other on their improvised cardboard seats and start to talk. A visitor from Finland, who accidentally drifted into the hall, is heard to say: "I have never experienced anything like this. It is lovely." She knows no German, and her English is scanty, but everyone understands her. Like many others, she is standing in a group, laughing, shaking hands, embracing. . .

Church Conventions are mass events. Young people with rucksacks on their backs, in jeans and tennis shoes, flock to these gatherings from all over Germany. They shun the church, they will not attend Sunday service, but they will come to the *Kirchentag*. These mass conventions are a thorn in the flesh of straight-laced theologians, and they often receive critical or cynical comments in the media, as a hodgepodge of everything—song, play, gospel, discussion of politics, economics, ecology, human rights, scientific and esoteric subjects, social issues, and what have you. The conventions are open to almost every subject. They are open to the world. This is why young people, and old people, too, like them so much. You see them standing in line patiently, waiting for admission, waiting for food or for the use of a toilet. They are friendly, they don't push, they communicate with each other. Life in Germany is chilling for many. Like everywhere else, it is the aggressive, competitive go-getters who win, and the social net, that proud achievement of post-war Germany, is seen to fissure under economic pressure. But for five days, well over a hundred thousand Germans and their foreign guests practice another way of life, another behavior, another set of values, and they love it.

Perhaps it is true that the future "church" will be of the spirit. It will leave the narrow boundaries of the formal churches and embrace all who are of kindred spirit, Christians and non-Christians alike.

Is this not the work of Sophia? It is growing in our midst, while we are still unaware of it.

Chapter Five

INTERRELIGIOUS SOPHIA

F OR AT LEAST A DECADE THERE HAVE been signs that Sophia is about to return. There is wide interest not only in the old goddesses of the Mediterranean world, but also in the Feminine Divine of more remote cultures. To some extent, these traditions have been able to preserve feminine Wisdom, as for example the culture of the indigenous people of the Andean region in South America.

Pachamama of the Andean Peoples

ALTHOUGH THE SOUTH AMERICAN Indians were forced by the Spanish conquerors to adopt the Christian faith, the peoples of the Andean highlands always maintained their reverence for the Great Goddess, whom they call Pachamama, Mother Earth. It is she who accompanies the cycle of the seasons and blesses the fields with fruitfulness. The popular festivals of the Virgin Mary with their lavish parades and celebrations that sometimes last for days, in reality honor Pachamama. She was the most powerful figure of Indian folk belief and was never supplanted altogether by the Christian Fathergod. On the outside walls of many a Christian church in Peru, she is represented in her natural environment. Indian stone masons covered the facades of magnificent churches in the Spanish baroque style with a profusion of animals, plants and human beings, and did not stop short of highly erotic scenes as a sacred symbol of the divine creative power, comparable to the suggestive sculptures of some Hindu temples in India.

Pachamama's concern is with the Earth. She *is* the Earth. Therefore the soil is sacred to Indios as the body of Pachamama, which man may work and cultivate, but on no account is he allowed to torture or exploit it. Indios traditionally have a close and tender relationship with their land, and suffer more than other peoples when they are forced to give up their plot, the *chacra*, which ensured their livelihood and made them recipients of the beneficent powers of Pachamama. In the language of the Quechua Indians, a man without land is an "orphan." He has lost his mother who provided everything, food, home, a sense of belonging, and the security that goes with it.

Before Spanish civilization changed the native customs, women had a high place in Quechua and Aymara society. They were respected, and their voices were heard in the village council. Under the local marriage law, the woman was allowed to choose her mate freely and separate from him during the time of probation, if she wished.[1] It was only during colonial times that women were subjected to men. In pre-Columbian civilization, woman was considered the human embodiment of Pachamama, the Divine Mother. There is a moving dignity still

---

[1] Even at a later time, after the couple has been properly married, a separation is possible according to Indian custom. Depending on the situation, the Council of Elders may even recommend a divorce, because marital strife is held to be damaging to the children and to the peace of the community.

in the women of the Peruvian Andes, despite their crippling poverty, in the loving tenderness of their treatment of children and animals, their strength and perseverance in the face of social and economic crisis. In Peru there is a women's movement from the "grass roots," which brought women together who migrated from the mountains to the slums of the big cities, mainly in Lima, for the survival of their families. Many of these women lost their husbands, and are left with numerous children, to fend for themselves. In some areas of the Andean region, it was the simple country women, poor *campesinas*, who enforced the land reform at the end of the 1960s by their sheer will power and determination. Indians were no longer willing to accept the norms of macho society, which did not exist in pre-Columbian village communities. They revived the values of their native Indian culture and recalled Pachamama, who is much more than an Earth goddess in the guise of the Virgin Mary. She is the source of their own strength that enables them to risk their lives in the struggle for liberation, as in the case of Rigoberta Menchú, winner of the Nobel Peace Prize, a woman from the Maya culture of Guatemala. Where do these women, who are often illiterate, get the courage to oppose military violence and to fight for a better future? They have a close affinity to the Earth; they know their task is the preservation of life.

> There is something important about women in Guatemala, especially Indian women, and that something is her relationship with the earth—between the earth and the mother. The earth gives food, and the woman gives life. Because of this closeness the woman must keep this respect for the earth as a secret of her own. The relationship between the mother and the earth is like the relationship between husband and wife. There is a constant dialogue between the

earth and the woman. This feeling is born in women because of the responsibilities they have, which men do not have.[2]

It is this reverence for the Earth as a "secret" or mystery which is the special obligation and privilege of women. In this mystery there is wisdom, the wisdom of the life-giving force, the wisdom of resistance and perseverance, of tenderness and harmony. The divine power which enables women to affirm life even under the most adverse conditions is experienced as feminine. As a Peruvian ethnologist, who grew up in a small village in the Andes with her Indian grandmother and her half-Indian mother, said:

> My personal vision of God the Mother incarnated in my mother and her mother, gave me, from childhood, the clearest certainty of woman as the truer image of Divine Spirit. Because she was a force living within me, she was more real, more powerful than the remote Fathergod. . . . I believed in her because I experienced her.[3]

Hindu Goddesses

PERHAPS NO OTHER CULTURE pays a higher tribute to the Goddess as a living presence than Indian Hinduism. Nowhere else but on the Indian subcontinent, where the social reality of women is generally oppressed and backward, exist more numerous and more powerful female deities.

[2] *I, Rigoberta Menchú. An Indian Woman in Guatemala*, ed. and introduced by Elisabeth Burgos-Debray (London, New York: Verso, 1984), p. 220.
[3] Communicated to me in a personal letter by Cristina Herencia, after we met in Arequipa, Peru, during the winter 1989/90. I owe to her much information about growing up in Peru as a woman with Indian background.

This is a startling paradox, which can only be explained by the complex history of India with centuries of invasion and dominance by foreign powers. Against this permanent threat to the cultural identity, religious tradition was upheld by a determined will to spiritual survival. In this ancient tradition, dating back to pre-patriarchal times, the Feminine always had an exalted position. To a pious Hindu, every woman represents the Divine Mother. This dignity can be manifested by a ragged woman of the slums, who steps from her ramshackle dwelling with the grace and majesty of a queen. Especially in the Dravidian South, the consciousness of the Great Goddess is still alive. The culture of the Dravidian tribes was mother-oriented, before they were gradually conquered by Aryan invaders from the North. Like everywhere else, women in India were subjected to patriarchal law, and the lawgiver Manu (who probably lived between 200 B.C. and A.D. 200) included women in the goods and chattels of the male, along with his slaves and herds of cattle. The misogyny of this Code of Law even outdoes that of the Bible:

> Woman is as foul as falsehood itself. When creating them, the lord of creatures allotted to women a love of their beds, of their seat and ornaments; impure thoughts, wrath, dishonesty, malice and bad conduct. . . . From the cradle to the grave a woman is dependent on a male: in childhood on her father, in youth on her husband, in old age on her son.[4]

But the lawgiver was not able to break the power of the Goddess. She continues to exist in the great goddesses Lakshmi, Parvati, Sarasvati, Durga, Kali, and countless others who are worshipped in India until today.

---

[4] Quoted in Elisabeth Bumiller, *May You Be the Mother of a Hundred Sons* (New York: Random House, 1990), p. 16.

The goddesses are praised in the Vedic hymns. They are of lesser importance than the great male deities, like Agni, Soma, or Indra, but after the 5th century A.D., there was a powerful resurgence of the Goddess, and ever since that time she maintained a central place in popular religion. As early as the Rig Veda, the Goddess Prithivi is mentioned, the female half of the cosmic parents. She is Mother Earth, whereas Dyaus, her male consort, represents Heaven.[5] In the hymns praising her, she appears as a great independent goddess, who brings forth all plants, nourishes all living beings, and maintains, by her loving kindness, the good and the bad. All Hindu goddesses are identified with *prakriti*, Nature in all her complexity. She is represented as affirming the world, in contrast with the ascetic Indian tradition of world renunciation. The Goddess is omni-present; there is not a particle of reality where she is not. Every male god has his female counterpart, either as a goddess in her own right with a name of her own, or as his female aspect. Every masculine figure in the Indian pantheon requires a feminine counterpart, a *shakti*, the female power which activates the male principle and sets it in motion. Even *Brahma*, the divine creator, depends on a *shakti*, so that ultimately every divine power of the universe reflects the highest world force, *Shakti*, the World Mother.[6]

As a universal life force the Goddess also has her dark aspect. She gives and preserves life, but she also takes it, as nature does. The whole range of the kind and the terrible, the bountiful and the destructive aspect is contained in the Goddess. The aspect of the terrible, devouring All-Mother is especially manifest in the goddess Kali of pre-Aryan origin. She is mostly represented as dark-skinned, with protruding tongue

---

[5] See David Kinsley, *Hindu Goddesses* (Berkeley: University of California Press, 1986).

[6] See Heinrich Zimmer, "The Indian World Mother," in *Eranos Yearbook* (1938), Bollingen Series XXX, no.6 (Princeton: Princeton University Press, 1968), pp. 70-102.

and dreadful fangs, adorned with a wreath of skulls, dancing on the prostrate body of Shiva, the powerful god of destruction. She is an independent goddess without a male counterpart, although sometimes Shiva is regarded as her consort. She feeds on blood, and in the temples dedicated to her, animal sacrifice is still performed today. Despite her ferocity, she is one of the most popular Indian goddesses, particularly in Bengal, where great festivals are held in her honor. This is of deep significance. The goddess Kali embodies a divine potency which is not only the source of good, but also of evil.

Jacob Boehme had a similar intuition when he saw both good and evil welling up from the Godhead, but Christian doctrine had no means to deal with this ambivalence. To the Hindu mind, this concept of the Divine was always familiar: God is conceived as light *and* darkness, kindness *and* ruin, life *and* death. The Divine embraces all polarities, and therefore never had to split off evil as did the monotheistic religions. The mother principle, like Nature, unlike the father principle, cannot be co-opted by goodness alone. The experience of both principles in the Divine Mother—birth and death, the splendor of life as well as indifferent cruelty—can lead to the realization of true reality beyond good and evil, and consequently to inner liberation, which is the goal of all Indian spirituality. In this way Ramakrishna, the great Hindu saint of the 19th century, experienced the goddess Kali as his path to illumination.

In her worship there is a kind of wisdom which is inconceivable to the Western mind so used to thinking in dualities. By defying *dharma*, the divine order, and breaking through social rules and conventions, the all-embracing female deity opens up a roadless space, where the human being is alone with the Incommensurable. She is the shocking opposite of narrow-minded virtue and conventional morality.

Sometimes Kali is associated with the goddess Durga, who is also from the indigenous, non-Aryan culture. On the one hand, Durga is the goddess of fertility, and on the other an awe-inspiring goddess of war, who destroys the powerful demon Mahisa. The male gods were not able to defeat him, and from their fiery energy sprang Durga, who then generated female assistants, such as Kali, and their combined female force defeated the demon. This myth seems like a reversal of the familiar heroic tales, in which it is invariably a male hero who is endowed with supernatural powers.

Kali and Durga contradict drastically the Hindu ideal of the submissive, obedient wife, as she is extolled by the great Hindu epic *Ramayana* in the figure of Sita. Also Lakshmi, or Shri Lakshmi, symbolizes the exemplary Hindu wife, associated with fertility, wealth, and worldly power. Her emblem is the lotus, the traditional Indian symbol of purity and spiritual strength. As the lotus has its roots in the mud, and unfolds its pure blossoms above the water, so does Lakshmi lend her pure luster to her male consort. At times she was associated with gods like Soma, the god of plants, or Indra, the king of the gods, but eventually she became exclusively the consort of Vishnu. From time to time he sends his incarnations, the *avataras*, to Earth in order to restore the divine order, but he can do nothing without her. No one can rule where Lakshmi is not. It is she who lends authority to kings and gives them power. Often she is represented with Vishnu as a hermaphrodite, like other divine couples, half female and half male. Her physical and spiritual features merge in one divine female-male unity. As one of the most popular mythical tales, the Vishnu Purana, says:

> Vishnu is said to be speech and Lakshmi meaning; he is understanding, she is intellect; he is the creator, she is the creation; she is the earth, he the support of the earth. . . . he is love, and she is pleasure.[7]

---

[7] Quoted in Kinsley, *Hindu Goddesses*, p. 29.

Lakshmi is mostly represented as smiling and radiant, the eternal source of delight. She is the joyous force without which a man cannot find fulfillment. The figure of Lakshmi illustrates what was lost in occidental Christian culture.

> The Hindus are right: Where Lakshmi, the feminine power of joy, lies fallow, the male becomes desolate—also in spiritual matters."[8]

Another complementary, though very different, couple are Parvati and Shiva. Their relationship expresses the tension between the ascetic ideal and the *dharma* of life in the world, marriage, and family. Shiva's element is fire, and in the flaming heat of his asceticism Kama, the God of Love, is burned to ashes. The fire of Shiva is destruction, and it requires the protective forces of Parvati to balance Shiva's fury of annihilation. His nature is excess, in his destructive power as well as in his sexual potency accumulated by asceticism. Parvati is the *shakti* of Shiva. She is the power at the basis of all creation. She is *prakriti*, nature; Shiva is *purusha*, pure spirit, but only by combining the feminine and masculine principle can the creation come into being. Their polarity does not lead to a hostile opposition or strife between the sexes, but it is a mutual complementation. God is masculine *and* feminine, father *and* mother, awful *and* kind.

Also Shiva and Parvati are often represented in a shape half male and half female. Most common, however, is their representation as *lingam* and *yoni*, the male organ of procreation and the female womb. The *lingam* is even revered in temples, but it never obliterated the fact that it is the *shakti* who is the source of all being, and therefore also of the procreative power. She is the universal force inherent in all female deities, and is often called by the name of Mahadevi, the Great Goddess. Traditionally, she is "the root of the world, she who transcends the uni-

---

[8] Walter Schubart, *Eros and Religion* (Munich: H. C. Beck, 1966), p. 57, translation mine.

verse, who has no equal, supreme ruler, she who pervades all, she who is immeasurable, she who creates innumerable universes, she whose womb contains the world, who is the support of all, she who is omnipresent, she who is the ruler of all worlds."[9] According to another text, she is the "life force in all beings . . . the only cause of the universe, to create Brahma, Vishnu, and Síva, and to command them to perform their cosmic tasks."[10] Mahadevi, or simply Devi, "Goddess," is at one with Being. She is life and fills the world with her life force. As we have seen with Durga and Kali, her features combine the beneficial and the terrible aspect, nature and spirit. She possesses supreme feminine beauty and erotic power, but at the same time she is the instrument of higher perception, of Wisdom herself, the redeemer and liberator from bondage.

Here Mahadevi merges with one of the oldest and most sublime goddesses of the Hindus, Sarasvati, the Goddess of Wisdom and the Arts. She makes her appearance as early as the Vedas and relates most closely to Sophia, as we know her in the Christian tradition. Originally, she was the Goddess of the holy river Sarasvati, which originates in heaven and flows down to Earth. The sacred power of the water, a feminine symbol since time immemorial, was transferred to all the rivers of India, as the ritual bath of pious Hindus, especially in the holiest of rivers, the Ganges, "Mother Ganga" in Indian usage, still bears witness. The image of the river and man's transcendence to another shore symbolizes purification and rebirth. Later, Sarasvati becomes associated with *vak*, speech, voice or language.

The gift of speech distinguishes the human being from the beast; it gives him a superior rank within the hierarchy of creation. *Vak* is the creative word, the medium of Vedic revelation and thus a close parallel to *logos* in the Bible. In Hinduism, the word is intuited as feminine, and as

[9] Kinsley, *Hindu Goddesses*, p. 133.
[10] Kinsley, *Hindu Goddesses*, p. 133.

such it is of extraordinary significance. From the sacred syllable *OM* the whole creation came into being, and *shabda-brahman*, the audible life stream, is the highest reality intuited as sound. The *mantras*, sacred syllables or sounds, are transferred from master to pupil in secret tradition, and their power to purify and spiritualize may be compared to the "prayer of the heart" in Eastern Christianity. Sarasvati is the vehicle of sacred speech and symbolizes thought and intellect. She is the Goddess of science, fine arts, especially music, the patroness of learning, of knowledge and all wisdom. Her nature is transcendence and purity, and her sacred animal the swan, the image of spiritual perfection. Brahma, the god of creation, is considered to be her father, sometimes her husband, but marriage and motherhood are ultimately not important to her. Sarasvati is the *shakti* behind every cultural achievement, the holy spirit of spiritual transformation. The arts and higher learning are a genuine way to God, as far as they have a share in the audible stream of creation. The intimate knowledge of this divine mystery belongs to Sarasvati.

Also Buddhism, which in its beginnings was hostile to women, could not but imagine a lofty female figure, especially Tibetan Buddhism. This is the White Tara as *prajna paramita*, "perfection of wisdom," as protectress and redemptress. Her name signifies that she leads the spirit out of anxiety and danger. Furthermore, she protects man against water, fire and wind, elephants, snakes, and demons.

> In her sacred gesture, as the initiating wisdom that redeems from the Samsara, she is archetypally related to the Christian-Gnostic Sophia.[11]

---

[11] H. Zimmer, "The Indian World Mother," p. 85. The "Green Tara" (Tibetan bronze statue, reproduced in Erich Neumann, *The Great Mother*, plate 185; also in Schipflinger, *Sophia-Maria*, p. 282) is Sophia in her most spiritualized form. The structure of the sculpture shows the synthesis of the female-male polarity, above which Tara is enthroned in the gesture of teaching and giving in complete harmony.

As perfection of knowledge or wisdom, she leads to illumination and Nirvana, to liberation from the wheel of rebirth. In Tantric Buddhism she is the mother of all Buddhas, i.e., of all illuminated beings, and in Nirvana she is represented as *shakti* in eternal embrace with the Buddhas. Thus, the Eternal Feminine is seen to triumph over the masculine, ascetic spirituality of Buddhist teaching.[12] However, she would not be an Indian goddess, if she did not have her dark aspects as well. These appear in the Blue, Yellow, and Red Tara. The important point is her female power, which even Buddhism cannot do without. In Chinese Buddhism, Tara is represented by the beneficent, loving figure of Kuan Yin (Kwannon in Japan), the goddess of compassion.

Heinrich Zimmer relates the Hindu myth about the fate of the gods who slighted the Great Goddess.[13] Once Vishnu was riding through the air on the sun bird Garuda, and in masculine arrogance disregarded the Goddess, the "Mistress of All Desires and Joys" enthroned in the mountains. Here she appears in the shape of the Great Maya, the material world of appearances, also in her function as mother of all beings. The God riding through the air literally removed himself from earthly reality, so that he is not aware of the Goddess. The punishment follows in due course: Vishnu and his bird are paralyzed, unable to move from the spot.

Similarly, all those who lose sight of concrete life from an overbearing sense of self are struck with paralysis. Maya casts a spell over Vishnu and throws him into the ocean of the world, where he loses consciousness. The message could not be more explicit: whoever fails to honor the *shakti* and splits her off from his conscious mental and emotional life, will literally be flooded by her in his subconscious. Brahma comes to res-

---

[12] H. Zimmer, "The Indian World Mother," pp. 86f.

[13] H. Zimmer, "The Indian World Mother," pp. 87-91.

cue Vishnu, but is also enchanted by the Goddess and turns rigid. Even the great Shiva must seek advice of Mahadeva, the Great God, to tell them what to do. Mahadeva instructs them that they slighted the Goddess and teaches the gods to fashion the magic armor against her. Only when they armor themselves with the force of the Goddess herself, and pay homage to her, are they set free. Vishnu performs the required ritual, and at last he is able to rise from the abyss of unconsciousness. When he approaches the Goddess, he worships her "as the mother of all worlds and beings, as primal substance and creatrix of the universe, and as the knowledge that confers redemption." Thereupon the Goddess confers her highest favor: she lets the gods drink and bathe in her womb. By immersing in holy communion in the source of life, the gods find rebirth and a higher form of existence in its waters.

Heinrich Zimmer interprets this ritual as "the solemn self-revelation of the veiled image at Sais." The Goddess does not unveil her face, as our more prudish tradition has it, but uncovers her womb, because there is no truly spiritual life without the creative female womb. It, rather than any spiritual flight soaring above earthly existence, contains the mystery of being. This is what Goethe had in mind when he sent Faust down to the "Mothers," in search of Helena and creative Eros in the depths of the archetypes.

Hindu tradition never abandoned the realm of the Mothers, as the West and the Islamic East have done. Despite modern distortions and a paralyzing stagnation of Indian society due to rigid social customs, despite an extreme, ascetic ideal as *one* possible way to salvation, the knowledge of the redeeming force of the *hieros gamos* was always preserved in India. According to the Hindu myth, the female element is endowed with greater power, because it is the primary force in this act of sacred union. It is she who dissolves the polarity in a higher wholeness. Without the *shakti*, nothing goes. Without her, even gods fall into a

Arya Tara, *or the* Golden Tara, *worshipped in Northern India since the 10th and 11th centuries. This Buddha in the shape of a divinely beautiful woman has all the attributes of a Buddha: the Third Eye in the middle of her forehead, the lotus seat, the sitting posture and the meaningful gestures of her* · *hands* (mudras). *She is the historical male Buddha's perfect female counter-part.*

state of stupefaction, and worldly power cannot be exercised, and Shiva and all "fiery" spirits like him are victims of their own excessiveness.

The wisdom of a mythical story like this cannot be stated in a formula. Part of this wisdom is its variability according to one's point of view. The divine figures are rarely without ambiguity. More often than not their polar features prevail, as the eternally playing, intuitive mind evokes them from the depths of the subconscious. This world of gods may seem quite bewildering and chaotic to the Western mind. This maze of proliferating, ambivalent parables may be uncomfortable, to say the least, to a mind used to clear distinctions. According to our way of thinking, wisdom is elevated and spiritualized, far removed from the "base" desires associated with the body. We have no difficulty recognizing Sophia in Sarasvati or in the White and Green Tara (see illustration, "The Golden Tara," page 184), but how are we to find her in Kali or in all those copulating gods and goddesses of the vast Indian pantheon? How can we recognize Sophia in the double-faced Goddess, who gives life and at the same time devours her creatures? What are we to make of a kind of wisdom located in a realm beyond good and evil? It seems to tell us that the higher perception of reality is to be found in this "beyond," as, for instance, in an encounter with Kali, provided the spirit is daring enough to dive into this realm with its terror and mind-blowing paradox.

This is a world necessarily foreign to rational thought, which insists on definite meanings in terms of "either-or." It allows no space for the variable play of polarities, but insists on boundaries and divisions. It clings to the separation of body and spirit and as a consequence to the inferiority of nature, woman, and matter, as opposed to a spirituality associated with male intellect. It is hypnotized by a model of linear development, in which the feminine (matriarchal) and "unconscious" prehistoric age was replaced by the masculine (patriarchal) era of consciousness and intellect. This model is invalidated not only by the glaring deficiencies of our "progress," but also by recent research in archeology and mythology. A different model of reality is emerging: feminine *and* masculine power in balance, none inflated at the expense of the other, so that both polarities may acknowledge their mutual dependence and fulfillment as complements to each other. With our acute experience of patriarchal arrogance, we search for Wisdom today, in order to regain the balance. We find it, among other places, in ethnic mythologies, because their wisdom is universal. It transcends time and space, and is not confined to cultural boundaries.

The Greek goddesses have been of help to modern women, in order to gain a better understanding of themselves and to find a more personal form of wisdom.[14] Likewise, we might meditate the different, partly paradoxical characters of Hindu goddesses. They, too, are part of the great Feminine Archetype, as it became consolidated and was handed down across vast periods of time as a pattern or structure of the psyche. It is not by accident that the archetype of the Great Goddess is increasingly turning up in the dreams and the imagination of women and men.[15] Moreover, it is the long-suppressed Goddess in her dark aspect who makes her appearance today, claiming integration in the household of the soul. The content and significance of this "dark" quality requires a different interpretation every time it becomes manifest.

Otfried Eberz, the remarkable prophet of Sophia in this century, has his own interpretation of the terrible aspect of the goddess Kali. He considers her ferocity the legitimate reaction to her overthrow as supreme Deity of the early Woman-oriented Age by the rising Masculine Age.[16] Eberz explains the insatiable lust for destruction

---

[14] Jean Shinoda Bolen, *Goddesses in Everywoman: A New Psychology of Woman* (San Francisco: HarperSanFrancisco, 1984).

[15] See previous discussion, pages 55-59.

[16] See O. Eberz, *S-L*, pp. 177f.; *SuL*, p. 547.

ascribed to her as a later distortion of what actually happened. In reality, it was "agnostic hominism" which got intoxicated with the blood of its victims, and forced them under the patriarchal yoke. In this view, the feminine archetype is simply responding to violence with counter violence, because in the hoministic world order it is denied the right to exist.

We cannot hope to elucidate the dark aspect of the Feminine completely. The important fact is that it is there; it does exist. It works like a reservoir of things suppressed by Logos, shoved aside, relegated to the "Shadow" or projected on women. This side is clamoring for attention for the sake of spiritual wholeness. If the "sacred wedding" is to take effect, it has to be consummated within the soul of individual men and women. For this end, many a thing will have to be brought to light that slumbered at the bottom of the subconscious a long time, until it started to assert itself and could no longer be suppressed. In the Gospel of Thomas, there is a saying attributed to Jesus:

> If you bring forth what is within you, what you bring forth
> will save you. If you do not bring forth what is within you,
> what you do not bring forth will destroy you.[17]

There is wisdom in the insight that the human being needs to express all the potentials of the soul to be whole. If one part is neglected, it becomes destructive and floods the subconsciousness, as we have heard in the Hindu myth.

---

[17] Quoted in Elaine Pagels, *The Gnostic Gospels* (New York: Random House, 1979; Vintage Books, 1989), p. 126.

Chinese Taoism

IF THERE IS A PHILOSOPHY OF BEING which sought the wise balance of polar opposites more than any other philosophy or religion, it is Chinese Taoism. The Taoist space is not filled with gods or goddesses. It is a philosophical rather than a mythological or religious space in any narrow definition, because the central intuition of Taoism, the concept of *Tao* itself, refers to pure Being. Many different words have been used to express the meaning of *Tao* in Western languages, but it is understood that these are only approximations: such as Meaning, Word, Reason, Doctrine, Path, Way of the World, Nature, World Order, Ground, *Urgrund*, Cosmic Law, the Absolute, the One. Ultimately, the *Tao* defies any definition or conceptualization. "Tao can be talked about, but not the Eternal Tao./ Names can be named, but not the Eternal Name," are the opening lines of the *Tao Teh Ching* of Lao Tzu, a Chinese sage who lived between 600 and 530 B.C.[18]

The principle of Taoism is illustrated by the well-known symbol of two intertwined halves, a light and a dark one, contained within a circle. At the point of the greatest expansion of one part, the other germinally appears as a tiny spot. The symbol represents the perfect balance of Yin and Yang, the central polarities of the Taoist worldview. The light part (Yang) is considered masculine, active and "positive," or Heaven; the dark (Yin) represents the feminine, passive and "negative," or Earth. Originally, there was no judgment or value attached to either "positive" or "negative." These were simply terms to symbolize polarity. This

---

[18] The existent translations differ widely from one another, as the Chinese original rather suggests than states the meaning. For German-speaking countries, the edition by Richard Wilhelm is the standard one (*Laotse. Tao Te King. Das Buch des Alten vom Sinn und Leben*, originally published in 1910). Addressing an English-speaking readership, I am using the translation by John C. H. Wu, *Lao Tzu. Tao Teh Ching* (New York: St. John's University Press, 1961; now also Boston: Shambhala, 1989).

changed with the patriarchal shift, which took place in China as everywhere else in prehistoric times, but the original intuition of equivalent polarities working together in harmony was not affected by it.

Behind the multiplicity of conflicting and ephemeral appearances there is the One, the Tao, which cannot be defined.

> There was Something undefined
> and yet complete in itself,
> Born before Heaven-and-Earth.
> Silent and boundless,
> Standing alone without change,
> Yet perceiving all without fail,
> It may be regarded as the Mother of the world.
> I do not know its name;
> I style it "Tao";
> And in the absence of a better word,
> call it "The Great."[19]

Thus, the Tao as primordial source of all things existent is experienced as feminine, the "Mother of the world." She is before creation, immovable, eternal, and perfect in herself. She is "silent" and "boundless" and "standing alone," the One without a Second. The All-Encompassing, in a state where she has not yet generated and set forth a Second, the Tao is nameless. Only when Something enters being, when it calls forth a second and a third, the "ten thousand things" come into existence, that is, the entire world in its complexity and polarity. If there is man, there must be woman; if there is light, there is also dark; as above, so below; if

---

[19] Chapter 25 (Wu, p. 51). The *Tao Teh Ching* is conceived in 81 short chapters or sections, some consisting only of a few lines. Henceforth I shall add to quotations the number of the chapter in brackets for easy reference, without further annotation.

justice, then injustice; if heaven, then Earth. However, the Tao takes precedence over all these pairs of polar opposites not in a temporal, but an ontological sense. The Tao as origin is described in Chapter 6 of the *Tao Teh Ching*.

> The Spirit of the Fountain dies not.
> It is called the Mysterious Feminine.
> The Doorway of the Mysterious Feminine
> Is called the Root of Heaven-and-Earth.

Differentiation is a necessity, in order to enter the state of being. The origin of being is considered feminine, and from this feminine principle the masculine and everything else in existence originate.

> Know the masculine,
> Keep to the feminine,
> And be the Brook of the World.
> To be the Brook of the World is
> To move constantly in the path of Virtue
> Without swerving from it,
> And to return again to infancy. [Ch.28].

Or, in the translation by Alan Watts:

> Know the male, but keep the female,
> so becoming a universal river-valley.
> Being the universal river-valley,
> one has the eternal virtue undivided
> and becomes again as a child.[20]

---

[20] Alan Watts, *Tao: The Watercourse Way* (New York: Pantheon Books, 1975), p. 41.

Human beings are called to incorporate and bring into harmony both the masculine and the feminine. Thus, every man and woman who contains the polarities and brings them to a higher unity mysteriously works toward the preservation of the world. The "Brook" suggests the riverbed in which all things flow and constantly change from one eternal moment to the next, as stated in the formula of Heraclitus: "Everything flows." The following stanzas of Chapter 28 name other polar opposites such as white and black, or the glorious and the lowly. They all have to be accepted and integrated as wholeness, if Man wishes to live in harmony with the Tao. This insight seems like an early intuition of Jung's concept of the "Shadow," which an individual striving for wholeness must integrate in his or her personality. The Chinese *Tao Teh Ching* suggests, like the Delphic Oracle or the Hindu concept of Being, as well as modern psychology, that wisdom consists of knowing oneself: "He who knows himself has insight"[Ch.33].

Throughout the book there are statements to the effect that the feminine, the passive and seemingly weak is in reality endowed with greater strength, as in Chapter 61: "The Feminine always conquers the Masculine by her quietness, by lowering herself through her quietness." The hard and rigid, the exclusively Masculine in the scheme of polarities will ultimately have to yield to the soft and the flexible principle, just as water in the course of time smoothes and polishes the hardest rock. The action of the wise person, following the cosmic law, is gentle "action in non-action," for which Taoism has a special term, *Wu Wei*. All merely activist and violent action is incompatible with it. Therefore, the wise ruler is he who stays in the background and rules little, yet everything is kept in order. The force of weapons, on the other hand, achieves nothing:

> A good soldier is never aggressive;
> A good fighter is never angry.

> The best way of conquering an enemy
> Is to win him over by not antagonizing him [Ch.68].

The superior strength of the person who lives in harmony with the Tao is the subject of many stories and legends of the Japanese Zen Buddhist tradition, which is rooted in Chinese Taoism. Thus, in the story of the "Miraculous Cat" it is not the greater physical strength or superior fighting technique which finally overcomes the vicious rat, but the serene poise within one's center of being, where all opposites are resolved.[21] The wise old cat sleeps all day and does not do anything, but her mere presence drives away all rats. They don't even come near her. Thus it is said in the *Tao Teh Ching*:

> Tao never makes any ado,
> And yet it does everything [Ch.37].

Similarly, the sage "sees without looking, and achieves without Ado"[Ch.47].

In this unperturbed resting in the Tao there is a nameless simplicity which the sage shares with little children. In various ways, the *Tao Teh Ching* suggests the simplicity of being as a state of grace. It affirms the truth of the paradox of the Gospel that "the first shall be the last," the wisdom of all-encompassing love and a number of other truths which might be called Christian. In our time, we are particularly susceptible to the warning against violence. Under any name and with any goal whatsoever, violence is damaging the truth and will be defeated in the end.

> Does anyone want to take the world and do what he wants
> with it?

---

[21] The story is admirably told in Karlfried Graf Dürckheim, *Wunderbare Katze und andere Zen-Texte* (Weilheim: O. W. Barth, 1970), pp. 61-72.

I do not see how he can succeed.
The world is a sacred vessel, which must not be tampered
    with or grabbed after.
To tamper with it is to spoil it, and to grasp it is to lose it
[Ch. 29].

These lines anticipate prophetically what is happening today. The perception is gaining ground that the world indeed is a "sacred vessel," an animated organism, which must not be tampered with or abused, but there is still a deficiency of right action following this insight. Consider the following lines:

There is no calamity like not knowing what is enough.
There is no evil like covetousness.
Only he who knows what is enough will always have
    enough [Ch.46].

We would be blind and deaf if we failed to get the message. The excessive desire to possess and accumulate wealth is a form of violence, which humanity at present is far from able to control. A radical change of thinking along Taoist lines is required. This can only come about if Wisdom, the sophianic insight in the mystery of being, is honored again.

As in Taoism, Sophia is the issue, albeit in a less personal, more abstract or "cosmic" way. As Tao, the "Mother of the world," she is in all things and works in them. Like Sophia, the Tao represents wholeness of being, interrelationship and harmonious balance, as opposed to a hierarchy of power and the principle that might is right. There are no explicit commandments in Taoism, because commandments necessarily cause their transgression. Whoever opposes Tao, or Sophia, upsets the cosmic balance and has to face the consequences. It is as simple as that.

M e d i t a t i o n

IN THE BEGINNING, there was water. It flowed from heaven to Earth in an eternal stream of grace. Water: it purifies, animates and fertilizes, it remains quietly where it is most deep. It is the source of all life; it gives nourishment to all. Without solid food we can sustain our lives for a while, but not without water. Water is the sap of the Earth, as our blood, for the most part a watery substance, is the sap of our veins. Through water, through the air we are connected with everything.

Left to itself, water is a gentle power. It glides over obstacles, it is supple and pliable, it follows the form of impediments, and overcomes resistance by constant movement. The hard and angular is polished off, imperceptibly, over a long period of time. Flowing water has any amount of time. It suspends time, as it is always at the beginning and always at the end. It flows toward the ocean, rises up in changed form, glides through the atmosphere in the shape of clouds and returns to the earth as rain in a never-ending cycle.

There has always been water, abundant in some places, scarce in others. Wells dry up, riverbeds are sometimes parched, but until recent times it was inconceivable that the Great Wellspring, itself, might dry out or that its waters might become poisoned. Once upon a time, when water was still held sacred, rites of sacrifice were performed along the river banks. The roaring or softly murmuring or inaudible sound of flowing water, inspired the word of reverence and worship of the Divine. The sacred Primal Sound was heard with the inner ear and was understood as creative power. As water unites with the air and the earth, so does sound unite with the light. It creates light where there was darkness; it transforms the nameless chaos of unshaped possibility into meaningful discourse, into the medium of inspired work, the animated sequence of sounds in music. In the beginning of all culture, there was the Word. It is born from the spirit of Love striving to become creation. Every meaning wrested from chaos is like a birth. Spirit and matter merge in indissoluble unity.

Behind every act of creation there is maternal Wisdom that brought it forth from her desire for union. From the One that she is she gives birth to manifold life and brings it back in the One, Vak—Logos, the creative primordial Sound, the nameless Tao. She sets in motion, yet remains tranquil. She sends her roots into the densest matter and transforms it into spirit. Thus, the Goddess is enthroned on the lotus above the nourishing waters, aware of her roots in the muddy ground. Real work is always aligned with nature, flowing like the current of a river, like the grain of wood or marble, the formation of clouds or sand dunes, matter in motion *and* creative spirit: the one merging with the other.

> *Labour is blossoming or dancing where*
> *The body is not bruised to pleasure soul,*
> *Nor beauty born out of its own despair,*
> *Nor blear-eyed wisdom out of midnight oil.*
> *O chestnut tree, great rooted blossomer,*
> *Are you the leaf, the blossom or the bole?*
> *O body swayed to music, O brightening glance,*
> *How can we know the dancer from the dance?*

—William Butler Yeats[22]

---

[22] William Butler Yeats, "Among School Children," verse VIII, p. 1040 in *A Treasury of Great Poems,* edited by Louis Untermeyer (New York: Simon & Schuster, 1942).

Chapter Six

FROM REVELATION TO REVELATION

S OPHIA, IN HER MULTIPLE TRANSFORMATIONS from time immemorial, would not resurge so powerfully today if her loss had not been such a disaster to our world. The suppression of Sophia, her co-option in Logos, her gradual absorption by the persons of the Trinity, go hand in hand with the marginalization of women in the church, after the living testimony of Jesus faded out from memory and the charisma of the original Christian community disappeared. Today, women reclaim their voice. It is especially women who are on a quest for the hidden, denied, forgotten, or distorted and mutilated Feminine Divine. They are searching for themselves when they follow the traces of Sophia. Whereas, in the past, authentic testimonies of Sophia mostly came from men, with the exception of Hildegard of Bingen and other female mystics of the Middle Ages, today it is mostly women who set out together in search of Sophia.

It is no longer the outstanding, single individual who gives expression to the Divine Wisdom of God, but the impulse has touched our time. It brings women together in seminaries and workshops, in conventions and private circles. Together they journey into the past and share their experiences. The search for a holistic vision of the Divine always includes the search for our own roots. It makes us face our individual past and brings into consciousness the hurt and humiliation received by a patriarchal religion. In the space of our churches, which until recently only addressed men, where every act of ritual was determined and performed by men, women were without speech. Their own experiences and intuitions of the Divine remained unexpressed, unheard, locked within their souls. The reality of their physical bodies with their cyclical functions and non-violent blood sacrifice, the changes and deep experiences connected with the flow of their blood, carried the stigma of impurity. Female blood was taboo. Woman in her role as mother was elevated and sanctified, yet her biology which gave her the capacity to produce life in her body was condemned as impure. Mary, the Mother of Jesus, is not much comfort in this predicament, because the church decreed that she was "not in the way of women" and gave birth as a virgin, not as a woman who had consummated *hieros gamos* with a man. This makes it difficult for women to identify with her. She is not a common woman of this Earth, and not quite Sophia, either.

Within few years and decades women have developed wonderful ways to share these experiences. In the beginning, an important part of this struggle was mourning. They included in their mourning the fate of countless women in the past who were burned at the stake as "witches." They also included women of the Bible who had suffered violence, or outstanding women whose achievements were disparaged and eliminated from memory. Women prophets and judges in the Old Testament were suppressed, the same as women who had been close to Jesus and were honored by him, especially those who had proclaimed the resurrected Christ. It was women who saw the risen Christ first. Women who held office as deaconesses in the early Christian community and gave their energy, and often their material resources, for the cause of Jesus, were soon deprived of their position and their offices were taken over by men. Thus, women were silenced in the church, and so Sophia, too, withdrew. She revealed herself from time to time to outstanding individuals, but she remained outside the mainstream of Christian life.

When women speak of their wounds, it is not only the mourning they share, but also their rage. They are also angry with themselves. Why did they tolerate it? Why did they suffer themselves to be shoved aside and forced to conform to the role of the eternal victim of male domination? Was Otfried Eberz not right when he spoke of "The Fall of Woman," as woman's betrayal of herself, the unpardonable sin against her Holy Spirit? Why did they not rebel against the emptiness of religious services and the irrelevance of sermons, in which the reality of women's lives was ignored? In fact, in the course of time the life reality of both men and women was ignored. What kind of a God is this "out there," who sits in state above human beings like a king, a Lord of the Universe, or, speaking in modern terms, like the Director of the Board, a Guru, the president of an institution, a kind of Supreme Judge?

> He is the eternal source of all that is above us, unlike us, not us. Out of our fear of death and fear of life and fear of the passion that enables us to experience either life or death, we weave a myth of divine-human alienation.[1]

Women experiment with what God might be. They examine the inherited images imprinted in their minds, and re-read and re-interpret the

---

[1] Carter Heyward, *The Redemption of God: A Theology of Mutual Relation* (Washington, DC: University Press of America, 1982), p. 158.

Bible against this background. They try to articulate what "holy" or "sacred" means to them and how they experience it. They sit together in small groups, talking. Even those who normally don't say anything for shyness now speak up. They sit in a circle, facing each other. There is none who dominates or tells the others what's what. Such conversations develop in a way not possible in the church, or in a lecture room, where people sit behind each other, staring at the back of each others' heads, where the speaker is elevated above the others and is thus separated from the group. They listen to each other carefully and humbly, so that everyone is encouraged to share.

American women call this kind of empowering, supportive, and protective attention "listening each other into speech." If you have ever experienced such an exchange, if you felt the healing power of merely paying attention to one another, listening in silence, you will not have any doubt that something new is underway. There is a new spirit in communication. This spirit is maternal, gentle, caring, understanding. It is non-exclusive and non-judgmental. It has no position to defend and is open to everyone and anything. It gives to strangers, to women with totally different backgrounds and life experiences, a sense of trust and familiarity. There is no need to keep anything back, because they feel that they are accepted with their hurts, their deficiencies, their inhibitions, their halting speech, as they grope for words which they never said to anyone before. In this spirit, women are beginning to feel empowered. In the healing dynamic of such sharing, mourning, anger, and anguish are transformed. Negative emotions, the accumulated weight of the past, may change into a positive force. This is empowerment. There is a sense of doors opening, just a small passage for one or a huge gateway for another, depending on the individual. In any case, they are discovering new territory, a vaguely anticipated or open and exciting freedom.

One group, about eighty women, is talking about "texts"—their own and alien, imposed and misunderstood "con-texts." They are concerned with "text-ure," the art of weaving, invented by women in the Neolithic Age, experiences woven into patterns. The room is decorated with scarves in bright colors. Everywhere in the house there are flower arrangements. The participants gather in small groups to discuss a particular topic. There is a great variety of topics, all of them having to do with "text" as applied to women's lives. In the groups, a lively, impassioned, heavy, and sometimes light-hearted exchange gets underway, which later in the plenary is shared with the other groups. Everyone has something to say; all contribute to shape the event. The groups could not be more heterogeneous: there are women wounded by the past, beaten, angry, resentful women, others are independent, self-assured and strong. There are women from various professions, callings, and age groups, academic women and others with little formal education, but plenty of practical experience of life. They succeed in finding a common language without discomfort to anyone, without imposing on others. There is no "pecking order"; nobody even "leads" the discussion.

In the afternoon, the talks continue with different topics in two sessions. There is a surge of new subjects that require investigation. There is such an abundance of ideas that the groups cannot handle everything and have to set limits. The uplifting spirit is contagious. There is not sufficient time to follow every thread, to weave every thought into the fabric. It remains unfinished, but it is rich in colors, durable, and resilient, like the bright scarves of Indio women in which they carry their children and other loads on their backs. Some women practice the capacity to find their voice in writing. There is a special workshop in speech, in which the Lord's Prayer is examined, tested, and *tasted* word by word. Many women find that they have difficulty with the *Lord's* Prayer. With the help of bibliodrama, an established technique to relate the deep meaning of biblical texts to one's own inner reality, the gospel is reinterpreted. Meditative dancing takes memory—the memory of the body—back to the rituals of an ancient feminine worldview. There are moon dances and dances of the seasons, spiral and labyrinth dances, dances of worship and affirmation. In one of the most popular dances, the women are led into a maze, and when two women meet face to face, they salute each other with the joyful cry, "Inanna, hey!"

A special workshop is devoted to Mechthild of Magdeburg, who was greeted in her 12th year "by the Holy Spirit in a most blissful flow," and after that "the loving-tender salute came all the days." How do women imagine the Holy Spirit? How would they wish to be saluted by her? Each woman selects a partner, and together they enact the salute of the Holy Spirit. First, one impersonates the Holy Spirit, then they change parts. One woman imagines a being who knows how to listen with attention and tenderness, so that the power which is in her sorrow might be released. Another simply wishes to be caressed, because in her old age she is not touched by anybody any more, and because she never knew how to be kind to herself. A third woman, silently weeping to herself, sits by herself on a chair, too anguished to participate. The other women draw their intuition of the Holy Spirit on large sheets of paper, which at the end they stitch together as a book. In the plenary, the various groups report, demonstrate, act, sing, and dance what they discovered in their work.

The draft of a new Credo is in the making. The various texts submitted by a number of women focus on issues like the sanctification of the body and the earth, and on love, which is at work throughout the universe, down to the very atoms, as the power of cohesion and attraction. Even matter is imbued with divine love. The Spirit is redefined, as *Ruah*, the feminine Divine Spirit, or Sophia, the source of the abundance of life, who guides all beings to their true nature in creativeness and strength. There are experiments with new prayers, because Sophia can only be a liberating force if her spirit is not smothered by obsolete formulas and customs.

In the evening an improvised festival takes place. The room is decorated, and there are flowers and trays with champagne glasses placed on small tables. There is music, and many women brought texts they composed, which they now read to the others. There is space for everything: joy and sorrow, anger and hope, differentiation and communion. A young woman is remembered who had come to these meetings for years. Here she had found understanding and healing for the greatest hurt of her childhood, sexual abuse by her own father. Gradually she was able to release her depression. She started to write poetry and opened up to the beauty of nature. Then the shadows closed in on her again, and she threw herself under a train and was killed. Many of the women knew her. Her photographs are pinned on a folding screen, her poems so sparkling and full of hope. She, too, is taken into the circle. Her pain is not shut out to preserve the festive spirit. Anguish is not shut out. The violated women of Bosnia are remembered. What would have to change that such crimes, mass rape as a normal part of warfare, become impossible? No legislation can be effective without a profound change of consciousness that outlaws violence of any kind. This primary act of violence, the rape of women by men, is committed every day, every hour and minute all over the world. It is still suppressed, still passed over in silence, although the taboo has been broken to some extent. What will have to happen, so that this nightmare will become a horror of the past?

The following morning, the plenary assembles once again. What will these women take home from the workshop? All their wishes are channeled in the desire for a full and meaningful life, a longing for wholeness, for the unfoldment of all their creative capacities, a kind of justice responsive to the larger cosmos. There is a prayer for courage to be able to carry out the work of justice—in personal relationships, in everyday work, in the church, in public life. After such a weekend of communion and intimate sharing, of healing and re-designing their lives, some women fall into a black hole after they have returned home. But isn't this time different from other times? Is there not a sense of a growing, sustaining network in the name of the Divine Spirit? This Spirit was always identified with Sophia. Sophia was right in our midst, as she has always been when she was called, when she was made welcome. She facilitates a new discourse of God. The Feminine has indeed become a source of revelation. This could not have happened with such urgency and irrepressibility, if the time had not been ready for the resurgence of Sophia.

A conspicuous feature of these workshops of feminist, or rather sophianic theology is that the initial planning is in the hands of a few women, that many take a part in the following preparation, and that all participants share in the actual shaping of the event and actively contribute their energy. There is no "leader" to announce the program and organize the discussion, and yet the event is not without leadership. Authority has given way to another form of cooperation. This "horizontal" style of leadership is gaining ground today also outside the feminist movement. It is a byproduct of sophianic consciousness. If God is relieved of his authoritarian, patriarchal mask, society is free for another concept and exercise of power.

The American theologian Carter Heyward coined the term "power-in-relationship" with reference to God. This is how she experienced God, because only in our relationships are we in God. God exists in relationship. The redemption of the world takes place *in* the world; justice and love must be realized *in* the world. It is time that we come of age and part with a "transcendental" God in the sense of a vertical power hierarchy. Humanity has to take responsibility for what is happening on the earth. Did Jesus not point the way? But we did not understand him. "To become 'like God' is to become human."[2]

We have turned God into an idol, instead of worshipping him (her) as transpersonal spirit and power-in-relationship. The power question is, in fact, the crucial issue. A God liberated from authoritarian power also liberates humanity. Since the beginning of a historical consciousness, power was always power *over* something or *over* other people, and this kind of power necessarily leads to violence. The power *over* controls by force and maintains itself at the expense of the weaker party. Anthroposophy, with its biblical roots, is based on this concept of power. According to this image of man, humanity, i.e., the male, is called by God to rule over the Earth, as well as over woman. He is created for his own sake, to achieve his ends; she is created for his sake, to serve his purposes. The power of Jesus was of a different order, but the norm was patriarchal power which by definition does not function without violence. At the turn of the century, when the rot of the patriarchal system began to disturb sensitive minds, Nietzsche in his despair about what he called the "slave morality" of Christianity was still upholding the negative ethics of the "Superman" (*Herrenmensch*) and legitimized a ruthless "will to power." We have not yet got rid of the evil spirits which this glorification of the power principle evoked. Nietzsche did not invent it, but he carried it to a perverse extreme, and unfortunately his giant intellect, his compelling argument in the language of revelation proved extremely influential.[3]

For some time a new concept of power has been emerging. In sophianic-feminist literature, this "other" power has been called

---

[2] Heyward, p. 151.
[3] See especially *Thus Spake Zarathustra* and *The Will to Power*.

"Power-of-Being."[4] It is supported by the sophianic movement as a central value of that new age at whose threshold we stand. The true transformation of all values means the revaluation of the "other" power, its emancipation from the stigma of weakness. In other words, it has to be given public credit. It must not go under in the doctrine of the "two kingdoms," the ancient Christian conviction that the earthly kingdom will always be subject to violence and the abuse of power, and that the "other" power will break through only now and then from the kingdom of God. In the '50s, at a time which was obsessed with official images of *the* enemy, the prominent theologian Paul Tillich thought that the "other" power could only have the significance of a signal, but would never be able to create new structures.[5]

This belief has changed. We have now reached a point where it *must* create new structures. Largely still invisible, something new is beginning to emerge, like the contours of a crystal in a saline solution. Like the crystal, new structures have to grow from within, expanding surfaces and volume simultaneously. When the sophianic consciousness reaches a critical mass of people, a palpable jump forward will be felt, like a surge of growth in the still hidden crystal. A new pattern of behavior acquired by a group of persons in one place will, by morphic resonance, be transferred to other groups. It enters automatically, as it were, into the experience of all humanity.[6]

That this new spirit is spreading, if almost imperceptibly, can be sensed at various places. In the summer of 1993, the Second Parliament

---

[4] American authors were the first to define this "other" power: Mary Daly, Carter Heyward, Elisabeth Schüssler-Fiorenza, Starhawk, to mention just a few. Of course, Riane Eisler's concept of a partnership society is based on the same idea.

[5] See Paul Tillich, *The Philosophy of Power* (German edition: *Die Philosophie der Macht*, Berlin: Colloquium Verlag, 1953).

[6] See Rupert Sheldrake, *A New Science of Life* (London: Blond & Briggs, 1981).

of the World's Religions took place in Chicago, and I was fortunate enough to attend. Six thousand persons, mainly from the United States, were gathering in this metropolis of commerce and crime, to participate in more than six hundred separate events. The overall theme was the mutual understanding of the world's religions, which the Hindu monk Swami Vivekananda had called for at the First Parliament of Religions. The stage for the earlier conference was also Chicago, a hundred years previously almost to the day. What was a revolutionary message then, is now a widely acknowledged necessity. If it had not been for Vivekananda, the earlier Parliament would have been entirely an intra-Christian affair.

This time, a great variety of non-Christian religions were represented, and everyone communicated in a spirit of harmony. An occasional strain of discord was far outweighed by sessions in the spirit of Sophia. Their variety and sheer bulk presented a model for the world of tomorrow. In many events, the need for a change of the traditional image of God was addressed explicitly. Sophia was mentioned surprisingly often in presentations, workshops, and discussions as the general symbol of the Divine Feminine. Feminists and authors, such as Riane Eisler, Charlene Spretnak, Eleanor Rae, Jean Houston and many others, designed their individual sophianic *oikumene*, drawing inspiration and strength from the return of the Feminine Divine.

In the new ecological-cosmological vision Sophia has a key position. Even when she was not mentioned explicitly—as in the keynote lectures by Robert Muller, the internationally acclaimed worker for global peace and leading figure in the United Nations, or the scientist Gerald Barney, author of *Global 2000*, a report on the Earth's resources; in lectures on Rudolf Steiner or Sri Aurobindo, in theosophical events, in interreligious discussions, in the sessions of the Taoists or the Bahá'ís (the youngest of the world religions), in the rediscovery of the mystical traditions, or the sessions, programmed or unannounced of the *wicca* cult—everywhere the Feminine Divine seemed to return for good, never to leave again the consciousness of human beings on this planet. This was, I thought, the most beautiful feature of the Chicago conference: Sophia was part of what was happening during these intensive eight days. She was palpably present.

One of the most significant results of the Conference was the ratification of a World Ethos.[7] It is clear that this consensus on basic ethical principles cannot be legally enforced, yet this document, which was signed during the Conference by more than a hundred leading figures from the world religions, will set a standard. Never before has a set of ethical principles been stated so succinctly and acceptably for all religions. What we have here is not a unified creed or a shared ideology, but a basic consensus on ethical values, as they are part of every religion. Any form of suppression is explicitly rejected. An entire section is devoted to the partnership of men and women in equality and a condemnation of the exploitation and abuse of women. Reverence for life and concern for the Earth are the basis of the whole document. It was presented and discussed throughout the Conference.

Much has been said about the United States as a "melting pot of nations," how it succeeded and how it failed. While it is painfully clear that North America did not produce the homogenous, peaceful society on the basis of human equality as envisioned by the Constitution, to a European view, America still provides prime opportunities as a laboratory for the future world society. It is an on-going experiment, and a discouraging phase in societal terms does not mean that there are not hope-

---

[7] The person largely responsible for drafting this document was Hans Küng of Tübingen, Germany. It will be remembered that Küng, one of the leading Catholic theologians of our time, was castigated by the Church for his critical attitude. He has done outstanding work to promote interreligious understanding.

ful signs in other areas. Under the high pressure of an interreligious dialogue, in which all the present problems of the world were addressed, something like an international sophianic platform took shape. Where so many people are striving to find a feasible way for the healing of the Earth, the spirit of Sophia is invoked. The whole World Parliament took place under the auspices of Sophia. She has her place and her own configuration in all religious traditions. She is the source where all streams and rivers come together.

Contrary to the first World Parliament of Religions, theology was definitely not the issue, for the theme here was a common effort to bring back to Earth the Wisdom that was lost. Any particular concept of God or religious dogma was not of interest, but people were interested in the holy spirit of Wisdom which blows wherever it is invoked. Wisdom is on the way to transform patriarchal Christianity. Sophia has touched ground in the least likely places, such as Tahlequah, Oklahoma, where more than ten years ago, a center of Sophianic Studies was set up by the intuition of a woman. Carol Parrish runs the Sancta Sophia Seminary as a training place for theologians and ministers with a difference. Esoteric Christianity, the wisdom of the Kabbalah and theosophical teachings are part of it. Creative new forms of liturgy, sacred dancing, the healing arts, meditation, yoga, are part of it. The wisdom of other religions, Eastern as well as native American religions, are appreciated as a matter of course.

The Chicago Conference served as focus for a great number of other sophianic initiatives and groups, such as the Center for Women, the Earth, the Divine, founded by Eleanor Rae, an unconventional Catholic theologian, in Ridgefield, Connecticut. There, I witnessed a remarkable day in celebration of Sophia in a group of about twenty-five middle-aged and older women. There was no difference whatsoever in the spirit of this group of generous, open-hearted and open-minded human beings longing for the bread of life, than I have experienced in Germany over the years. There, too, are women reluctant to break allegiance with the Church, or who have left the Church, and who look for something new. They all reach out for Sophia.

Everywhere in the world, Sophia is celebrating her resurrection. Her spirit is present in mass events like the church conventions in Germany, in symposia and seminars of Catholic and Protestant Academies, in the Parliament of the World's Religions in Chicago, which brought together representatives of all religions, in the revived old and new goddess cults, in feminist theology in the USA and in Germany, in the curricula of theological seminaries and institutions of adult education, in small centers which were founded in honor of Sophia, in private discussion groups, and last not least in those numerous dance circles, which invoke Sophia with the body. I believe there is no country in the world at present, where sacred or meditative dancing in the spirit of Sophia has become a popular movement as it is in Germany. Although most of these groups are open to anyone, they are attended almost exclusively by women. The leaders are women who often devote years to research ethnic dances, of our own folk tradition and that of other nations. Often, dances—choreography and music— are passed on personally from one teacher to another. Some inspired "Dance Women," as they are called, create their own elaborate choreographies on the basis of ancient myths and symbols. They travel a great deal, leading dance retreats all over Germany as well as abroad. The dance movement brought back an awareness of the human body as a sacred vessel. Worship expressed in dance, so long condemned as sinful and heathenish, is admitted even in churches, and thrives as an independent affirmation of the new sensuous quality in worship, the new Eros of the sophianic movement.

Sophia gave to the women's movement an impulse to go beyond the struggle for equal rights and to reclaim their divine heritage. In her sign we ask for the healing of the Earth from patriarchal exploitation and destruction. The perception of her, which is never a theological knowledge of the mind, but an intuitive heart knowledge, put us in touch with the sophianic stream of other religions. As this is often misunderstood, let me affirm once more that this approach will not lead to any syncretistic "world religion" as a summary or substitute of all religious traditions. Something else is happening today which can only be understood in terms of Sophia. The openness and love, with which the truth in all religions is received in our time, does in no way discredit the love of Jesus Christ. This love is one and indivisible. It is not diminished by the encounter with other spiritual traditions. On the contrary, it may grow in strength and conviction on the part of the individual believer. The same principle is in operation as with the concept of the "other" power: it takes delight in the power-of-being, the vitality and fullness of life of another. From non-Christian religions and the old goddess myths we learn today that no religion is viable without Eros. Tragically, the magnificent love mysticism of our Judaeo-Christian tradition did not succeed to infuse Eros into our churches, because the patriarchal suspicion against uncontrollable, sophianic heart knowledge and the wisdom of the body resisted it. It would have had to admit the erotic power of the Feminine, but it had cut itself off from the source right at the beginning. The divine *hieros gamos* can only take place if it mirrors an earthly one. In the entire cosmos, in the human and the subhuman realm down to the mysterious inner structure of matter, there is this drive of an elemental attraction. It is part of creation, or shall we say, the very secret of creation? It is, in the words of Faust, "that which holds the world together innermost." Had Faust really been a loving man, he would have known the answer to his quest. However, Faust, this proto-type of Western man, was most deficient as a lover. The fiery energy of cohesion, of a loving relationship, can only manifest concretely. In the human dimension, which differs from the elemental one, it needs to be personalized in responsible action, and elevated beyond the level of the senses. It is not only a physical, but at the same time an emotional and spiritual drive. The union of man and woman in physical love aspires to a spiritual union with God. The love mysticism of all cultures affirms that sensual love has a metaphysical goal. Men like Soloviev, Rudolf Steiner, Walter Schubart and Otfried Eberz understood this, and women and poets of all times knew it. Especially Otfried Eberz realized how much the feminine capacity for love is rooted in the relationship with the Divine. Christian doctrine, however, had nothing to say about this. Today's feminists generally avoid the issue, because woman's capacity for love was defined too long in terms of male needs. The time has come for an all-embracing erotic vision of life in the sign of Sophia.

If our brief excursion through the configurations of "Lady Wisdom" in the Judaeo-Christian tradition and in an interreligious context is of more than historical interest, its meaning is to bear witness to the omnipresence of Sophia, in whatever form she may appear. Even the patriarchal estrangement and her exclusion from the persons of the Trinity ultimately could not harm her. Throughout the ages, she convinced those who were overwhelmed by her presence of her genuine divinity. Her return today has no traffic with theological hairsplitting. Whether created or uncreated, emanation or hypostasis, helpmate of creation or divine creatrix, projection of Jesus or the Virgin Mary or the Church—these intellectual differentiations and theological niceties have lost all meaning. The deeply ambiguous terminology concerning the nature of her divinity is of no interest any more. Sophia is here, a fully empowered presence. She followed the call in this time of emergency and put an end to the gender definition of the Divine as male. She responds to the need of our age as anticipated in the Revelation of John and the old, eternally young myths. She is the ever-present origin and there is no end to her transformations. As the French philosopher and translator of Jacob Boehme, Louis-Claude de Saint Martin, wrote at the end of the 18th century:

> The ways of Wisdom are so prolific that she changes every moment to adapt to all conditions and circumstances. If she embraces all times and spaces in the fullness of her capacities, she will never let the wellspring of her gifts run dry, in whatever situation we may find ourselves.[8]

Sophia is Divine Wisdom, which is inseparable from the love of God: the love which heals every discord, resolves all dualisms, turns with tenderness to the Earth and to human beings, and bestows the freedom of empowerment inherent in all beings. As Hildegard saw the true love of God in one of her visions: "constantly circling, wonderful for human nature, and such that is not consumed by age . . . everlasting until the end of time."[9]

---

[8] Translation mine.
[9] Hildegard of Bingen, *Book of Divine Works* (Sante Fe, NM: Bear & Co., 1987), p. 26 (Vision II:2).

AFTERWORD

THIS WOULD NOT BE A BOOK ABOUT Sophia if it were not allowed to end with an address of homage.

It is well that women discover their freedom today in the name of Sophia, and many have become empowered by her return—reborn in the holy spirit of Divine Wisdom. Many of us have found support in the strength and encouragement of other women, and our common search for Sophia was to me one of the happiest experiences in the past, when so many certainties seemed to crumble. Wounded by patriarchal society and a patriarchal religion, as many of us have been, I wish to acknowledge that I also found Sophia within the Church. I found her spirit in men representing the Catholic tradition, which clings tenaciously to male privilege and continues to deny the priesthood to women. Yet there are men in the Church who cherish Sophia and serve her with devotion and enthusiasm. They encouraged me to start my work and helped me to overcome the scruples I had with patience and gentle persuasion.

Since our shared interest in Sophia brought us together years ago, Thomas Schipflinger, a Roman Catholic country priest, never tired of stimulating and assisting me with his resources. While pursuing my studies, I drew from his encyclopedic work *Sophia-Maria: A Holistic View of Creation*,[1] which no amount of reading can exhaust, and I shall continue to use it as my most reliable standby. Thomas Schipflinger is a sophianic savant of a very special kind. Ever since his soul was stirred when, as a young soldier, he saw an icon of Sophia in a Russian village devastated by the German army, Sophia never left him again. After his return from the war, he settled down as a parish priest and devoted all his spare time to the investigation of Sophia. In the course of his life, he collected the materials published in *Sophia-Maria*, and studied Chinese and Sanskrit, so that he might also follow Sophia in the spiritual traditions of the Far East.

When we met in his parsonage out in the Bavarian country, Sophia was always with us. And because she has a way to reconcile the dichotomy of spirit and matter, body and soul, the mundane and the divine, she bestowed on us all the benefits conducive to a spirited conversation. When, after mass, I cooked our lunch in the spacious, modestly furnished kitchen of his parsonage, he merrily set the table and fetched an exquisite bottle of wine, which one of his parishioners had presented him. Then we enjoyed our meal, and after a siesta, which in the summer I preferred to spend stretched out on the lawn of his rose garden, we went into his study for work. What a study! It contained a veritable sophianic cosmos. There were books in profusion, precious pictures and sculptures, antique works of art, modern designs, portfolios with preliminary studies for further work on Sophia. On one of the walls there hung a mandala he had commissioned an artist to do according to his design—a combination of Christian symbols and the sacred symbols of

---

[1] Thomas Schipflinger, *Sophia-Maria: A Holistic View of Creation*, to be released by Samuel Weiser, York Beach, ME, November, 1997.

other religions—the *OM*, the *Yin-Yang*, the lotus. He shared with me all he had and all he knew about Sophia. He looked up quotations, rummaged source material, and loaded me with books and photocopies to take home.

In these busy, animated hours in his country parsonage a joy sometimes welled up from deep within—a promise that the paths of Sophia will never end, but spread and grow richer all the time, opening up new possibilities of a creative life. At present we only have words from the past, all the testimonies about Sophia in history, but the time will come when she is restored and will make all things new. This has to happen in the consciousness of individual women and men. Only then will she be able to effect the necessary change. Father Schipflinger carried her in his heart ever since he set eyes on her image in the house of a poor Russian priest. The higher significance of this event dawned on me when he first told me about it. Sophia, rooted in the Russian soil as nowhere else, persecuted during the Communist regime and the savagery of the Second World War as nowhere else, took refuge in the middle of ruin and destruction in the consciousness of a young man, who brought her to the country that had betrayed Sophia in this century more than any other nation. She was destined to reappear in the work of Thomas Schipflinger.

His vision infected me, and for this I am even more grateful than for all the practical help he gave me. A lot of inside noise calmed down when I left the parsonage. I came away in higher spirits than I had when I arrived. His example, among other considerations, saved me from signing off from a Church which had neglected its sophianic heritage for so long. As a Protestant I experienced this loss even more deeply.

The truth is that there have always been sophianically inspired individuals, women and men, in the West and in the East, who kept the spark of Sophia alive and rekindled it when it was all but extinguished.

We need Sophia *today*, so that the *kairos* may be fulfilled. We need the living witnesses, the companions on the way, the personal relationship with Sophia-oriented individuals, we need exchange and sharing. Next to the network of women it was Thomas Schipflinger to whom I owe this impulse.

There are still men in the Church who are blessed with Sophia. They are her faithful servants. They rescued her—sometimes with difficulty and pain—from the ruins of history. This is still happening, and therefore Christianity is still a space where the miracle of an experience of the Divine can take place. I am grateful to have witnessed this dimension of the Church. The spirit of Sophia bloweth where it listeth, in men and women alike, and happy is she who has found it in both.

BIBLIOGRAPHY

Arnold, Gottfried. *Das Geheimnis der göttlichen Sophia.* Facsimile reprint of the edition of Leipzig 1700. Stuttgart-Bad Cannstadt: Frommann, 1973.

Boehme, Jacob. *Aurora. That is, the Day-Spring or Dawning of the Day in the Orient. . .* Reprint of the edition of 1656. Edmonds, WA: Holmes Publishing Group, 1992.

———. *Six Theosophic Points and Other Writings.* New York: Alfred A. Knopf, 1920.

———. *The Threefold Life of Man.* London: John M. Watkins, 1909.

———. *The Way to Christ.* John Joseph Stoudt, trans. New York & London: Harper Brothers, 1947.

Bolen, Jean Shinoda. *Goddess in Everywoman.* San Francisco: HarperSanFrancisco, 1985.

Bumiller, Elisabeth. *May You By the Mother of a Hundred Sons.* New York: Random House, 1991.

Cady, Susan, Marian Ronan, Hal Taussig. *Sophia: The Future of Feminist Spirituality.* San Francisco: HarperSanFrancisco, 1986.

Campbell, Joseph, and Charles Musès (eds.). *In All Her Names*. San Francisco: HarperSanFrancisco, 1991.

Cantor, Aviva. "The Lilith Question," in: *On Being a Jewish Feminist*, ed. by Susannah Heschel. New York: Schocken Books, 1983.

Christ, Felix. Die Sophia-Christologie bei den Synoptikern. Diss. theol. Zurich, 1970 (dissertation).

Daly, Mary. *Beyond God the Father: Toward a Philosophy of Women's Liberation*. Boston: Beacon Press, 1973.

―――. *Gyn-Ecology*. Boston: Beacon Press, 1990.

Dürckheim, Karlfried Graf. *Wunderbare Katze und andere Zen-Texte*. [Miraculous Cat and Other Zen-Texts] Munich: O. W. Barth, 1970.

Eberz, Otfried. *Vom Aufgang und Niedergang des männlichen Weltalters*, ed. by Annemarie Taeger and Lucia Eberz. Bonn: Bouvier, 1990.

―――. *Sophia–Logos und der Widersacher*, publ. by Lucia Eberz, Nigerstr. 2, D-81675 Munich. 2nd printing: Munich, 1978.

―――. *Sophia und Logos oder die Philosophie der Wiederherstellunq*, publ. by Lucia Eberz. 3rd printing: Munich, 1983.

Ehrenberg, Margaret. *Women in Prehistory*. Norman, OK: University of Oklahoma Press, 1989.

Eisler, Riane. *The Chalice and the Blade*. San Francisco: HarperSanFrancisco, 1988.

Empedocles. *The Extant Fragments,* ed. by M. R. Wright. New Haven-London: Yale University Press, 1981.

Engelsman, Joan Chamberlain: *The Feminine Dimension of the Divine*. Philadelphia: Westminster Press, 1979.

Evdokimov, Pauel. *Woman & the Salvation of the World: A Christian Anthropology on the Charisms of Women*. Crestwood, NY: St. Vladimirs, 1994.

Faludi, Susan. *Backlash: The Undeclared War Against American Women*. New York: Doubleday, 1992.

Fester, Richard (ed.). *Weib und Macht. Fünf Millionen Jahre Urgeschichte der Frau*. Frankfurt: S. Fischer, 1979.

Florensky, Pavel. *An den Wasserscheiden des Denkens* [A Florensky-Reader] ed. by Sieglinde and Fritz Mierau. Berlin: Kotext, 1991.

———. *Iconostasis*. Donald Sheehan and Olga Andrejev, trans. Crestwood, NY: St. Vladimir's Seminary Press, 1996.

Fox, Matthew. *The Coming of the Cosmic Christ*. San Francisco: HarperSanFrancisco, 1988.

France, Anatole. "Die Tochter Liliths," in: *Novellen*. Munich: Musarion, 1922.

Friedan, Betty. *The Feminine Mystique*. New York: Dell Publishing Co., 1963.

Galland, China. *Longing for Darkness: Tara and the Black Madonna*. London: Penguin, 1990.

Gebser, Jean. *The Ever Present Origin*. Columbus: Ohio University Press, 1985.

Gimboutas, Marija. *The Goddesses and Gods of Old Europe. 6500–3500 B.C.* Berkeley: University of California Press, 1982.

Heyward, Carter. *The Redemption of God: Theology of Mutual Relation*. Washington, DC: University Press of America, 1982.

Hildegard of Bingen. *Book of Divine Works, with Letters and Songs*, ed. by Matthew Fox. Santa Fe, NM: Bear & Co., 1985.

———. *Scivias*. Santa Fe, NM: Bear & Co., 1986.

Hurwitz, Siegmund. *Lilith: The First Eve*. Santa Rosa, CA: Daimon, 1991.

Jung. C. G. *Answer to Job, Collected Works, Vol. II, Psychology and Religion: East and West*, R. F. C. Hull, trans. Bollingen Series

No. 20. Princeton: Princeton University Press, 1958.

Kinsley, David. *Hindu Goddesses*. Berkeley: University of California Press, 1985.

Koltuv, Barbara Black. *The Book of Lilith*. York Beach, ME: Nicolas-Hays, 1986.

Kurz, Isolde. *Die Kinder der Lilith*. Stuttgart-Berlin: Cotta'sche Buchhandlung, 1908.

Lao Tzu. *Tao Teh Ching*. John C. H. Wu, trans. Boston: Shambhala, 1989.

Lovelock, James. *Gaia: A New Look at Life on Earth*. Oxford: Oxford University Press, 1987.

Mack, Burton Lee. *Logos und Sophia*. Diss. theol. Göttingen, 1967 (Dissertation).

———. *Wisdom and the Hebrew Epic*. Chicago: University of Chicago Press, 1986.

Mechthild of Magedburg. *Das fließende Licht der Gottheit*. Margot Schmidt, trans. Zurich: Benziger, 1955.

Mulack, Christa. *Im Anfang war die Weisheit*. Stuttgart: Kreuz, 1988.

Neumann, Erich. *The Great Mother*. Bollingen Series, Vol. 47. Princeton: Princeton University Press, 1964.

Nigg, Walter. *Heimliche Weisheit: Mystisches Leben in der evangelischen Christenheit*. Zurich-Stuttgart: Artemis, 1959.

Pagels, Elaine. *The Gnostic Gospels*. New York: Random House, 1979.

Pflüger, Peter Michael (ed.). *Wendepunkte Erde Frau Gott*. Olten-Freiburg: Walter, 1983.

Riedel, Ingrid. "Wandlungen der Schwarzen Frau," in: Pflüger (ed.) *Wendepunkte Erde Frau Gott*.

———. *Die weise Frau in uralt-neuen Erfahrungen*. Olten-Freiburg: Walter, 1989.

Rilke, Rainer Maria. *Letters to a Young Poet*. M. D. Herter Norton, trans. New York: W. W. Norton, 1934.

Rimbaud, Arthur. *Rimbaud: Complete Works, Selected Letters*. Wallace Fowlie, trans. Chicago: University of Chicago Press, 1966.

Roebling, Irmgard. *Lulu, Lilith, Mona Lisa–Frauenbilder der Jahrhundertwende*. Pfaffenweiler: Centaurus, 1989.

Schaup, Susanne. *Wandel des Weiblichen*. Freiburg: Herder, 1988.

Schipflinger, Thomas. *Sophia–Maria: Eine ganzheitliche Vision der Schöpfung*. Munich-Zurich: Verlag Neue Stadt 1988. (English edition, *Sophia–Maria: A Holistic View of Creation*, York Beach, ME: Samuel Weiser, November 1997.)

Schipperges, Heinrich (ed.). *Hildegard von Bingen*. Olten–Freiburg: Walter, 1978.

Schubart, Walter. *Religion und Eros*. Munich: C. H. Beck, 1966.

Seuse, Heinrich. *Büchlein der ewigen Weisheit*. Stein am Rhein: Christiana-Verlag, 1987.

Sheldrake, Rupert. *A New Science of Life*. Los Angeles: J. P. Tarcher, 1988; London: Blond & Briggs, 1981.

Soloviev, Vladimir. *The Meaning of Love*. Jane Marshall, trans. London: Geoffrey Bles, 1946.

———. *Russia and the Universal Church*. Herbert Rees, trans. London: Geoffrey Bles, 1948.

Solowjews Leben in Briefen und Gedichten. Ludolf Müller and Irmgard Wille, eds. Munich: Erich Wewel, 1977.

Starhawk (Miriam Simos). *Dreaming the Dark*. Boston: Beacon Press, 1982.

Stein, Gerd (ed.). *Femme fatale–Vamp–Blaustrumpf: Sexualität und Herrschaft*. Frankfurt: S. Fischer, 1985.

Steiner, Rudolf. *Die Suche nach der neuen Isis, der göttlichen Sophia* [The Search for the New Isis, the Divine Sophia]. Dornach: Steiner, 1980.

Stone, Merlin. *When God Was a Woman*. New York: Harcourt Brace/Harvest, 1978.

Teilhard de Chardin, Pierre. "The Eternal Feminine," in: *The Prayer of the Universe*. Selected from *Writings in Time of War*. New York: Harper & Row (Perennial Library), 1965.

Tillich, Paul. *Die Philosophie der Macht*. Berlin: Colloquium Verlag, 1953.

Voss, Jutta. *Das Schwarzmondtabu: Die kulturelle Bedeutung des weiblichen Zyklus*. Stuttgart: Kreuz, 1988.

Wasson, R. Gordon, Albert Hofmann, Carl A. P. Ruck. *Der Weg nach Eleusis: Das Geheimnis der Mysterien*. Frankfurt: S. Fischer, 1984.

Watts, Alan. *Tao: The Watercourse Way*. New York: Pantheon Books, 1975.

Wedekind, Tilly. *Lulu, die Rolle meines Lebens*. Munich-Berne-Vienna: Scherz, 1969.

Wehr, Gerhard. *Die deutsche Mystik*. Munich-Berne-Vienna: Scherz, 1988.

Weiler, Gerda. *Ich brauche die Göttin: Zur Kulturgeschichte eines Symbols*. Basel: Mond-Buch, 1990.

———. *Der enteignete Mythos: Eine feministische Revision der Archetypenlehre C. G. Jungs und Erich Neumanns*. Frankfurt-New York: Campus, 1991.

———. *Eros ist stärker als Gewalt*. Frankfurt: Ulrike Helmle, 1993.

———. *Der aufrechte Gang der Menschenfrau*. Frankfurt: Ulrike Helmle, 1994.

Whitmont, Edward. *Return of the Goddess*. New York: Crossroad, 1984.

Wodtke, Verena (ed.). *Auf den Spuren des Weisheit*. Freiburg: Herder, 1991.

Wöller, Hildegunde. *Ein Traum von Christus*. Stuttgart: Kreuz, 1987.

Zimmer, Heinrich. "The Indian World Mother," in: *Eranos Yearbook*, 1938. Bollingen Series XXX, no. 6. Princeton: Princeton University Press, 1968.

INDEX

S USANNE SCHAUP WAS BORN IN VIENNA. She studied languages, psychology, and philosophy at Vienna University, continued her studies in the United States on a Fulbright scholarship, receiving her B. A. from Milwaukee Downer College, an M.A. from Auburn University, returning to Germany to complete her Ph.D. at Salzburg University. She spent two years at the University of London as a language assistant, then moved to Munich, where she worked independently as an editor for two Munich publishers from 1970 until 1977. Since then she has been writing, lecturing, and working with German radio stations. Two highly successful series of broadcasts were turned into books—"On the Transformation of the Feminine," and "Alternative Life Styles in America," both published in German. Recent publications (in German) include a short monograph on the life and work of Elisabeth Kübler-Ross (*Ein Leben für gutes Sterben,* Kreuz Verlag, 1996) and an anthology of H. D. Thoreau's journals in a new translation (Tewes Verlag, 1996). She lectures widely on the feminine aspect of God and related subjects. Dr. Schaup also conducts workshops and seminars for women who are tracing their roots.